THE POTTER QUEST

Christine Stearns

"You are the light of the world. A city set on a hill cannot be hid. Nor do men light a lamp and put it under a bushel, but on a stand, and it gives light to all in the house. Let your light so shine before men."

Matthew 5:14-15

"My words itch at your ears till you are ready to understand them."

Walt Whitman in Song of Myself, Section 47

Table of Contents

Introduction

If you have been secretly convinced that the Harry Potter series is really fine writing—and definitely not just for children, rest assured. You are right. It is absolutely clear that J. K. Rowling has written a classic piece of quest literature, one that will stand the test of time, because she has, in her own wonderfully creative fashion—found her way right into the "heart of the matter," to borrow a phrase from Hamlet. Her journey takes us right to the heart of the quintessential questions about the nature of the human condition. Along the way, we confront some of the most difficult and challenging questions that any writer has ever faced—the nature of our life here on earth; the battle between good and evil; the complexity of human nature; the difficulty of determining the truth of a situation; the possibility of life after death; and the way to live your life with honor and integrity in the face of overwhelming odds against you, and in the face of terrible loss. J. K. Rowling has woven a story filled with wonderfully imaginative settings, but the funny thing is—in many ways, we find many of the incidents of the stories feel very familiar. That is part of the magic that invites us into Harry's world. → relatable!

In other words, although much of the action takes place in a setting where we Muggles are not likely to ever find our way, the plain truth of the matter is that our battles are very much like the battles that Harry and his friends face, and we have much in common with him. In the course of our discussion, I will be talking about what happens in the stories, book by book, walking you through the plot as it develops, and pointing out interesting thematic connections. Although I will be careful about the order that J. K. Rowling uses, I may be talking about something that happens much later in the quest, even in these earliest stages of our discussion. So, if you have not finished the story, beware! Nonetheless, the seven novels that J. K. Rowling has written are quest literature, in the finest tradition, and we will explore those themes. Now, please don't think that I am saying that my discussion here will be in any way a final statement of the themes and literary value of these novels. I would never presume to imply that. Mostly, what I would like it to be is almost a classroom discussion, and you should feel free at any moment to interrupt the discussion and digress...for as long as you like. That would make me very happy.

In literature, there are essentially two master plots, or master narratives. Something has to happen to upset the status quo that we are initially presented with. Basically, a writer has two kinds of destabilizers that will be certain to get things moving. First, there is the plot line that essentially springs from "a stranger comes to town." The story opens with a glimpse of life, and then, a stranger comes to town and destabilizes everything. The journey of the novel thus begins. The second very famous basic plot line is quest literature; it could be called "the hero goes on a journey." This is not to say that a piece of literature is either one or the other of these narratives. Frequently, a story contains both elements. However, they are both exceptionally good ways of getting a story started. Either incident unsettles or destabilizes the opening situation, and the story begins.

A scholar named Joseph Campbell wrote the most famous study of the heroic quest narrative. His study can be found in his brilliant book entitled The Hero with a Thousand Faces. He discovered that this pattern is almost universal, occurring in almost every culture in the world, and crossing all boundaries of time. The essential elements go something like this: Life is a heroic quest. Everyone is potentially a hero at the moment of birth. There are four basic stages to the journey—leaving home, the searching or the tasks that must be performed, returning, and benefiting humanity with your knowledge, or passing the torch. This myth could be said to be an allegory, or an attempt to understand the human condition. In the course of the journey out, the young hero faces many tasks. The young hero is marked for greatness, although he may not know it at the time he receives the call. He will experience doubts about his worthiness as he faces his trials. Oftentimes, there is an old man who is the wise adviser. He sometimes gives the young hero a weapon, which is something, some object with magical powers. But the most important thing he gives the young hero is a transformation of consciousness, a stronger sense of self and a commitment to good. The saga often concludes with a cataclysmic battle, and the young hero eventually crosses the threshold back to the world of family obligations. During many quest stories, we are given a glimpse of the hero as a grown man or woman. We realize, therefore, that the larger human quest will go on, even though this particular hero has completed his mission or quest successfully. Sometimes, but not always, we see the torch being passed to a young champion; in other stories we are quietly aware that our young hero has settled down, and the next set of battles will be championed by someone younger, maybe many years later. In some famous quests, the hero dies, but there is sometimes the promise that he will come again. One of the most famous novels about the legendary King Arthur is therefore called The Once and Future King.

We never have the sense that evil is completely eradicated, but we do have the sense that the good people have beaten it back for a while. When evil rears its ugly head again, another hero will arise— another time, another place. Another quest. Life is a battlefield, and peace is always only temporary. Still, the hero knows that he has completed his mission. There will be a "season of grace," or a time of quiet. That is not to say that the war is done. It is never done. In time, the torch will be passed, and a new hero and a new quest will take the stage. Life is always in the stage of "becoming" and not in the stage of

8

"having become." At least far as we are able to see. One very famous quest saga that you may be familiar with is the Star Wars story. If you think about the qualities we have just discussed, you will realize that it too is a classic quest narrative.

The Harry Potter story is a brilliant and imaginative quest. Harry is the young hero that goes on a journey, and he takes us with him. It will be our goal to watch as the lessons unfold, book by book on Harry's wonderful journey, and to explore the connections to the quest lore that lies just under the surface of Harry's epic battles. Perhaps, underneath it all, we will come to realize that Harry's journey is our journey. Each of us is living our own personal quest right now. We are the heroes of our own quest narratives, and our "opening situations" are destabilized every morning with either going on a journey or a stranger coming into our lives. We try to do the right thing, as best we understand it, and we try to protect those who are too weak to defend themselves. We face losses and disappointments and have to rethink how to attack a problem or struggle on when the odds seem to be overwhelmingly against us. As we study the message of the Potter quest, we will come to realize how very much it has to say to us about how to live our lives so that, at the end of the day, we can say, with Harry, "All is well." → we are on a quest

Harry Potter and the Sorcerer's Stone

Rowling has our attention right from the opening chapters as we meet "the boy who lived." There is something that pulls at your heartstrings about an orphaned child. In fact, as soon as we meet the boy who lived, we see something of ourselves in Harry. Children, of course, immediately sympathize with Harry, and wonder if they would ever be able to be as brave under similar circumstances. However, for those of us who are parents, the idea of an orphan is even more complex and more troubling. First of all, we consider the possibility of our own children without our guidance, and every parent knows that they would do exactly what James and Lily Potter did. There is no question. You would die to protect your child, even if it meant leaving your child orphaned. Secondly, at some level, many adults have faced the possibility of being an orphan themselves. Many of us are. When your parents die, no matter how old they are and how rich and full their lives have been, you feel a little bit orphaned yourself. The world has been diminished. So, on many levels, we can identify with young Harry Potter.

Even his name asks us to do this. In the Old Testament we get these words: "Yet, O Lord, thou art our Father; we are the clay, and thou art our potter; we are all the work of thy hand"(Isaiah 64: 8). It is possible that our hero's name, Harry Potter, suggests heir of the

Bible!

Potter, or God's son. Now, this of course, leads us to the possibility that Harry is a Christ figure, and we could certainly defend that.

compares to Jesus

Like Jesus, Harry suffers to make other children safe. In fact, as we shall see in book seven, Harry would even die, sacrificing his own earthly happiness, to save those around him. We will speak about this in much more detail later. However, it is possible that Rowling is probably intending for us to think of this connection in another way as well. In a way, we are all Harry Potter, and we are all God's sons and daughters…we are his children. Abba Father. The word comes to us from the Old Testament. Abba means God, and it suggests a loving and almost intimate relationship with our heavenly Father. He is the Potter. We are the clay, the work of His hands. And this interpretation works because Harry's journey is our journey in very many ways. The Christian tradition holds that we are all God's children. This is a core belief, and therefore, Harry's story could be said to be our story as well.

we are God's children

And so, our journey begins.

It is very impressive that J. K. Rowling has so many ideas in place, right from the beginning. There is that wonderful scene in chapter two where Harry sets the snake free, and Dudley's friend Piers notices that Harry was talking to the snake. We know that Harry's ability to speak this snake language, which Rowling calls parseltongue, becomes very important later on in the epic. This episode fits perfectly with classic hero quest literature. Often, the young hero has certain exceptional abilities, things he or she can do that even they cannot explain. At these early stages, the young hero may notice the ability, but certainly not understand its significance.

When Harry's obnoxious uncle, Vernon Dursley, cannot stop the letters written in green ink from inundating his Muggle house and cannot even escape them in the desolate shack, Hagrid strides into the story, bigger than life, and demands that Harry be allowed to leave for Hogwarts, the school of magic. And Harry Potter finds out a little bit about who he is. Certainly, his journey will get much more complicated. However, in hero quest literature, the young hero typically must answer three questions—remember, by extension then, these are questions that each of us face in trying to understand the purposes of our lives:

3 essential ?s

1. Who am I, and who is my father? (Actually, these two questions are just different ways of saying the same thing. You can't know who you are if you don't know who your father is, and vice versa. The word mother can be used instead of father, because knowing who our parents are helps us to know who we are—at least in part.)

2. Why am I here?

3. Is the course of my life determined by free will or by fate?

It should become readily apparent that these are the very questions every person must answer in his or her life. So, once again, we see the link to Harry. While Harry must answer these questions in the course of his quest, we all must answer them for ourselves as well.

Through his conversation with Hagrid, Harry learns the truth about how his parents died, and how he got that scar on his forehead: "Never wondered how you got that mark on yer forehead? That was no ordinary cut. That's what yeh get when a powerful, evil curse touches yeh—took care of yer mum an' dad an' yer house, even—but it didn't work on you, an' that's why yer famous, Harry. No one lived after he decided ter kill 'em, no one except you"(55). When Harry doubts that any of this could be true, that he could have magical powers, Hagrid asks him if he has ever made something happen when he was scared or angry. At this point, J. K. Rowling draws all of us into the story, because we believe that, at least at some level, this kind of behavior is possible. Almost every person has experienced that time in their life when, with the adrenalin surging, we could do something we might not have been able to do under ordinary conditions. When we are scared or angry, we become just a little bit super-human, and we all know it. So, we are ready to journey with Harry, and, to some extent, recognize his journey as our own.

As Harry first enters the breathtaking magical world when visiting Diagon Alley, more Biblical parallels emerge. Hagrid's presentation of Harry to several residents of the magical world is vaguely reminiscent of the scene where Mary and Joseph present

13

Jesus in the temple. This moment is described in Luke: "And when the time came for their purification according to the law of Moses, they brought him up to Jerusalem to present him to the Lord...Now there was a man in Jerusalem whose name was Simeon, and this man was righteous and devout...and when the parents brought in the child Jesus...he took him up in his arms and blessed God"(Luke 2:2-27). Probably, most parents who have presented their child for baptism or some other rite of initiation can identify with this moment. Hagrid is the surrogate father for Harry in this scene, and he proudly presents him to the magical world, represented by the patrons of the Leaky Cauldron. "Bless my soul," whispered the old bartender, "Harry Potter...what an honor"(69). We meet, in passing, the strange Professor Quirrell, who has changed dramatically since he has been possessed by the Dark Lord, although, so far, no one else knows that this has happened. However, Hagrid offers the observation that Professor Quirrell seems to be afraid of his own subject, the Dark Arts, and scared of his own students. This observation seems to be born out by Quirrell's constant stuttering. He will be much more important later in the novel.

Harry and Hagrid approach Gringotts, which contains the vault that holds Harry's money. On the walls of the wizard bank is engraved a warning against greed: "So if you seek beneath our floors / A treasure that was never yours, / Thief you have been warned, beware

/ Of finding more than treasure there"(73). This engraving reminds us of Chaucer and "The Pardoner's Tale." The moral of that famous story is…Greed is the root of all evil. Sometimes people misquote this line, thinking that what Chaucer had written was…."Money is the root of all evil." But he was wiser than that: the sin is greed, which is closely tied to the sin of pride. The ancient Greeks had a name for it…hubris. And for them, it was the unforgivable sin. There is a connection between greed and hubris. Greed involves thinking you deserve more than you have, thinking that you are better and more important than you are. When a man considers himself an equal to the gods, when he puts his own welfare above all others, even if he must act unethically to preserve it, if he considers himself more important than everyone else, if he believes he is a law unto himself and he need not bother with questions of right and wrong, he is guilty of hubris. Already, we have a glimpse of the sins that will bring Lord Voldemort down in the end.

In the course of this first visit to Diagon Alley, we meet Lucius and Draco Malfoy. Rowling is giving us a clear indication of their predilection toward evil in the way she has named them. First of all, let us look at their surname--Malfoy. It comes from the Latin for bad or evil (mal) and foy for faith. Bad faith. Hence, this is the first connection with the ultimate Dark Lord--Satan. Remember that the word "Lucius" comes from the Latin word "lux," or light. So, in its earliest etymology, the name Lucius Malfoy is connected to images of light. However,

HUBRIS

his surname, taken with his given name, would seem to indicate that he has rejected the light. To the true light, he has shown bad faith. Furthermore, Lucius' name connects with Lucifer, and this connection works well because Lucifer, the Light-bearer, also rejected the light, supposedly when he was guilty of the sin of hubris. There are many different interpretations of the Lucifer myth, but perhaps the most important thing to remember here is that Lucifer had a chance to be involved with the light; he was the light bearer. And yet, he turned away from it. It comes down to choice. The idea of choosing to believe will be an enormously important idea as we move on.

Furthermore, Lucius' obnoxious son Draco, who will be a foil for Harry throughout his quest, has at least two interesting etymologies for his name. First of all, he may be named for Draco, an infamous Athenian lawgiver whose name has become synonymous with cruelty. Secondly, his name links to dragon. And most dragons in classic literature would just as soon attack you as look at you. It is interesting to note that even when Harry is talking with him for the first time, he is oddly reminded of Dudley, another spoiled child and chronic bully(77).

Shortly after this encounter, comes the memorable scene in Ollivander's wand shop. Ollivander will be an important character in the quest, even playing a crucial part in the final book. A portentous feeling surrounds his first meeting with Harry. After trying several wands unsuccessfully, Ollivander hands Harry the one that will be his: "I remember every wand I've ever sold, Mr. Potter. Every single wand. It so happens that the phoenix whose tail feather is in your wand, gave another feather—just one other. It is very curious indeed that you should be destined for this wand when its brother—why, its brother gave you that scar...Curious indeed how these things happen. The wand chooses the wizard, remember...I think we must expect great things from you, Mr. Potter...After all, He-Who-Must-Not-Be-Named did great things—terrible, yes, but great"(85). What an important moment this is. We are put on alert that a great battle, with mighty implications, is waiting in the wind. And the battle will be between Harry Potter and He-Who-Must-Not-Be-Named. The wand chooses the wizard, and will not give its truest allegiance to a wizard that it does not honor or respect. It will perform better for its true owner. It is fun to think of applications for this idea in our own world. The wand chooses the wizard, and in time, we see the majestic consequences of this interesting statement. We who have followed Harry on his journey, know that it will be a battle of mighty opposites. Mr. Ollivander seems very prescient in this scene.

After this interesting scene, Harry must unfortunately return to the Dursleys for the rest of the summer, and Rowling introduces an interesting pattern that she carefully follows--after an exciting scene, a crisis of sorts, comes the deflation. Back to the ordinary. Time to catch your breath. Isn't that very much like life, so many times? Harry heads back to the dreadful Dursleys, but there is a new song singing in his head: "Everyone thinks I'm special"(86). A lovely song indeed.

Eventually, it is time for Harry to leave for Hogwarts, and the scene of departure takes place at Kings Cross. It is hard to miss the religious symbolism involved here, for the name Kings Cross suggests Jesus' cross, since he is the King of Kings. Those readers who have seen the quest all the way through know that a very important scene will take place at Kings Cross in the last book. Suffice it to say right now, that this is where the magical Platform 9 and ¾ is found. It is a testament to how beloved the Harry Potter story is that the real Kings Cross now marks the location of this platform, with a trolley pushed half way into the boundary wall. Any child can go up to it, hang on to the trolley, and imagine being whisked through to the platform where the beautiful Hogwarts Express is waiting. Rowling is using a time-honored technique here. We are about to enter the magical world, and remain there for almost the rest of the novel. She creates two co-existing worlds, operating, for the most part independently of each other. However, she always reminds us that what happens in the magical world often spills over into the Muggle world.

To their delight and surprise, the children make it through the barrier, and fate seems to bring them together on the Hogwarts Express. Once again, young Draco, now in the companion of the ever-obnoxious Crabbe and Goyle (whose names conjure up the images of a crab and a gargoyle and therefore are just perfect!) threatens Ronald Weasley, who in the beginning of the series is a timid soul, languishing in the shadow of successful and popular older brothers. Throughout his association with Harry, he will grow into a fierce warrior—no longer a weasel but a lion. However, he tells us early on that his father, Arthur Weasley, does not trust the Malfoys at all, and with good reason, as we shall see: "I've heard of his family," said Ron darkly. "They were some of the first to come back to our side after You-Know-Who disappeared. Said they'd been bewitched. My dad doesn't believe it. He says Malfoy's father didn't need an excuse to go over to the Dark Side"(110). The Malfoy's surname, bad faith, is unfortunately appropriate. They place their faith in evil, they are not people you can trust, and repeatedly, they prove themselves to be cowards. Bad faith, indeed.

When the children arrive at Hogwarts, they are introduced to the Sorting Hat and the Sorting Ceremony. Now we learn more about the four houses of Hogwarts, and are given a quick description of the kind of person that we will typically find in the various houses. This is, of course, an oversimplification, as we will find the characters are much more complex than that. Nonetheless, the first characterizations are as follows:

Gryffindors—brave at heart

19

Hufflepuff—just and loyal

Ravenclaw—ready minds

Slytherin—cunning folk

Hermione, who is named for the wonderful, spunky, and wise character in William Shakespeare's play entitled The Winter's Tale, is named to the house of Gryffindor. Hermione Granger's name is no accident, nor is this connection to the play by Shakespeare. It will be more appropriate to explore this connection in the seventh book of the series, so we will come back to this idea later. However, at this early stage, we can at least pay some attention to the word Granger. In Shakespeare's time, a grange is a farm, and a granger is therefore a farmer, or someone connected to the earth. This is another connection that becomes even more important in the last book, when Hermione must forage for food to keep the young heroes alive.

Ron is also named to the Gryffindor house--everyone in his family has always been in Gryffindor. That, by the way, is an early hint to us that their surname, Weasley, might be misleading. After all, according to the Sorting Hat, the Gryffindors are all "brave of heart." The idea that we define ourselves through the choices we make and the complexity of human nature are illustrated when the Sorting Hat placed on Harry's head. The hat has some reservations about which house to place Harry in. We hear the hat thinking its way through the complex vibrations that Harry apparently gives off. Harry sits there, engaged in his own internal struggle. He expresses his desire very succinctly in two words: "Not Slytherin"(121). Perhaps Harry associates the house of Slytherin with evil, and secretly fears that he might have evil tendencies too. Perhaps he knows that the Malfoys are Slytherins, and he has already met them and found them to be obnoxious. No matter what the motivation is, Harry does not want to be named to that particular house…"Not Slytherin!" The hat hears Harry's request and honors it, but not before telling Harry that he might be making a mistake, suggesting that the house of Slytherin could help him on his way to greatness. The very fact that Harry has to say over and over his all important two words suggests the possibility that, at least at some level, Harry suspects that he might be cunning or evil, and that he does not want to be. We will revisit this all-important moment at the end of the second book in the series. Suffice it to say, at this moment, that Harry voices a strong desire not to be placed in Slytherin House, and his choice is honored by the Sorting Hat. Rowling has just introduced an idea that will become a key theme in the quest narrative: the idea that our choices matter. They determine the course of our lives.

Soon we meet the potions master, Severus Snape, who is the head of Slytherin House. He will be one of the most important characters in the entire series, continually revealing more and more complex associations. He is the most famous example of the brilliance of Rowling's choice of a limited third person narrative style. All of the

21

novels are written in a third person point of view, but the narrator holds us at arm's length. She limits our perspective to Harry's point of view. In other words, we experience the quest with Harry as the central consciousness. In doing so, she takes us along on the quest, making us think things out with Harry. And, Harry is very wrong about Severus Snape, many times throughout the novels, in spite of many hints that he is much more complex than he might seem. Harry identifies Snape as evil, but the truth is, it is always much more complex than that. People are complex. There is the potential for good and for evil in all of us. Harry does not see even the remote possibility that there could be anything good about Severus Snape. But he is wrong. The most famous illustrations of this, of course, come in the sixth and seventh novels. But we will get to that in time.

In this early novel, Harry feels that Snape hates him, but he does not know why. Snape is the head of the Slytherin house, and therefore seems to favor his own students, but he strikes fear in many of the children's hearts...especially poor Neville, whom Snape continually refers to as an "idiot." The truth is, Snape is not very likable. But, we should pay some attention, at least briefly, to the etymology of his name. First of all, Snape sounds very much like snake, of course, and that works because a snake is the symbol of the Slytherin house, for which Snape is the headmaster. However, his first name ought to catch our attention. Severus sounds very much like "sever the"—so his name becomes "sever the snake." Let us bear that in mind. Right from the beginning, Rowling has given us a pretty powerful hint about his true nature. And there are many other hints to follow, including, and perhaps most important of all, Dumbledore's unfailing patience with him, defense of him, and trust in him. The Harry Potter saga will explore the idea, over and over again, that people are very complex, and Snape is one of the most difficult characters. He seems to have hated Harry's father and his friends, and this bad blood goes back to the days of their childhood. However, he loved Lily Potter, Harry's mother. It will be interesting to watch and see the battle between these two powerful emotions in Snape.

Shortly after this, we meet Madame Hooch, and we see the children get their first flying lesson. Harry defends Neville from a nasty trick played on him by Draco Malfoy, and accidentally discovers that he is a natural born flyer, and here is one of Rowling's most clever little twists. Harry has terrible vision. He can never see very well in the morning until he gets his glasses on, and yet he is a Seeker. Professor Minerva McGonagall discovers Harry's abilities, and Harry becomes the youngest player on the Quidditch teams, representing his house as a Seeker. How perfect for Harry. He is a Seeker in many ways--a seeker of truth and a seeker of the golden snitch on the Quidditch field. The golden snitch is the little golden ball that Harry must try to catch, while dodging the other team's players and nasty balls that are trying to knock him off his broom. The snitch is described by Oliver Wood, Harry's team captain as "very hard to catch because it's so fast and difficult to see"(169). It is pretty clear to us that the snitch is a metaphor for the truth—it too can move very quickly and be very hard to see. But Harry is a persistent, and rather fearless seeker. If we pursue this metaphor a little further, then your Quidditch opponents could represent either people that attempt to conceal the truth or place obstacles in your way as you try to understand the truth. Harry will have to deal with both of these things in the course of his quest, as do we. Once again, Malfoy's trick ends up backfiring on him. He had hoped to get Harry in trouble; instead, he ends up getting Harry noticed for his abilities as a flyer. Malfoy is, to borrow another phrase from Hamlet, "hoisted on his own petard." That is an ammunitions metaphor—it means that the bomb backfires, taking out the bomb maker rather than the intended target. This is not the only time that Malfoy's "bad faith" tricks will backfire on him. Sometimes, it takes a little longer, but in the Potter Quest, right triumphs. At least temporarily, and that is all we can hope for. The story goes on, and as another challenge evolves, another hero will emerge. Again, that is the nature of the human condition.

From whispered hints that they have overheard, Harry, Ron, and Hermione have become convinced that something important is hidden down in the bowels of Hogwarts Castle. Hermione goes home for the Christmas holiday, and she leaves Harry and Ron an assignment—they are to get into the "Restricted Section" of the library, and find out what they can about Nicholas Flamel, whose name they have heard. Harry is on a search when he suddenly hears Snape and the caretaker Filch approaching. He ducks into an abandoned classroom to hide, and comes upon the mysterious Mirror of Erised. This whole incident gives rise to a brilliant and gentle lesson for every reader.

First off, we should notice that the weird word, Erised, is really the word Desire spelled backwards. And that's important. The mirror does not show us a healthy desire. Instead it shows us an unhealthy desire—desire inside out, wrong, jumbled, backwards. Let us explore this idea. As Harry stands before the mirror, transfixed, he sees his family for the first time since he was a baby: "They just looked at him, smiling. And slowly, Harry looked into the faces of the other people in the mirror, and saw other pairs of green eyes like his, other noses, like his, even a little old man who looked as though he had Harry's knobbly knees—Harry was looking at his family, for the first time in his life. The Potters smiled and waved at Harry and he stared hungrily back at them, his hands pressed flat against the glass as though he was hoping to fall right through it and reach them. He had a powerful kind of ache inside him, half joy, half terrible sadness"(209).

We are right at the heart of a very human, very powerful longing here. Anyone who has lost a loved one knows exactly what

25

Rowling is talking about with this powerful ache that is half joy and half terrible sadness. Sometimes, when we have lost a loved one, they seem to come to us in our dreams, and we awaken, wanting to claw our ways back into their presence, back into their arms. But we cannot do it. And neither can Harry. And, Rowling's point is that we must not try to do so. It is an empty longing with dangerous consequences.

However, it is an almost addictive desire. And, night after night, Harry sneaks back to the wondrous, "terrible" mirror. Ron Weasley warns Harry against going back to the mirror. He tells Harry that he just has a bad feeling about it, and his instincts are, at least at this particular moment, very good. When Harry sits rapt in front of the mirror one night, filled with this terrible longing, Dumbledore saves him from himself. He guides Harry to articulate what the mirror shows us: "nothing more or less than the deepest, most desperate desire of our hearts"(213). It is important to pay attention to the diction that Rowling uses in describing this mirror. It is surrounded by words that certainly have an ominous connotation—dark, terrible, deep, desperate. Then, Dumbledore explains to Harry, and to us, why the mirror is dangerous: "This mirror will give us neither knowledge or truth. Men have wasted away before it, entranced by what they have seen, or been driven mad, not knowing if what it shows is real or even possible....It does not do to dwell on dreams and forget to live, remember that"(213-214). In the classic hero quest, the journey and

26

the tasks will sometimes overwhelm the young hero. It is important to give yourself time to rest and to recover, but then, the young hero must get back into action. It is good to dream, but not at the expense of action. And this is exactly what Dumbledore tells young Harry. We cannot dwell on the past at the expense of the present.

Hemingway's novels echo a similar warning. He has an interesting central metaphor that guides his stories—life is a battlefield, and everyone is eventually wounded, either physically or spiritually. This wound, this sacred hurt, causes you to reevaluate everything. Things that were once possible no longer are. The world is forever changed, diminished. Hemingway would say that it is only at that point that a person really becomes interesting, for the question is— how will he or she handle themselves from that point on? Hemingway presents us with the quintessential battle in his first novel, The Sun Also Rises. The protagonist there is Jake Barnes, and he has suffered a wound in the war that has left him unable to have children of his own, or to make love to a woman. Denied this quintessential physical pleasure, and denied the love of the woman of his dreams, how can he go on? The novel is essentially a portrait of Jake as he comes to terms with his loss, and decides to live. He says that he isn't sure that he cares to figure out what life is all about, but he would certainly like to learn how to live in it.

This whole idea is very closely related to what Rowling is

telling us with the Mirror of Erised. We cannot allow ourselves to dwell on that which cannot be. There is an abyss out there that can whisper seductively to any of us—longing for loved ones who have passed beyond our reach. We can drive ourselves crazy if we are not careful, worrying about things we wish we would have said or done differently, when it is all beyond our reach. At some point, we have to trust. We have to turn our faces to the life that lies before us. Treasure the memories of the ones we love, and live the life we have now. In so doing, we honor them. And that is just what Dumbledore teaches Harry here, who learns this important lesson at the ripe old age of eleven. That is one stroke of genius on Rowling's part. She is never condescending. She respects young people. As a careful reader will certainly have noticed, it is Dumbledore's approach too.

This longing to be once again in the presence of our lost loved ones is a seductive desire, a Siren song, and it is an abyss in which we can lose our lives if we are not careful. Still, anyone who has lost a loved one, anyone who still aches from that loss, and hears their voice in the back of their head knows exactly the pull of the Mirror of Erised. At the end of this scene, Dumbledore is really quite stern with Harry, telling him that he is moving the Mirror, and asking Harry not to go looking for it again. He further tells Harry that if he ever runs into it again, he must now be prepared. That sounds like the mirror is an enemy, an adversary of sorts. In fact, it is. The message is clear. Live your life. The rest will take care of itself. In time.

Harry tries to put the mirror out of his mind—it still seems to haunt him, but thankfully, he is distracted by Neville. Malfoy has been making poor Neville's life miserable, in every possible way. When he stumbles into the Gryffindor common room, he has his legs locked together because of a curse that Malfoy sprung on him. Once again, he has not defended himself, and he refuses to tell Professor McGonagall. Ron and Harry speak at some length to Neville, and between the two of them, help him to feel a lot better about himself. Ron tells Neville: "You've got to stand up to him, Neville! He's used to walking all over people, but that's no reason to lie down in front of him and make it easier"(218). He is teaching Neville, and by extension us, a very important lesson here. It is the same lesson that Hamlet articulates in his moment of epiphany in Act 4, scene 5. He suddenly realizes that he has been over thinking everything, and that when a man's honor is on the line, he has got to stand up for himself. Hamlet says, "Rightly to be great is not to stir without great argument, but to find quarrel in a straw when your honor's on the line"(4.4.56-59). It is the same idea that Ron is expressing—no one should fly off the handle at every whim, but you have got to stand up for yourself when your honor is attacked. If you don't, you are already as good as dead. Neville doesn't hear the wisdom of what Ron is saying at that moment. He only cries out that maybe he should not be in Gryffindor,

29

the home of the brave. Harry quietly answers that question, with wisdom he is still struggling to believe himself: "You're worth twelve of Malfoy. The Sorting Hat chose you for Gryffindor, didn't it? And where's Malfoy? In stinking Slytherin"(218). Then, he hands Neville a chocolate frog, having learned the benefits of chocolate when you are hurting spiritually. In earlier chapters, we have seen Harry battle with this idea himself, and experience his own doubts about his right to be in Gryffindor, the home of the brave. So, it is especially poignant that he is able to reassure Neville when he has doubts about his own courage. The Sorting Hat, as we will discover, is right on both counts.

It is quite by accident that Harry and Ron, helping themselves to a chocolate frog, notice that the package includes a Dumbledore card, just like the first one he ever saw. And suddenly, the epiphany happens all at once. Waiting right there on the back of the card, is the information they have been seeking—the fact that Dumbledore had worked on uncovering the secrets of alchemy with his partner, Nicholas Flamel. Often in the stories there comes a moment of accidental discovery—a helpful serendipity that brings a sudden light of understanding where there had only been darkness and confusion. And we often find it in life as well. Isaac Asimov refers to the "Eureka Phenomenon" where we suddenly have a breakthrough when we least expected it. It is as if our minds were working even when we did not know it, and the problem seems to solve itself. This frequently

eureka!

happens in quest literature, where the hero just suddenly figures it out; something that had eluded him becomes suddenly clear. That is what happens here, and Harry and Ron are able to trace the name Nicholas Flamel further. Flamel is the only known maker of a Sorceror's Stone, a "stone that makes gold and stops you from dying"(220). And Harry rightly guesses that this is what is being guarded in the dungeon below the castle.

Harry and Hermione are given a detention for being where they ought not be, and this detention is to be served with Hagrid. In the course of Harry's quest, it often seems like everything happens for a reason, even though that reason may not be readily apparent at the time. Now that is a difficult idea. If we say that everything happens for a reason, then we are talking about fate—not free will. Perhaps we ought to say that almost any turn of events can be a source of more information for us as we pursue our own quest, but we must constantly be willing to make adjustments. At any rate, Hagrid takes them, along with Draco Malfoy, into the forbidden forest at night, where Hagrid is trying to figure out what has been killing unicorns. Here, we meet the first centaurs of the story, and they will prove to be even more important later on.   centaurs

Talking with a centaur is apparently kind of a mind-bending experience. When Hagrid asks Ronan if he has seen anything unusual tonight, Ronan replies, "Mars is bright tonight. Unusually bright"(253).

Centaurs apparently move in different psychic circles than humans, and there is only an uneasy truce between the two groups. Still, since Mars is the god of war, it does seem as if Ronan is warning us of the great battle to come. After thanking Ronan for his "help," they move deeper into the forest, where they come across a terrible thing, a beautiful unicorn slain: "Harry had never seen anything so beautiful and sad. Its long, slender legs were stuck out at odd angles where it had fallen and its mane was spread pearly white on the dark leaves"(256). Several things come to mind because of this striking image. First of all, the unicorn is a classic symbol for Jesus Christ—too beautiful for this world, having almost an ethereal or otherworldly beauty. Here, the unicorn has fallen into a position that is reminiscent of Christ crucified. Suddenly, "out of the shadows, a hooded figure came crawling across the ground like some stalking beast...The cloaked figure reached the unicorn, lowered its head over the wound in the animal's side, and began to drink its blood...Then a pain like he'd never felt before pierced his head; it was as though his scar were on fire"(256). Voldemort, the hooded figure, is closing in on Harry, who cannot even defend himself. Harry collapses, and when he regains consciousness, he is in the care of a new centaur, a younger one whose name is Firenze. How appropriate this imagery too. After Jesus died, he sent the Holy Spirit, who appeared in tongues of flame to the apostles. Harry is one of God's disciples, as are we, whenever we minister to each other. Firenze, whose name suggests fire, might be said to represent, at this moment in the story, the presence of the Holy Spirit. We remember that the Holy Spirit once appeared in tongues of flame to the apostles.

Firenze then explains why the "hooded figure" had attacked the beautiful unicorn: "It is a monstrous thing to slay a unicorn. Only one who has nothing to lose, and everything to gain, would commit such a crime. The blood of a unicorn will keep you alive, even if you are an inch from death, but at a terrible price. You have slain something pure and defenseless to save yourself, and you will have but a half-life, a cursed life, from the moment the blood touches your lips"(258). Harry, with the wisdom and clarity of a child, cannot understand why anyone would want to do such a thing. He says, "If you're going to be cursed forever, death's better, isn't it?"(258). Harry, with these words, illustrates the wisdom of the Book of Psalms: "Out of the mouths of babes and infants, you have drawn a defense against your foes, to silence enemy and avenger"(Psalms 6:3). Sometimes, the wisdom of a child approaches the highest possible wisdom. Certainly, Harry has already made a choice, and it is a choice that clearly separates him from Voldemort. As Harry says, if you are going to be cursed forever, death is better. It really is just that simple. No Faustian bargain ever comes to joy. J. K. Rowling will have a lot to say about death before the quest narrative is completed.

33

Harry comes out of this encounter with a new understanding of the importance of his scar when it burns and with a respect for the centaurs. He believes that his scar hurts when danger is approaching—danger and evil. Harry is now fiercely determined to get down into the dungeon and find the Sorceror's Stone, convinced as he is that Severus Snape is trying to steal the stone to give it to Voldemort. There are many, many times in the quest when Harry, brilliant though he is, gets it wrong. That happens frequently, and, it might even contribute to our feeling of genuine affection for and identification with Harry. We all know what it is like to be very certain, only to find out in time that we were also very wrong. At any rate, this is one of the times when Harry has analyzed things very carefully, and come to an incorrect conclusion.

Harry, Ron, and Hermione slip under the invisibility cloak and set off on this dark journey. Like knights on the Grail Quest, they are presented with a series of tasks and tests…a drooling three headed dog, Devil's Snare, flying keys, and Wizard Chess. When we encounter the scene with the Wizard Chess, we realize that this is Ron's moment to shine, and we, as readers, begin to understand that it is no accident that he is along on this quest. He directs Harry and Hermione through the life size chessboard, knowing that he must call the moves because neither one of them is as good at chess as he is. He sacrifices himself to free Harry up to take the last leg of the journey, knowing that in chess, as in life, "You've got to make some sacrifices!"(283. Let us not even for one minute underestimate the importance of Ron's decision here. As far as he knows, his "death" in the game of wizard chess may really be his death, as far as he knows. And, he is willing to sacrifice his life to help Harry defeat Voldemort, whom they agree is the embodiment of evil. As much as this is Harry's story, it is always Ron's and Hermione's too. Throughout the quest we will realize, time and again, that the friendship these three young people share is sacred. It takes all three of them, supported by a whole host of other good and brave people, to finally defeat Voldemort.

When Harry gets down into the dungeon, he encounters the odd Professor Quirrell, whom he had earlier disregarded as weak and ineffective. Now, Quirrell reveals to us that he is quite literally possessed by Voldemort, who has taken over his body and whose serpent-like face is concealed beneath his turban. And here, in the dungeon, they come face to face with the Mirror of Erised, with which Harry has had some experience. Harry cleverly tries to use the mirror to see himself finding the stone, without Quirrell knowing what he is up to. It is what he wants most at that moment, and that is what the mirror shows him. And it works. Harry then bravely demands the right to speak face to face with his enemy, like a knight of old. Voldemort is also desirous of speaking with Harry, arrogantly believing that he is about to kill his he reveals his terrible snake like face and hisses at Harry, and we hear the voice of evil incarnate: "How touching…I always value bravery… Yes, boy, your parents were brave…I killed your father first, and he put up a courageous fight…but your mother needn't have died…she was trying to protect you…Now give me the Stone unless you want her to have died in vain"(294). Instead of debilitating and unmanning Harry, this statement gives him strength. This testimony of his parents' love, even from the mouth of evil, emboldens and strengthens Harry, as only love can do. Although Voldemort orders Quirrell to grab Harry, Quirrell finds that he cannot lay a hand upon him. Instead, Harry touches the weird professor's face, as if by accident or instinct, and the half-man crumbles at his feet, screaming in pain. The fight nearly costs Harry his life, a second time, but once again, love triumphs. It takes us a while to understand that love is the power that was working here, but Dumbledore will help us to understand this idea.

Here, in the closing pages of this chapter, we get three very important lessons and explanations from Dumbledore. First of all, when Harry hesitates to use Voldemort's name, Dumbledore says, "Always use the proper name for things. Fear of a name increases fear of the thing itself"(298). This is a lesson that Harry will hold dear for the rest of the battle. And it is an important lesson. Let us call evil what it is. Voldemort's name comes from the Latin for "turn to evil." Turn to death. Let us call it what it is. And then, turn away from it.

Secondly, Harry asks Dumbledore to tell him the truth

about his past, and Dumbledore has these gentle words of caution: "The truth…it is a beautiful and terrible thing, and should therefore be treated with great caution"(298).   Caution…and reverence. Throughout the quest, and throughout our lives, we are in pursuit of the Truth. And we ought to be, but it is not an easy thing. The quest requires patience and perseverance. That is an undervalued quality in our time—perseverance. It takes a brave heart to soldier on when you are exhausted, to keep going, to do the next thing, to do the right thing, and to trust that it will all make sense in the end. Our modern world often fails to recognize the importance of this kind of courage. Not J. K. Rowling. She values persistence--dogged persistence. She values admitting when you are wrong, correcting your direction, and trudging bravely on, even through the darkness. And so should we.

Finally, this first little book closes with some of the most important words in the whole Potter quest. Harry asks Dumbledore why Quirrell could not touch him. And Dumbledore says, "Your mother died to save you. If there is one thing Voldemort cannot understand, it is love. He didn't realize that love as powerful as your mother's for you leaves its own mark. Not a scar, no visible sign perhaps….but, to have been loved so deeply, even though the person who loved us is gone, will give us some protection forever. It is in your very skin. Quirrell, full of hatred, greed, and ambition, sharing his soul with Voldemort, could not touch you for this reason. It was agony to touch a person marked by something so good"(299).

We are right at the heart of it here. In this very early book, we learn something very important--if we are listening. Love is the most powerful magic of all. It is so easy to run right by that idea and miss the brilliance. Love is the most powerful magic of all. And we are all capable of giving and receiving it. It is God's greatest gift. It is why He walked among us. And today—we are God's hands and feet and mouth and eyes. We are the possibility of love. And once you have been loved like that, you are marked with it forever. Like Harry is marked with James and Lily Potter's love. Like we are all marked with the love of someone.   And we have the power to give and to receive this mark of love.

This is old magic—the most powerful kind. And it is so simple that it is easy to not give it the high regard, the solemnity it deserves. But it is very, very powerful stuff. Listen to St. Paul on love: "Love is patient and kind; love is not jealous or boastful; it is not arrogant or rude. Love does not insist on its own way; it is not irritable or resentful; it does not rejoice at wrong; but rejoices in the right. Love bears all things, believes all things, hopes all things, endures all things. As for prophecies, they will pass away…as for knowledge, it will pass away. For our knowledge is imperfect and our prophecy is imperfect, but when the perfect comes, the imperfect will pass away. When I was a child, I spoke like a child, I thought like a child, I reasoned like a child;

38

when I became a man, I gave up childish ways. For now we see in a glass darkly, but then face to face. Now I know in part; then I shall understand fully, even as I have been fully understood. So faith, hope, love abide these three; but the greatest of these is love"(I Corinthians 13: 4-13). The greatest virtue is the greatest magic—love. We are marked with love. Not with a scar, but with a power from within, something so strong that it changes everything forever. Lily gave her life for Harry. That is love. And there is no dark magic that can ever defeat that. Love will triumph over hatred and evil, and that is the lesson of the Potter quest. And we hear that, very clearly, in this first book. We will come back to this idea over and over again. As we should.

And, ever so quietly, Dumbledore says another amazing thing. He explains to Harry that the Sorceror's Stone is not such a wonderful thing after all. We should not try to live forever in this earthly incarnation; that is not the way it is supposed to be. And then he adds, "After all, to the well-organized mind, death is but the next great adventure"(297). Well, now we have another definition of faith--an unconventional one for sure. Faith is having a well-organized mind. We have been told this before. Death is just a moment, a transition to the next life. We cannot know, not yet and not now, what that next great adventure will hold, but we can trust that it will be wonderful. We have been told that every tear will be wiped away: "And I saw the

holy city, new Jerusalem, coming down out of heaven from God...
and God himself will be with his people; he will wipe away every tear
from their eyes, and death shall be no more, neither shall there be
mourning no crying nor pain any more, for the former things have
passed away"(Revelation 21:2-4). We walk by faith in our earthly
quest. We must walk by faith. We cannot know the answers to some
of the questions that burn deep in our hearts. We do the best we can,
we try to keep our hearts centered on the present, and continue on
our quest.

The first book closes shortly after this wonderful conversation
between Harry and Dumbledore, with a change in the dining hall
decorations as final points are awarded, and the Gryffindors claim the
House Cup. Harry goes to bed on that final night at Hogwarts aware
that he is very happy, happier than he has ever been. And there's
a simple little bit of wisdom in that too. The secret to happiness is
to take the time to realize that you are happy when you have that
opportunity. Learn to be satisfied with small victories, know that
you are loved, know that you are doing the best you can, and that is
enough.

There is a rather lengthy short story written by Stephen Crane
called "The Open Boat." It makes an interesting analogy to life for us.
Crane writes: "A singular disadvantage of the sea lies in the fact that
after successfully surmounting one wave you discover that there is

another behind it just as important and just as nervously anxious to do something effective in the way of swamping boats"(Crane 58). This is a very apt metaphor for life. Borrowing a little from Nietzsche and Schopenhauer here, let us pursue the imagery. [Each of us is in our own little boat, from the moment we are born. We are sailing along on this unpredictable body of water, which is sometimes sun dappled and calm and sometimes raging, threatening to overturn our boat at any moment. We must steer our craft the best we can, and even then there are no guarantees. And when we survive one wave, we will probably find another one coming for us. Still, every now and then, there will be moments of relative calm--what the poet of the Psalms calls a season of grace. And when those moments come, we ought to take time to realize that we are in the midst of one of those beautiful seasons of grace, or periods of calm, lift our faces to the sun, feel the warm wind on our backs, and just breathe. For the storm will come again—that is for certain. Still, we have this moment.]

And Harry Potter seems to understand this idea. At the close of this first novel, he takes time to realize, to recognize, that he is happy. As should we. For as Feste says at the close of William Shakespeare's play entitled Twelfth Night, "the rain it raineth every day"(5.1). On any given day, at any moment, it is raining for someone. And yet, we may be having our moment in the sun. That is the beauty and the mystery of life. And so, for a moment, Harry has a season of grace. He has held

our journey . . .

the powers of darkness at bay, and he arrives at King's Cross Station, momentarily safe and sound.

In conclusion then, the first book introduces us to the major characters in the quest narrative, and it introduces the very important idea that the most powerful magic of all is love. Throughout the entire quest, this idea is sacred.

Harry Potter and The Chamber of Secrets

Evil is a seductive and powerful presence. The stakes are higher from here on in, and the quest gets ever more dangerous. As this second novel opens, Harry is back at the Dursley residence, suffering through an interminable summer, believing that all of his Hogwarts friends have forgotten him. In the early chapters, we meet Dobby, the house elf who adores Harry Potter. House elves are frequently treated as filth by members of the wizarding world. But not by Harry. In spite of Dobby's annoying tactics that often get Harry into trouble, Harry treats him as an equal. It never occurs to Harry to treat him any other way. Harry has a remarkable and refreshing innocence about him— he has no prejudices or condescension—and treats every person and creature with respect. This attitude will eventually play a huge role in defeating Voldemort in book seven. Dobby tries, unsuccessfully, to keep Harry from returning to Hogwarts because he is afraid that Harry will be hurt there. They are working at cross-purposes here because there is nothing Harry wants more than to get back there.

Luckily, Harry is rescued from the horrible Dursleys, who are certainly not representative of most Muggles, by Fred, George, and Ron Weasley. They are able to accomplish this in spite of Dobby's best efforts to prevent Harry from leaving Privet

Drive. The Weasley men arrive for Harry in a flying Ford—a Muggle car that has been bewitched by their father. They are equally puzzled about what might have been motivating Dobby's strange behavior, but in passing, Fred tells us something that will be very important later on: House elves have got powerful magic of their own. And it is different from witch and wizard magic; different rules apply and they have certain powers that will prove very helpful to Harry in his quest. The Weasley men hustle Harry off to the Burrow, the most beautifully dilapidated house Harry has ever seen. The Burrow is practically bursting with magic, and everything about it fascinates Harry, but what makes it the most wonderful place he has ever seen is that everybody there seems to like him. We see time and again how smart J. K. Rowling is. What makes a house beautiful is the presence of love.

When the students are buying their schoolbooks, they meet the new Defense Against the Dark Arts teacher, Gilderoy Lockhart. It is pretty clear that J. K. Rowling is having some fun with names here. Gilderoy is a "gilded" fool, in love with his own appearance. He gives the impression that he is full of knowledge and courage, but he is not. He is not true gold; he is gilded metal, a cheap imitation of the real thing. And certainly, like Narcissus of old, his "heart" is "locked" on his own importance. He will provide a good deal of comic relief

44

in the course of this second novel. When he meets Harry, Lockhart immediately fastens on him, hoping to augment his own stardom by linking himself up with Harry. It is interesting to note that both Harry and Ron smell a rat as far as Gilderoy is concerned, right from the beginning. On the other hand, the women—Hermione, Ginny, and even Mrs. Weasley—are all smitten. It is one of the few times where Hermione is a bad judge of character, and this makes her all the more human and real to her readers. Many women have been deceived by an attractive outside. However, when push comes to shove, Lockhart shows his true colors, and Hermione will eventually wonder how she could have ever been so deceived. Ah! It happens.

The last month of summer goes sailing by, and since Harry is at the Burrow, it is the happiest time of his life. When it comes time to leave for school, Harry is again thwarted by Dobby, who is trying to protect Harry from the danger that most assuredly awaits him at Hogwarts. However, in doing so, he causes Harry a great deal of difficulty. This time, Ron is along for the ride, and the two of them find themselves confronting a sealed barrier at Platform 9 and ¾. So, the boys hop in the flying car and begin their journey to Hogwarts, under their own power. What seems like a great adventure soon turns into drudgery, and then into danger as they crash into the notorious Whomping Willow, a tree that guards an important portal. The willow clobbers the poor magical car, which dumps the boys unceremoniously on the lawn, and then escapes into the Forbidden Forest. In their tumble, Ron's wand is broken, and this event will have some interesting and comical consequences. Ron knows that he is going to be in trouble with his parents for using the car without their permission, but at least they are safely back at Hogwarts. The car will appear later in the novel, at just the right moment. As we have said before, in the Potter saga, and maybe in life too, sometimes things happen for a reason, a reason which often eludes us at the time.

Having survived a scolding from Dumbledore and Snape, the young students begin their classes. There, we get to see Gilderoy Lockhart in action. First, Gilderoy struts around his classroom, flashing his award-winning smile at his students, charming the girls, and bragging about his accomplishments. Then, he unleashes their first classroom experiment, by setting free a gaggle of Cornish pixies, which prove to be devilishly difficult to recapture—so difficult that Lockhart exits the room rather hurriedly, leaving the kids to fend for themselves. We get our first hint that we are looking at a confirmed coward. When Hermione tries to defend him, having read his books about what he has supposedly done, Ron points out to her that there is a difference between what a person does and what a person says he has done. Amen to that.

Harry is joyfully looking forward to the new Quidditch season, but the stakes are definitely going to be higher this year. The

Slytherin team announces that they have a new seeker, and it is Draco Malfoy. This announcement intensifies the competition between Harry and Draco, who will meet on the Quidditch field in a most highly anticipated match. It seems that Draco's father has bought his son's way on to the team, by providing the entire Slytherin team with expensive new brooms. You could almost feel sorry for Draco sometimes. Almost. When Draco snidely refers to Hermione as a "mudblood," which is a pejorative term referring to the fact that her parents are Muggles (non magical people), Ron tries to defend her. It is hard to say what would be an equivalent in our terminology for the term mudblood. Certainly, it would be equivalent to a racial or an ethnic slur. Suffice it to say that using the term indicates that you think you are better than someone else, just because of your bloodlines. The underlying assumption of the use of the term involves a terrible hubris. It could be said that Draco Malfoy, with all of his false pride, is "gilded" too. He believes that the purity of his blood makes him superior in personal worth, skill, and power. However, none of this is true. On many different occasions, he proves himself to be a coward and a follower. Again, it is not our abilities that determine what we will be; it is our choices. At any rate, Ron whips out his broken wand, tries to defend Hermione, and the wand backfires, sending Ron sprawling on the grass, belching out slugs. This broken wand will backfire again, with comical consequences, later on. Immediately thereafter, Harry and Ron are cornered by Professor McGonagall, who says that they must serve detentions that evening. For his detention, Harry will be helping Gilderoy Lockhart answer his fan mail.

Poor Harry. The hours crawl by as slowly as snails, or slugs. Lockhart spends the time telling Harry how wonderful he is, and he is fond of saying, (as though it makes any sense at all) that "Celebrity is as celebrity does"(120). What nonsense! It is no small wonder that Harry tunes his voice out. However, when he does so, a weird thing happens. He picks up the presence of a strange hissing voice, whispering, "Come to me…let me rip you…let me tear you…let me kill you"(120). Harry is understandably terrified, but Lockhart can hear nothing. Although Harry doesn't understand what has just happened, we, as readers, wonder if we have heard the voice of the monster of the Chamber of Secrets for the first time.

The next day, Harry politely listens to Nearly Headless Nick's sad story, about how he cannot be admitted to the Headless Horseman's Hunt because he is not exactly headless. No matter how silly this discussion might seem to us, there is an important lesson underneath it all. Harry listens respectfully to Nick's story. Although he has a lot of other things on his mind, and troubles of his own, and even though Nick kind of gives him the creeps, he listens and sympathizes. He stops what he is doing, turns his full attention to Nick, and listens. This behavior is something that endears Harry to many people along his journey. And perhaps he knows that he should do this for others because it is important to him too. One of the things that Harry treasures most about the Weasley family is the feeling that everybody there likes him, cares about him. We all crave having someone think we are special, having someone to be a witness to the moments of our lives, someone to share our secret hopes and disappointments with, someone to sit quietly with, not even having to speak. Harry understands this, and he also understands the obligations of friendship. The sacredness of true friendship will be one of the most important and universally applicable lessons of the quest. We will keep an eye on this very important theme. So, when Nick asks Harry to come to his Deathday Party, Harry says he will be there, even though it might be the very last thing he feels like doing. When the day comes, and Harry considers the possibility of missing the event, Hermione reminds him that a promise is a promise. So, she and Ron accompany Harry to this strange little party. Hermione and Ron also clearly understand the obligations of friendship.

The three of them, filled with apprehension and a longing to be anywhere but there, walk into a room full of ghosts. They are careful not to walk through anyone, because doing so feels like stepping into an ice cold shower. Besides that, they suspect it might be bad manners, or at least disrespectful. It is here, however, that they meet Moaning Myrtle, who proves to be very important later in the story on several occasions. Having fulfilled their obligation to Nick, they start off to the dining hall and the Halloween feast, and once again Harry hears the hissing voice: "rip...tear...kill...sooo hungry...for so long...kill...time to kill"(137). He stops dead in his tracks, begging Ron and Hermione to listen with him. The voice is moving, growing fainter and fainter, but he can still hear it. Here we learn that neither Ron nor Hermione can hear this hissing voice, and we get our first hint that it may be parseltongue. Suddenly, they come upon a blood chilling sight—in letters four feet high these terrifying words are scrawled on the wall: "THE CHAMBER OF SECRETS HAS BEEN OPENED. ENEMIES OF THE HEIR, BEWARE"(138). Not only that, Mrs. Norris, who is the beloved cat of Filch, the bad-tempered caretaker of Hogwarts, has been petrified. Filch quickly accuses Harry of the deed, and Snape is eager to jump on the bandwagon. He is stopped by Dumbledore who insists that Harry is innocent until proven guilty, and Harry is dismissed for the night. Before they go to bed, Harry asks Ron and Hermione if he should tell Dumbledore about the voice he heard, and Ron advises against it. He says, "Hearing voices no one else can hear isn't a good sign, even in the wizarding world"(145). Harry learns, very clearly here, that no one else can hear this hissing voice. This fact gives him pause, and he cannot as yet make any sense of it. It is another dark secret that haunts him and troubles him when he is alone with his thoughts.

The next day, during History of Magic, taught by a ghost

named Professor Binns, Hermione asks him for an explanation of the Chamber of Secrets. Although he seems very skeptical of the whole thing, he answers her question as best he can, surprised to find his usually bored students startled into attention. Professor Binns tells the children that the Chamber of Secrets was supposedly built by Salazar Slytherin, one of the four founders of the school. He believed that only pure blood witches and wizards should be taught magic at the school. According to legend, when the true heir of Slytherin arrives at Hogwarts, he will be able to unseal the chamber, set the monster free who is imprisoned within, and purge the school of those who are unworthy to study magic—that is, anyone descended from Muggles. As history has shown us, inbreeding has been tried in many different cultures, with disastrous results. J. K. Rowling is cleverly making us realize, once again, the folly of this kind of thinking.

After the students hear this " legend," Harry is once again haunted by self-doubts. He remembers that the Sorting Hat had considered the possibility of putting him in Slytherin House. Harry had already heard the reputation of Slytherin House for turning out wizards connected to Dark Magic, and had desperately thought to himself "Not Slytherin!!" He has already comforted Neville with the importance of this decision, as Dumbledore had comforted him. However, it is such an important idea, it bears repeating. It is not our abilities that make us what we are—it is our choices. We have free will,

☀ choices > abilities ☀

and we should choose to do what is good, as best we understand it.

Desperate for more information, and convinced that Draco knows something because of his smug way of strutting around the castle, sure of his pureblood status, they decide to use some Polyjuice potion to transform their appearances into three Slytherins so they can get into the Slytherin common room and question Draco. Hermione starts concocting the potion although Ron professes his skepticism about the wisdom of the plan.

While it is brewing, we are treated to the big quidditch scene of the novel, and here we encounter the rogue bludger, a ball that has had a spell put on it, and which therefore is determined to attack Harry. Draco Malfoy gets too caught up in belittling Harry to focus on his job as seeker. His pride and self-assurance have gone unchecked once again; this time it costs him the game. It will cost him much more later on. In contrast, Harry has a broken arm and a rogue bludger chasing him; yet, in spite of this, he does not lose his focus and does all he can to win the game, that is, to catch the snitch. Throughout the quest, Harry faces terrible challenges and setbacks, but he usually does not surrender to pain or self-pity, and he keeps doing what he needs to do to emerge victorious. Again, we are reminded that the snitch may be a metaphor for the truth. Harry is a seeker of truth, and it often seems to be just out of reach. Life is filled with small victories and defeats, like goals for and against us, but you truly are victorious when you understand the truth, even a small portion of it. Plato argued that truth is always ultimately good. That too is an interesting idea.

The match ends with Harry, passed out on the turf from pain, still clutching the snitch in his good hand, and Professor Gilderoy Lockhart once again proving his ineptitude by stupidly insisting he can mend Harry's arm. Although Harry tries to stop him, Lockhart persists, and ends up removing all the bones from Harry's arm instead of mending them. That night, as Harry lies alone in the hospital, with Madame Pomfrey's potion for regrowing bones slowly working, Dobby shows up and confesses that he had set the bludger on Harry, trying once again to warn him away from Hogwarts. Harry barely keeps his temper in check this time, telling Dobby that his love and friendship are going to kill him if he is not careful. Later that night, as Harry lies awake in pain, another patient arrives in the hospital. Poor little Colin Creevey, the youngster who so adores Harry, is carried in, and he has been petrified. Dumbledore sadly says that this proves that the chamber is indeed open, and Harry feels a chill run through his whole body. We do not understand the connection between victims being petrified and the chamber, but we soon will.

Because of the increased threat level, the professors decide to start a "dueling club," so that the students can practice their defensive skills. Perhaps this is the precursor to the much more important Dumbledore's Army that we will see in the fifth book. The students are all very excited about this idea until, much to their dismay, they see the pompous Gilderoy Lockhart stride proudly on to the stage. Dressed in fancy robes of plum velvet, gilded as ever, and foolish as ever, he addresses the young students, twinkling his eyes and flirting with himself. His opponent in the practice match is none other than Severus Snape, and this gives the duel some kind of an interest factor for the observers.   Ron fantasizes about the possibility of the two of them finishing each other off, Lockhart teasingly promises not to hurt Snape too much, and the duel begins. It is incredibly stupid for Lockhart to get into the ring with Snape because in his secret heart of hearts, he knows he is way out of his depth here. So, of course, Snape easily blasts Lockhart off of his feet with the disarming charm of "Expelliarmus!" which we students of the Potter quest instantly recognize as Harry's signature move. Even at this early point in the series, J. K. Rowling is subtly suggesting a link between Snape and Harry, a link that each of them would patently reject, if suggested to them at this moment in their lives. They will come to this awareness and make peace with it eventually.

The scene builds to its highly anticipated climax, a "practice" duel between Draco and Harry. As they take the stage together, Snape whispers some advice about a spell that would be useful for Draco to use, who smirks and calls out "Serpensortia!" He doesn't even wait until the count of three, thereby cheating Harry of a fair chance in the fight. A huge black snake explodes out of his wand, and Draco enjoys watching the terrified look on Harry's face as it heads right for him. As readers, we start to wonder if Draco might be the true heir of Slytherin. Young though he is, we notice how quickly he has summoned a gigantic snake, which is the mascot for the Slytherin House. However, what happens next is even more important. As the snake suddenly turns his attention to Justin Finch-Fletchley, Harry moves to defend him, and in so doing, he speaks to the snake, telling it to move away from Justin. Without knowing that he is doing so, he is speaking parseltongue. Everyone is astonished; most are also frightened. Could Harry be the heir to Slytherin? Everybody knows that Salazar Slytherin was a parselmouth, and that is a very rare gift—and rather a dark one, at that. This incident gives us an important insight. We see how a presumed dark power can be used for good. Being a parselmouth is a quality typically associated with dark wizards, but here, it is used for good, not for evil. Once again, it comes down to choices, not abilities.

Nonetheless, after this rather public display of his ability to speak parseltongue, even Ron and Hermione regard him with suspicion, and Harry finds himself once again wracked with doubts about his identity, and his right to be a true Gryffindor. Harry wonders how in the world he can speak a different language when he does not even know that he is doing it. In time, we will get our answer to that question—but not yet. Harry finds himself surrounded by classmates who are now regarding him with a wary eye, and a couple days later, the monster of the chamber attacks two more victims—Justin Finch-Fletchley and Nearly Headless Nick! Not even ghosts are safe from the petrifying attacks, and the castle is in an uproar!

When the attack is discovered, and Harry is found nearby, Professor McGonagall wastes no time at all. She ushers Harry up to Dumbledore's office, and we are given our first glimpse of the inner sanctum of the wonderful Albus Dumbledore, who could be said to represent the aging Fisher King of the Grail quest. Albus Dumbledore's name translates roughly to white bumblebee. White is a color used for the imagery of resurrection, and J. K. Rowling has told us in an interview that she chose bumblebee because she pictures Dumbledore humming happily to himself, left to his own devices. Certainly, Dumbledore is in tune with the music of life, and this seems to be an apt metaphor for him.

In the Grail Quest, the whole journey begins with the Fisher King. He is, according to legend, a descendant of one of the guardians of the Holy Grail. Now, there are many different interpretations as to what the Grail is. Some say it is the royal blood, and therefore, by extension, the Eucharist which we can receive into our hearts and bodies at every Mass. The most popular legend has it that the Grail is either the chalice or the platter used at the Last Supper, used by Jesus Christ himself to serve the bread and wine to his apostles on that final

56

night on earth. After Jesus was crucified, the Grail was supposedly taken by Joseph of Arimithea to a secret hiding place, about which there is still a good deal of dispute. One version of the story suggests that eventually the Grail made its way to England, where it is still hidden. Perhaps for our purposes here, it is most important to understand that the Grail is much more important as a symbol than as an actual object, and what it symbolizes is God's grace.

According to the classic legend of the Grail Quest, the Fisher King has been grievously wounded; often the wound is thought to be in the area of his groin, because that is the seat of his seed and therefore new life. Because of this wound, he is suffering, and his impotence renders his homeland impotent as well. The people are suffering as they see their land turned into a wasteland, and the Fisher King commissions several young and noble knights, more powerful and better warriors than he, to go on a quest to recover the Holy Grail. If the Grail can be recovered, the land will be healed, or so he thinks. It is easy to see the link to Albus Dumbledore. Dumbledore was once a great warrior himself, and he is still a brilliant man, but his time on earth is coming to a close, and he knows it. In the course of the Potter quest, he will be an adviser to Harry, and he will eventually pass the torch to his young disciple.

It is important not to press this analogy too far, because if we do, we will compromise the integrity of both the Grail lore and the

57

Potter saga. However, if we can let the imagery echo somewhere in the back of our heads, it can enrich our reading of the Harry Potter novels. Handled in this way, the following scene becomes even richer. Let us take a look at chapter twelve of The Chamber of Secrets. The first thing Harry really notices in Dumbledore's amazing office is the old Sorting Hat. It seems to guess the nature of Harry's doubts, and it reaffirms that it was right in suggesting that Harry would have done well in the Slytherin House. And just as determinedly, Harry reaffirms his insistence on Gryffindor. Again, we are reminded of Dumbledore's wise words. Then, all of a sudden, Dumbledore's phoenix bursts into flames. Surrounded by disasters, Harry gasps an apology to Dumbledore, saying that he could not save the poor bird. Dumbledore smiles and says, "About time, too. He's been looking dreadful for days; I've been telling him to get a move on"(207). He goes on to explain, when Harry expresses astonishment, "Fawkes is a phoenix, Harry. Phoenixes burst into flame when it is time for them to die and are reborn from the ashes...Fascinating creatures, phoenixes. They can carry immensely heavy loads, their tears have healing powers, and they make highly faithful pets"(207). With these words, J. K. Rowling is giving us a good deal of resurrection imagery. Furthermore, she suggests a connection between people and phoenixes.

First of all, we are told that phoenixes can carry immensely heavy loads. This ability will, of course, be very important in one of the closing scenes of the novel. However, we start to suspect that J.K. Rowling is telling us something more. We are all phoenixes. We can carry immensely heavy loads. There is nothing more wonderful and resilient than the human spirit. Every single one of us has survived days when we did not think we could take another step, so burdened were we with grief, or we have seen someone else miraculously do this. Every single one of us has witnessed the quiet acts of courage that ordinary, anonymous people do every day, not because of any recognition they will receive, just because it is the right thing to do. That is not to say that all people behave in this way all of the time, sadly. But we can and we do, on many occasions. We are all potentially phoenixes.

Secondly, we are told that the tears of a phoenix have healing powers. Although this will quite literally be brought into play in the amazing scene that is coming down in the chamber, again, we are working on multiple levels. I am convinced that tears are sacred— that they are, in effect, a kind of holy water. They come from a source deep down within us, a place beyond words. In sorrow, there is the potential for learning. Think of the last time you were privileged enough to witness someone crying for the loss of a loved one, and you will know what I mean. Tears are involuntary, and they spring from deep within us, in that place that goes even deeper than language or reason. They communicate the power of hurt much more eloquently than any speech can. Next time you see someone crying, think of this. Tears have healing powers. They can, in time, bring the person who is hurting closer to healing, and for those of us who witness someone weeping, we ought to be humbled. To be alive and human is a difficult thing, a quest that is sometimes overwhelming. But we dry our tears, and we soldier on. There is great nobility of spirit in that decision.

Thirdly, we are told that phoenixes make highly faithful pets. Again, we have the potential to be like phoenixes. We can be very faithful. If we are true to our promises, we will be faithful to the people who have a right to our love and respect. If we stray from that faithfulness, we most often hasten our own pain. Finally, we re reminded that phoenixes rise from their own ashes, reborn. This is, of course, very powerful Christian imagery. Over and over again, Jesus spoke of the promise of resurrection: "Truly, truly, I say to you, he who hears my word and believes Him who sent me, has eternal life; he does not come to judgment, but has passed from death to life"(John 5:24). This imagery of resurrection is at the very heart of the Christian religion; in fact, it is at the heart of most religions. There is something about us that is eternal. This life is a time of trials and tribulations. It is a series of tests, a quest or a journey, and we will pass through death into life. The Potter quest is underscored with this powerful imagery.

Although Dumbledore asks Harry if there is anything Harry would like to confide in him, Harry declines, therefore not seeking help with his worries about the hissing voice. A couple days later, the polyjuice potion is ready, and the three young warriors decide to try out their ruse, to get into the Slytherin common room and question Draco Malfoy about the chamber of secrets. Of course, there is the awkward mishap with the potion, and Hermione turns herself into a catwoman, so Harry and Ron go on alone. There they are able to draw Draco into a conversation where he, as he usually does, speaks disrespectfully of Dumbledore and Arthur Weasley, both of whom, to his disgust, love Muggles. It is important to notice that two of the wisest people in the whole quest story love Muggles. No question about it.

When Draco smugly expresses his hope that Hermione Granger will be the next Muggle to be attacked by the monster of the chamber, Harry can scarcely control Ron, and they almost blow their disguises as the loathsome Crabbe and Goyle. While Hermione is healing up from her cat features, Harry makes a visit to the girls' bathroom where the ghost named Moaning Myrtle has taken up residence. Harry always treats her politely and patiently, in spite of her annoying propensity for whining dramatically. And this time, he picks up some very important information. Someone had tried to flush a diary away, and Moaning Myrtle shows it to Harry and Ron. Ron instinctively draws back from the thing, but Harry is mysteriously drawn toward it. Again, we notice that J. K. Rowling is reminding us that we all have the potential for good and for evil, and that there are some occasions when evil can be very seductive. We are all human and therefore flawed. We can all be tempted, and so can Harry. He picks the diary up and discovers that the little book is fifty years old, and that it once belonged to a person named T. M. Riddle. And now, we have made physical contact with Lord Voldemort.

Although Ron urges Harry to throw the thing away, or let it lie, Harry pockets it. He cannot quite explain his fascination with it, but right away, he finds himself strangely attracted to it, as if T. M. Riddle might have been a friend from long ago. One night, Harry sits in bed with the diary, and driven by some kind of instinct, writes in the diary. Instantly, the thing writes back to him—and Harry has opened the door to the chamber of secrets the diary holds. The diary's voice is seductive, a kind of Siren song whispering to Harry of forbidden knowledge. When the diary offers to show Harry an important memory about the chamber, Harry gives his permission, and immediately finds himself whirling through time and space, back fifty hears ago. Harry witnesses a scene between a wizard who was then the Headmaster at Hogwarts, Professor Dippet, and the young Tom Riddle, whom Harry admits looks quite a bit like Harry himself. And the similarities don't stop there. Tom Riddle is also an orphan.

Then, Riddle shows Harry a scene that suggests that Harry's dear friend Hagrid may have been the one that opened the chamber of secrets fifty years ago. Harry is saddened and worried by this suggestion, and he "half wished he hadn't found out how to work Riddle's diary"(249). The next day, he returns to his room to find that it has been searched, and the diary is gone.

We are given a short reprieve with a quidditch match, but just before the match, Harry hears the hissing voice again. This time, Hermione lights up, says she has just figured something out, and disappears to the library, which she believes to be the keeper of all human knowledge. Harry and Ron shrug their shoulders at her and go to the match. As Harry and the Gryffindors are ready to take the field, Professor McGonagall's voice comes on the magical public address system, announcing that the match has been cancelled, and that Harry and Ron should report to her immediately. She escorts them to the hospital wing where Hermione lies, petrified. But not dead.

Harry and Ron, desperate to do something, take off to see Hagrid and find out the truth of what happened so long ago. There, they are witnesses to a scene including Hagrid, Dumbledore, Lucius Malfoy, and Cornelius Fudge, the Minister of Magic. Malfoy wants Dumbledore fired, calling him incompetent and incapable of protecting the students of Hogwarts. Dumbledore seems unfazed by his threats and accusations, and although he is looking at Malfoy, he seems to be speaking to Harry and Ron, who are cowering nearby, concealed by the invisibility cloak. He says, rather pointedly: "You will find that I will only truly have left this school when none here are loyal to me. You will also find that help will always be given at Hogwarts to those who ask for it"(264). Once again, we hear a strong echo of an important passage in the Bible. In teaching his disciples, Jesus has this to say: "Ask, and it will be given to you; seek, and you will find. Knock, and it will be opened to you. For everyone who asks receives, and he who seeks finds, and to him who knocks, it will be opened"(Matthew 7:7-8). We receive two important messages here—help will always be given if you ask for it. Seek and you will find. The quest goes on. We are never truly alone. And, even more important than that—our loved ones never really leave us. Dumbledore says he will only be gone when no one at Hogwarts is loyal to him. Think about that. If you are missing someone you loved and lost, remember this. As long as you hold him or her in your heart, as long as you are loyal to them, they are with you. Keep their picture nearby. Talk to them when you are on a long walk. Know that they can hear you and they are near you. As long as your heart is loyal, they are near you. In many ways, this idea can be kind of empowering. They will come to you if you call, whenever you call. You have to train yourself to listen more closely. You will hear their answers to our pleading, but it may not come in the way you expect it. Consider the possibility of guardian angels. Consider the possibility that they are speaking to you through someone you meet in the course of the day. Listen more closely. Ask for help. Our loved ones never leave us. Remember—your tears are sacred. Do the best you can, and be true to the code of what you know to be right. You are not alone on your journey, your quest.

In the scene in the shack, both Dumbledore and Hagrid had said strange things before being taken into custody by Fudge and Malfoy. We have spoken about what Dumbledore had said, and now we turn our attention to a hint that Hagrid left for Harry. He told him that if he wanted to know what was going on in the chamber, all he had to do was follow the spiders. Oddly enough, later that day, Harry notices a long parade of spiders seemingly bound for some destination. This sight is less than thrilling to Ron, since he suffers from arachnophobia, but he goes with Harry, reluctantly following the spiders with Harry into the Forbidden Forest. When Ron expresses his fear of the forest, saying that it contains many evil things, Harry reminds him that the forest also contains unicorns and centaurs. There is a lesson here for us. Even in the midst of evil, beauty and innocence can be found. You just have to be open to the possibility.

Deep in the forest, they come upon a colony of spiders ruled by their king, the mighty Aragog. Fearfully, Harry asks him if he can tell them about the chamber of secrets. Oddly enough, Aragog knows quite a bit about it. He tells Harry that Hagrid was wrongly accused of having opened the chamber, that he is innocent. He tells him further that Hagrid saved his life, saved him from the monster that haunts the chamber, a monster which he describes for Harry: "The thing that lives in the castle…is an ancient creature we spiders fear above all others. Well do I remember how I pleaded with Hagrid to let me go, when I sensed the beast moving about the school…We do not speak of it! We do not name it!"(278). Interestingly, we hear in those words an echo of the terms often used for Voldemort, and we are therefore prepared for the connection between the two. It is not very specific information, but Aragog's words impress Harry and Ron with the idea that they are going to come face to face with evil incarnate, and they are. When Aragog's descendants move to attack Ron and Harry, the beat up old Weasley car, which has been hiding in the forest, and which has now "gone rogue" comes to rescue them. Everything happens for a reason. Sometimes we just have to trust and wait and see what it is.

As Harry is falling asleep that night, it suddenly hits him who the little girl must be that was killed in the chamber so long ago—Moaning Myrtle! Once again, we see the Eureka principle at work. Sometimes, we puzzle and puzzle over an idea, struggling with it, and getting nowhere. And then later, if we can just let go, our subconscious mind finds the way, shows us the light…Eureka. Watch and see. It may happen to you.

eureka!

The next morning, Ginny Weasley shows up, and she is more troubled and frightened than Harry has ever seen her. She insists that there is something she must tell him, but they are interrupted, and she does not get to confide in Harry. When we next see Ginny, she will be in mortal peril, gripped in the dark magic of the chamber. When they go to visit Hermione, still in the hospital wing and still petrified, Harry suddenly notices a paper clutched in her hand. It is a page torn from an old library book; the passage tells about the King of Serpents, a basilisk, a monster that can live for hundreds of years. According to legend, it has a murderous stare, and all who are fixed with the beam of its eye die instantly. Spiders flee from a basilisk, as do all other creatures, save one: "The basilisk flees only from the crowing of the rooster, which is fatal to it"(290). How brilliant of J. K. Rowling to add this little bit of information. It flees from the rooster! Of course it does. **Rooster!**

The basilisk is evil incarnate, and the rooster is the time-honored symbol of a divine or a heavenly interruption. There is a great deal of folklore surrounding this idea. The first thing that comes to mind, of course, is Peter's denial of Jesus in the Garden of Gethsemane. According to Matthew: "Jesus said to him, 'Truly, I say to you, this very night, before the cock crows, you will deny me three times"(Matthew 26:34). As the story goes, Peter did just that. Ever since then, the rooster has been used as a signal from heaven, a divine interruption, a signal of the coming of dawn, a new day, and an affirmation of life and the presence of God. There is a moment in the play Hamlet when the Ghost is coming to visit his son, to tell him of his murder, and he is about to speak when the rooster crows: "It faded on the crowing of the cock. / Some say that ever 'gainst that season comes / wherein our Savior's birth is celebrated, / the bird of dawning singing all night long; / and then, they say, no spirit dare stir abroad /...so hallowed and so gracious is that time"(1.1.173-178). So, Shakespeare echoes the time-honored tradition; the rooster is a heavenly interruption, a sign from heaven.

Furthermore, in the final section of T. S. Eliot's important poem entitled "The Waste Land," the rooster crows and signals the beginning of understanding, the amelioration of the feeling of desperation that has almost conquered the narrator's soul. These lines come right after the allusion to the Chapel Perilous, in the section of the poem entitled "What the Thunder Said." We will come back to these very important lines when we discuss the final book in the series. Suffice it to say, right now, that the rooster signals the beginning of understanding: "Dry bones can harm no one. / Only a cock stood on the rooftree / Co co rico co co rico / In a flash of lightning. Then a damp gust / Bringing rain"(The Waste Land, lines 391-396). Having heard the rooster call out the morning, the narrator of the poem listens to the voice of the thunder, and hears wisdom, perhaps even the voice of God. Of course the basilisk fears the rooster! And perhaps he fears phoenixes too, with good reason.

Then Harry notices something else. Hermione had scribbled

the word "pipes" just before she lost consciousness, and suddenly Harry puts it all together: "Pipes...Ron, it's been using the plumbing. I've been hearing that voice inside the walls"(291). And now we are ready for the amazing climactic scene that the novel has been building toward. Soon after Harry puts it all together, it is announced that Ginny has been taken into the chamber, and the school is under attack. Snape challenges Gilderoy Lockhart, the supposed Defense against the Dark Arts master, to go to the chamber and do battle with the monster. Gilderoy immediately sneaks off to his office and starts frantically packing, because he knows he is a fraud. Words can only get you so far. Gilderoy had built himself a reputation out of nothing, boasting of his alleged accomplishments. This technique is a dangerous one for anyone to pursue. When you put yourself on a pedestal, boasting of your alleged accomplishments, you may gain admirers temporarily. Eventually, however, your story will be tested. If you cannot deliver on your promises, your pedestal of words collapses like a house of cards, and you, your credibility, and your reputation crash. Hard.

However, not yet knowing just how inept he is, Harry and Ron grab him and force him to come with them. They head straight up to the girls' bathroom and question Moaning Myrtle. She tells them about the attack where she lost her life fifty years ago, and they know what they have to do. Harry conjures up parseltongue and tells the chamber, whose portal is marked on one of the taps in the bathroom, to open, which it does. Harry's ability to speak parseltongue has now served an important purpose. It allows him to get into the chamber, and to save Ginny's life. Once again, Harry uses his ability to speak parseltongue not for evil, only for good. Remember, in the Potter quest this ability to speak parseltongue is thought by many to be a dark gift, but Harry uses it for good. It all comes down to choices. You have certain abilities; what matters is how you choose to use them.

The three of them—Harry, Ron, and Gilderoy Lockhart—are whisked down a portal that feels like a slimy, dark slide, and Harry reminds them that if they see any sign of movement, they must close their eyes right away, so as not to be killed by the basilisk's deadly stare. Instead of preparing to pitch in, Lockhart is looking for a way to escape. The minute he gets his chance, he tackles Ron, steals his broken wand, and shouts "Obliviate!" It is the one charm that Lockhart is good at, because he often has to wipe people's memories from remembering how inept he is. Usually, these people were the ones who had done the courageous acts that Gilderoy subsequently took credit for. However, the one thing that he had not counted on was Ron's damaged wand, which causes his spell to backfire. That is exactly what happens to Lockhart, and he has, in effect, worked the obliviate spell on himself, rendering him even more of a blubbering idiot than he already is, but certainly removing him as a threat. He now has

70

no idea where he is, or what he is doing, or even that he might be in danger. However, the explosion has one more consequence, and it at first seems very ominous, but it is also very necessary for the narrative at this point. A wall of rock crumbles, effectively separating Harry from Ron and Lockhart, and Harry must go the final distance alone.

But that is at it must be. When all is said and done, there are many moments when Harry must face the dangerous task alone. Harry is the central hero of this quest, although many other characters are also very heroic. Now, he must face the monster of the chamber alone. He comes to a gigantic door, marked with serpents, and hisses his command in parseltongue: "Open." He enters a long, dimly lit chamber, glowing eerily with a greenish light. Green is the color associated with the death of his parents in Harry's memory, and we are now about to be in the presence of that killer, so the greenish glow is appropriate. In the distance, he sees a small black-robed figure—Ginny Weasley—and she is only barely alive. As he kneels at her side, he is approached by a tall, black-haired boy, and suddenly Harry realizes that he knows this young man—Tom Riddle. Harry has met him before, and he asks him if he is a ghost. Riddle tells him that he is a memory, preserved in his diary for 50 years. He looks to be about 16 years old, so at this point in the story, we know that Lord Voldemort is really 66.

At first, Harry does not suspect him of evil intentions; in fact, he asks him for help with Ginny. However, Tom does not move to help and instead demands that he and Harry have a talk immediately. Suddenly, Harry's instincts catch up with his concern for Ginny, and he understands that he is in the presence of evil--an evil that he does not quite understand, but evil nonetheless. Riddle brags to Harry that he has possessed Ginny's mind, controlling her through the diary. He boasts further that he has forced her to act for him, to open the chamber of secrets, kill the roosters in the schoolyard, scrawl with blood upon the walls of the castle. And now, as she lies at Harry's feet, he is slowly draining her soul out of her. He feeds on other people's soula—he is evil incarnate. He will do anything to remain alive, even sacrifice his own soul as well as those of others. This foreshadows Voldemort's willingness to make so many horcruxes. He will shamelessly take others' lives, the lives of innocents, so that he can keep himself alive. He values his own life here on earth above absolutely everything else. This is the sin of hubris, and it proves to be his fatal error.

And then he tells Harry that Ginny has now done him the biggest favor, for she has brought Harry to him, and Harry is his real target. Then comes the extraordinary moment where he reveals the connection that Harry has not yet figured out. He scrawls the words "Tom Marvolo Riddle" in the air with the tip of his wand and magically rearranges the letters to read: "I am Lord Voldemort"(314). He tells Harry that Tom Riddle is no more; he has become Lord Voldemort. He has rejected his earthly parentage and given himself a new identity. Lucifer became Satan. Riddle became Voldemort. Tom Riddle, the boy whose name means puzzle, has solved his puzzle with a Faustian bargain with death and evil. In his search for immortality, how ironic that he would name himself "turn to death." Perhaps he meant "turn away from death," but then—that is not the province of this earthly life. His hubris will be punished—in time.

When he declares himself the greatest sorcerer that has ever lived, Harry rejects that claim. Even though he is being threatened with death by Voldemort, once again, Harry immediately denies his boast, saying that Albus Dumbledore is the greatest wizard in all the world, and everybody who has any judgment at all knows that. Voldemort laughs at Harry's words, saying that Dumbledore is gone, and Harry says, "He's not as gone as you might think!"(315). We remember what Dumbledore had said, that as long as his students are loyal to him, he would never be gone from Hogwarts. Harry tells us that he was, at this point, speaking at random, just saying words that seemed to pour from him, almost without thought or analysis on his part, perhaps engaging in a desperate kind of wishful thinking. We are reminded of a passage in the Bible where Jesus tells his disciples that He is with them always. They are not to worry. When the moment of trial comes, they will open their mouths, and the right words will come out, almost unbidden, as He speaks through them.

This idea is expressed in this memorable passage from Mark: "And these signs will accompany those who believe; in my name they will cast out demons; they will speak in new tongues; they will pick up deadly serpents, and if they drink any deadly thing, it will not hurt them; they will lay their hands on the sick and they will recover"(Mark 16:17-18). J. K. Rowling never lectures, and certainly she does not ever limit her story to only a Christian interpretation. This is a universal story, a quest for all. Still, there are so many moments where the Christian imagery underscores what is going on. Remember, we are the hands and feet of our heavenly Father today. We are made in His image, and we do the work of His kingdom. And Harry is clearly in this vein at this point in the story. He will cast out demons, and he is speaking in new tongues. He will lay his hands on the sick, and she will recover, and he will most certainly strike down this vicious serpent. It will injure him, but it will not "hurt" him. At this moment, it might be wise to explain the distinction between these two words. injure / hurt

Once again, we go back to Ernest Hemingway, and his brilliant metaphor for life. Life is a battleground, and everyone is eventually wounded, either physically or emotionally. At that moment, we begin to get the measure of a man or a woman. How will they handle themselves after they have suffered this wound or loss? If they soldier bravely on, doing their best to do what they believe to be the right thing, conducting themselves with dignity even in the face of danger

74

and disappointment, then they have not been diminished any further. Once a person has achieved the status of an exemplar in Hemingway, it is unlikely that they will lose their balance for very long. They have figured out what is sacred to them, what they believe in, and who they are as people. They know what they must stand up for, what they must die, if necessary, to protect. Someone for whom they have no respect cannot "hurt" them. They can be injured, wounded, and betrayed, but someone for whom they have no respect does not have the power to "hurt" them or make them lose their way. And so it is with Harry. The basilisk, an agent of Voldemort, will injure Harry, but it will not "hurt" him. Even if you die, you may do so without being "hurt"--remember what Harry said earlier. If a person were going to live a cursed life as a result of a sinful action, wouldn't death be preferable? Yes, it would. Harry, who is a good man, thinks this way; Voldemort, who is evil, does not.

But it does not come to death for Harry in the chamber. As he finishes speaking his words of affirmation for Dumbledore, music enters the chamber, at first from very far away. Harry does not know the source of this ethereal music, but it fills his heart with joy, and with courage. Suddenly, Fawkes appears—Dumbledore's beautiful, mighty phoenix, and he drops a gift on Harry's lap—the old Sorting Hat! We cannot imagine, at least for a moment, how this could possibly be helpful, and neither can Harry. We do remember, however, that

Dumbledore told Harry that if someone at Hogwarts were to ask for help, help would certainly be given. Ask, and you will receive. Seek, and you will find. Still, a phoenix and an old hat do seem like strange assistants, and Tom Riddle scoffs at them.

However, the hat conceals a mighty weapon, and we have already talked about the majesty of phoenixes. We have learned, as has young Harry, to trust, and to keep fighting. Harry, filled with a sense of returning power, knowing that he is not alone, and trusting that this will all make sense somehow, prepares to do battle with Voldemort. He tells him that although he seems to be gaining strength right now, Harry has seen the real Voldemort, whom he describes as ugly, foul, and barely alive. Nonetheless, at the moment, Voldemort does seem to be getting stronger, as he draws the lifeblood from young Ginny. He laughs at Harry's bravado, and then he sets the basilisk loose, commanding it to kill Harry.

This terrible monster, green of course, starts slithering toward Harry. Harry runs from it, but he cannot outrun its strength and speed. Suddenly, the snake is distracted, and Harry sneaks a look to see what is going on. Fawkes is attacking the basilisk, gouging out its venomous eyes with its sharp beak. The deadly might of the basilisk is at least compromised, but it still pursues Harry, urged on by Voldemort's screaming. Harry, exhausted, whispers sacred words: "Help me, help me...someone, anyone...please help me"(319). There is an important lesson here for all of us, and it is a lesson about how to pray. Speak from your heart. Ask, and it will be given unto you. Seek, and you will find. Praying is talking to your heavenly Father. At Hogwarts, when someone asks for help, help will always be given. And here we are—at Hogwarts, every day of our lives. And help arrives.

Suddenly, the Sorting Hat pushes something at Harry: "Something very hard and heavy thudded onto the top of Harry's head, almost knocking him out. Stars winking in front of his eyes, he grabbed the top of the hat to pull it off and felt something long and hard beneath it. A gleaming silver sword had appeared inside the hat, its handle glittering with rubies the size of eggs"(320). Here, we are deeply within classic quest lore. In the master narrative of the hero's quest, a young hero leaves home, goes on a journey or a quest, and faces many trials of his courage and heart. There sometimes comes a moment when he is at the end of his strength—he simply has nothing left to give. When he cries out in his desperation, help is given. Frequently, the help comes in the form of a magical sword. From Morte D'Arthur we have the most famous sword of all—Excalibur. There are different versions of this heroic quest, but frequently, this is the sword that Arthur receives from the Lady of the Lake as a replacement for his first sword, that one that only he could pull from the famous stone. When Arthur is finally mortally wounded, and we remember that all heroes must die eventually, he arranges to have the sword returned to the Lady of the Lake. In most versions, Arthur's faithful knight, Bedivere, reluctantly throws the sword back into the lake, where it is caught and brandished in a blessing before disappearing below the surface of the lake.

Then again, there is the character of Beowulf, who in the great Anglo Saxon poem of the same name, is battling with Grendel's mother, in the second monumental battle of the quest. He has descended mysteriously into the depths to fight her, and she is far more terrible and vicious than Grendel ever was, and that's saying something! When Beowulf is at the end of his strength and about to be killed, a majestic and mighty sword appears, a sword made by giants, and with the help of this mighty sword, he finally kills her.

So, Harry is in good company at this particular moment of his quest, but he is also in mortal peril. The basilisk, although blinded by Fawkes' attack, is still deadly, and in a final thrust, Harry kills the terrible snake, but one of its venomous fangs pierces Harry's arm. Tom Riddle gloats that Harry is dying, and he mocks the beautiful Fawkes who is weeping tears into Harry's wound. Once again, and this is characteristic of his deadly hubris, Voldemort underestimates his adversary and the power of good. He has forgotten the amazing healing power of phoenix tears, and, with Fawkes' help, Harry is able to fight off the venom long enough to save himself, and beat back evil once again.

It is interesting that at crucial moments, Harry often acts on instinct, and he does so here. Fawkes drops the evil diary in his lap, and Harry, without thinking, stabs it with the basilisk fang: "Then, without thinking, without considering, as though he had meant to do it all along, Harry seized the basilisk fang on the floor next to him and plunged it straight into the heart of the book. There was a long, dreadful, piercing scream. Ink spurted out of the diary in torrents, streaming over Harry's hands, flooding the floor. Riddle was writhing and twisting"(322). And then he was gone. As the energy drains out of Riddle, Ginny slowly comes back to life. We do not know it at the time, but the first horcrux has been destroyed. Ah, we have much to learn about horcruxes—in time. But, take a look at the etymology of the word right now, and you get a hint…the crux of horror. The horror. The horror. Sounds familiar, doesn't it? We find ourselves listening to a distant echo of the end of Joseph Conrad's Heart of Darkness.

Ginny, slowly regaining her strength, is sobbing, so embarrassed that she was possessed and used by Voldemort. Harry and Ron support her, and with Fawkes leading the way, they begin to exit the chamber. They march side by side with Fawkes, like battered, but victorious warriors of old exiting the field of battle. Then, a wondrous thing happens. Fawkes seems to indicate that they should hang on to him, and so they grab Lockhart, who is still babbling senselessly because of the Obliviate Charm he accidentally worked on himself. Then, they fly out of the chamber, carried by the strength of Fawkes' magical wings. After all, this is no ordinary bird!

Again, we are just a little bit like phoenixes. Just as Fawkes can do extraordinary things, so can we. Motivated by Harry's loyalty to Dumbledore, Fawkes did far more than anyone ever expected of any bird. We can surprise ourselves by finding untapped reservoirs of patience and courage that we never knew we had. Motivated by love, compassion, and loyalty, we too can successfully carry loads that seem much too heavy for us to bear. When they get out of the chamber, they are ushered into Dumbledore's office, and Ginny is mortified and worried that she will be expelled for her part, however unwilling, in this near disaster. Of course, Dumbledore is way too wise for that, and with his godlike wisdom, he understands everything all at once. He tells them that Tom Riddle was probably the most brilliant student that Hogwarts had ever seen, and we are reminded of the myth of Lucifer and his fall. He was once one of the most trusted of the archangels. Supposedly, his sin was hubris, vowing not to serve or respect his heavenly Father. This sounds like Voldemort. Tom Riddle used to be a handsome boy, but Voldemort is ugly. Having conversed with evil for so long and having pursued the dark arts for all these years, Voldemort is now twisted and hideous in his appearance. A commitment to evil can make you ugly. Probably most of us can think of someone we have met along the way that would make us see the wisdom of that

80

statement. True beauty comes from within, and it cannot be painted on or bought.

Mr. and Mrs. Weasley are there to receive their daughter back from Harry's rescuing arms, and Arthur Weasley delivers what is one of the most unique speeches of the novel: "Ginny!...Haven't I taught you anything? What have I always told you? Never trust anything that can think for itself it you can't see where it keeps its brain"(329). Now, there's an interesting observation, and it is fun thinking of ways to apply that bit of wisdom to our own world. The Weasleys fear that there will be some punishment for Ginny, but Dumbledore is quick to put them at ease, saying that many people older and wiser than young Ginny have been hoodwinked by the sweet talking Tom Riddle. It is clear to us that he includes himself in that list. He orders instead two very good remedies—a cup of hot chocolate and a good night's sleep. But before that—a feast. We are reminded of the wisdom of the book of Ecclesiastes from the Old Testament: "Go and eat your bread with enjoyment, and drink your wine with a merry heart, for God has already approved what you do"(Ecclesiastes 9:7). There is another famous passage from this same book from the Old Testament that I am sure you can think of, and it too applies here....there is a time for war, and a time for peace. This is a time for peace.

We who are on this quest with Harry know that peace does not last forever. In fact, it does not ever last all that long, but we learn, along with Harry, to enjoy the reprieve—the season of grace, when it comes. In the wonderful closing scene, Dumbledore fills Harry in on some of the things he does not know, helps him fit things together into a larger, clearer vision or understanding. In this moment of quiet, Harry confesses his fears that he is too much like Tom Riddle, and he is embarrassed to admit that he can speak parseltongue, an ability which makes him fear he might have been meant for Slytherin House after all. Dumbledore calmly explains that Harry can speak parseltongue because Voldemort inadvertently transferred some of his powers to Harry on the night, long ago, when he gave him his scar. At first, this revelation does not comfort Harry. He thinks, once again, that the Sorting Hat might have made a mistake, that he had forced his will upon the hat. Dumbledore uses Harry's own words and reinterprets them, saying that he is correct, but he has not quite understood the import of his own words: "Exactly!...Which makes you very different from Tom Riddle. It is our choices, Harry, that show what we truly are, far more than our abilities"(333). *choices vs. ability*

We have spoken of this passage before, but the words bear repeating. This is one of the most important lessons of the Potter quest. These are sacred words. Powerful words. We are born with God given abilities, or talents. What makes all the difference is what we do with them. We are reminded of the parable of the talents in Matthew. Our heavenly Father has given us gifts, each of us a different set of gifts. But He will hold us accountable for having put those gifts to good use to further the work of His kingdom. We will want to hear these words, when all is said and done: "Well done, good and faithful servant; you have been faithful over a little, I will set you over much; enter into the joy of your master"(Matthew 25:23). Each of us is potentially a good and faithful servant, but we must use our abilities, whatever they are, for good. Dumbledore then shows Harry the sword that he had wielded down in the chamber. He shows him the name inscribed just below the hilt: Godric Gryffindor. Enough said.

Dumbledore is about to send Harry off for food and bed when they are interrupted by an irate and self-righteous Lucius Malfoy, accompanied by Dobby, his house elf. Dobby, against the rules of proper conduct for house elves, is trying to warn Harry that Lucius is the one who planted the Riddle diary in Ginny's bookbag back in September, beginning the seduction. Suddenly, Harry understands. He accuses Mr. Malfoy of having slipped the diary into her bag in Flourish and Blotts. Although Lucius does not deny it, he says that no one will be able to prove that he did, in fact, do this terrible thing, putting Ginny's life at risk. He storms out of Dumbledore's office, dragging a wailing Dobby with him, and we get this interesting passage: "Harry stood for a moment, thinking hard. Then it came to him"(337). Interesting. Sometimes, Harry seems to be gifted with a kind of intuitive response. Sometimes, he has to think hard and figure it out, as we all do. This is one of those moments when he has to think hard—quickly.

But he outfoxes Mr. Malfoy. He rips off one of his filthy socks, stuffs it into the damaged diary, and chases Malfoy down. He tells him that he has something for him, hands him the diary, which Malfoy throws disgustedly at Dobby. Just like Voldemort, Lucius Malfoy tends to underestimate his adversary. In throwing the diary and the sock at Dobby, a sock that Dobby quickly catches, he accidentally sets Dobby free. Whenever a master of a house elf gives his elf human clothing, this symbolic act represents giving this slave his freedom. This act of cleverness and kindness on Harry's part will be repaid a hundred fold as the quest moves on.

The rest of the term passes in a happy daze, days filled with sunshine and laughter. Soon enough, the term is up, and Harry must return to Privet Drive and the dreadful Dursleys. However, he is becoming a seasoned warrior, and a man. That much is clear.

Harry Potter and the Prisoner of Azkaban

Harry Potter and the Prisoner of Azkaban is the third book in the series, and it is the book where the story kicks into another gear, a higher gear. It has an interesting title; we will find out a great deal about Azkaban, a notorious witch and wizard prison, in time. First of all, the novel opens with a scene of departure from the Muggle world, and this time it includes a hilarious, if rather irreverent, scene where Harry launches Aunt Marge, after she insults him and his dead parents, into the London twilight. Not that she doesn't deserve it. Aunt Marge says vicious and hateful things about James and Lily Potter, and Harry's rage boils over. He sort of turns her into a hot air balloon, like the enormous balloons that fill the sky on the day of the Macy's Thanksgiving Day parade. This is certainly appropriate for her, since she is full of hot air. After Harry storms out of the Dursley residence, he is picked up by the Knight Bus, and the adventure begins.

The operator of the Knight Bus, a young man named Stan Shunpike, senses that Harry is in trouble and announces, "Welcome to the Knight Bus, emergency transport for the stranded witch or wizard. Just stick out your wand hand, step on board, and we can take you anywhere you want to go"(33). As they squeal through the streets of London, performing amazing feats with this invisible double decker bus, Stan tells us that most Muggles never notice anything—that they don't look properly and they don't listen properly either. A gentle lesson for us all. There is magic all around us. Furthermore, we need to listen with our ears and with our eyes when someone is trying to communicate with us. Young Stan is full of gossip, and the news of the wizard world right at this moment is all about Sirius Black, a notorious criminal who has just escaped from Azkaban, a wizard prison on an island somewhere in the North Sea. The name Azkaban is inspired by the notorious prison Alcatraz, from which it was supposedly impossible to escape. However, nothing is ever impossible, is it?

Stan delivers Harry to Diagon Alley, in London, and to a rather dodgy looking pub, the Leaky Cauldron, where Cornelius Fudge, the Minister of Magic, is waiting for him. Harry is very much afraid that he is going to be expelled from Hogwarts for using magic on Aunt Marge, but, to his surprise, all is forgiven. Fudge says: "Circumstances change, Harry…We have to take into account…in the present climate…Surely you don't want to be expelled?"(45). This is not the only time that Fudge will prove himself to be rather Machiavellian in his methods and his thinking. In The Prince, Machiavelli says that the main objective of the man who rules, the prince, is to hang on to his power: "To preserve the state, he often has to do things against his word, against charity, against humanity, against religion. Thus he has to have a mind ready to shift as the winds of fortune and the varying circumstances of life may dictate. And as I have said above, he should not depart from the good if he can hold to it, but he should be ready to enter into evil if he has to"(511). Although Cornelius Fudge is often cowardly, he is definitely trying to maintain his position as the Minister of Magic throughout much of the quest. He seems to be a man who enjoys the trappings of power, and he will do whatever seems politically expedient in order to hang on to it. Although he may seem to be a friend to Harry at this particular moment, he is not a reliable friend. We will see Fudge demonstrate the kind of behavior that Machiavelli is describing many times during the story.

Harry spends a couple of blissful days, enjoying his relative freedom at the Leaky Cauldron, and soon Ron and Hermione show up. Hermione has purchased this big tabby cat whose name, Crookshanks, suggests his bandy legs, and who will be found to be a pretty good judge of character as the story moves on. Right from the moment they meet, Crookshanks does not like Ron's pet rat, Scabbers, who is definitely not what he seems to be, and Crookshanks seems to know that. Shortly afterwards, the students board the train for Hogwarts, and our three heroes find themselves in a compartment with a shabby and exhausted looking professor, a man named Lupin—a name that is very suggestive etymologically, bringing to mind images of the wolf. As he sleeps and they gossip merrily, a sudden chill sweeps over the train, and it grinds to a halt somewhere in the deserted English countryside. Here we get Harry's first personal encounter with a Dementor, and a chilling encounter it is.

The word dementor is of course related to dementia, and these terrible creatures have the ability to cause this if their attack on someone goes unchecked. On the train, one of them attacks Harry: "An intense cold swept over them all. Harry felt his own breath catch in his chest. The cold went deeper than skin. It was inside his chest, it was inside his very heart…Harry's eyes rolled up into his head. He couldn't see. He was drowning in cold…and then, from far away, he heard screaming, terrible, terrified, pleading screams. He wanted to help whoever it was"(84). When Harry comes to, the shabby professor is handing him a piece of chocolate, imploring him to eat it. Harry is embarrassed and bewildered, wondering why the dementor affected him so much more powerfully than the others.

Nonetheless, they eventually make it to Hogwarts, and Harry feels like he is home. One of the first new courses this year is Divination, with the weird Professor Sibyll Trelawney. Her name is appropriate, of course. A sibyl is someone who is said to speak for the god Apollo, and who therefore can see the future. Our Sibyll will be an important presence in this quest, more important than we could possibly know at this point in our reading. She proudly proclaims the importance of her course: "So you have chosen to study Divination, the most difficult of all magical arts. I must warn you at the outset that if you do not have the Sight, there is very little I will be able to teach you. Books can take you only so far in this field..."(103). During the first lesson, Sibyll frightens the whole class, and Harry especially, by pronouncing that the "Grim"—a terrible death omen, is hiding in Harry's tea leaves. After this nonsense, the much more logical voice of Professor McGonagall is a welcome relief to Harry's ears: "Divination is one of the most imprecise branches of magic. I shall not conceal from you that I have very little patience with it. True seers are very rare..."(109). Although Harry is relieved to hear her say this, he cannot quite dismiss Trelawney's warning; it hovers just below his consciousness. So it is with all predictions. Once the words are spoken, it is as if they have a life of their own.

This year, Hagrid is their teacher for the Care of Magical Creatures, and he has excitedly planned his first lesson to be very impressive. The third years are introduced to a rather scary looking creature, a hippogriff: "They had the bodies, hind legs, and tails of horses, but the front legs, wings, and heads of what seemed to be giant eagles, with cruel, steel-colored beaks and large, brilliantly orange eyes. The talons on their front legs were half a foot long and deadly looking"(114). Pretty intimidating! Hagrid is anxious for a student to volunteer to interact with the hippogriff, and understandably, no one is very much inclined to do that. Fearing that Hagrid's lesson plan will be a disaster, Harry volunteers. This shows us, once again, how good of a friend Harry is. We saw his good heart when he attended Nearly Headless Nick's Deathday party, although it certainly wasn't anything he wanted to do. Now, he volunteers to interact with the hippogriff, even though he is afraid of it. He wants to protect his friend Hagrid from dejection and humiliation, so he does something he doesn't want to do. His volunteering to help Hagrid shows his loyalty to his friends and his willingness to place himself in danger to protect them. While this is only a small risk at this time, it still gives us insight into Harry's character, and to this altruistic quality which will become much more important later in the quest. Hagrid instructs Harry to bow respectfully to the hippogriff, to not blink too much, and to wait for an invitation from the animal to come any closer. Harry respectfully does these things, and the hippogriff rewards Harry with a startlingly wonderful ride on its back. Harry is hailed as a hero by his classmates, and Draco Malfoy, angry at seeing Harry get so much attention, then decides that if Potter can do it, so can he. Draco lacks humility and modesty, and, once again, his hubris is going to get him in trouble.

He approaches the hippogriff rudely, with disastrous results. Perhaps because Draco knows nothing about manners and politeness, having been raised to be an arrogant young man by his equally arrogant father and mother, Draco insults the hippogriff who then injures him. Once again, we see that, in spite of his bluster and bravado, Draco Malfoy is a coward and a crybaby. He is all talk, and he is completely lacking in true courage. What a fall is in store for him. At this point, he is planting the seeds of that fall with his rudeness and mean-spirited behavior. As Hagrid carries him into Madame Pomfrey for some medical attention, he wails that his father will see Hagrid fired for this. His approach to Buckbeak contrasts in every possible way with Harry's characteristic kindness. At this moment, it seems like it really doesn't matter very much. However, acts of kindness are almost always rewarded in the Potter quest, and perhaps in life, and Harry's respectful treatment of Buckbeak will be important later in the novel.

It is as if J. K. Rowling is quickly moving a lot of pieces into place in the early stages of this novel, and that is certainly true with what happens in the next chapter. We have our first Defense against the Dark Arts class with Professor Lupin, the kindly professor who assisted Harry on the train. He introduces the students to a boggart, which is a shape shifter that can take on the shape of whatever it thinks will frighten the person his is facing the most. The etymology of this word comes from the old word bogeyman that we all grew up with, and he too, could be considered to be a shape shifter. Ask anyone what the bogeyman that haunted their childhood dreams looked like, and you will find that, although he retains some similar characteristics, he comes in many different appearances. The thing that can defeat a boggart s very powerful magic--laughter! Professor

Lupin tells his students: "The charm that repels a boggart is simple, yet it requires force of mind. You see, the thing that really finishes a boggart is laughter. What you need to do is force it to assume a shape that you find amusing"(167). This scene with the boggart gives us a very comical moment with Neville, when he causes the shape-shifter to look like Professor Snape dressed up in his grandmother's terrible clothes. And then, Lupin tells him that, with all the force he can muster, he must shout "Riddikulus!" How brilliant is that. Think of the times when you were frightened, by whatever your personal bogeymen were. This fear can be defeated by laughter. There are enough things to be genuinely frightened about in this world without imagining more. J. K. Rowling reminds us about the importance of laughter, and the importance of being able to laugh at yourself too.

When the rest of his classmates take off for their first ever Hogsmeade visit, Harry must stay behind, since he did not have a signed permission slip. Remember—everything happens for a reason, and this event provides an opportunity for Harry to talk to Professor Lupin about the boggart lesson. Lupin had arranged for Harry not to fight the boggart in front of his classmates, and Harry has felt a little embarrassed about that, wondering if Lupin did not regard him as man enough to handle even a bogeyman after his episode of fainting on the train. Instead, Professor Lupin proves that he respects and knows quite a bit about Harry. He says that he was afraid that Harry

92

might cause a Lord Voldemort boggart to appear in the classroom, and he didn't want to frighten the other students. When Harry says that he was actually thinking about a Dementor, Professor Lupin is impressed: "That suggests that what you fear most of all is—fear. Very wise, Harry"(155). After all, in Harry's mind, he has already faced Lord Voldemort twice, arguably three times, and he has survived the encounter on each occasion. However, perhaps this moment is important enough that we ought to look at it a little further.

Lupin says that Harry is wise to be wary of fear. Having faced Voldemort and death on several occasions already, Harry knows fear and danger. However, during his most difficult challenges, his courage, hope, faith, and positive thinking enabled him to overcome his fear, to persevere and eventually succeed. The dementors strip away all these positive attributes and leave Harry alone with fear and hopelessness. Harry does not really fear fear itself; he fears that this kind of hopelessness or despair can encompass his entire being and block out the power of his innate love, hope, and courage. At the end of this scene, we see that Professor Snape has brewed a special potion for Lupin. We are not told what the potion supposedly treats. We will find out later in the story. Harry is worried about Lupin trusting Snape, but Lupin indicates that he trusts him implicitly. And this is exactly what Dumbledore always says about Snape. We should be paying attention. However, J. K. Rowling cleverly keeps us within Harry's central consciousness. That is to say, we experience and see the story from Harry's perspective, and like Harry, we are suspicious of Snape until the very end of the quest. Truthfully, it is hard not to distrust Snape. He frequently seems sinister and evil. We don't blame Harry for being suspicious of him. Still, in retrospect, it is a good idea to note the clues that J. K. Rowling has given us.

In spite of the fact that Dumbledore does not want the Dementors on school grounds, they show up at a Quidditch match, while Harry is playing seeker for the Gryffindor team. He has no chance against a hundred of them, and he is overwhelmed: "At least a hundred dementors, their hidden faces pointing up at him, were standing beneath him. It was as though freezing water were rising in his chest, cutting at his insides. And then he heard it again...Someone was screaming, screaming inside his head...a woman. 'Not Harry, not Harry, please not Harry...Not Harry! Please have mercy...have mercy'"(179). But there is no mercy in the heart of evil. No mercy at all. And Harry finally realizes that when the dementors overwhelm him, when sorrow conquers him, what he hears over and over again is the moment of his mother's death, when Lily Potter sacrificed herself to save him. No wonder the experience can bring him to his knees.

Harry is hard on himself, as we all can be. He is sickened and humiliated that the dementors have such power over him, when they do not seem to have as much power over some of his classmates.

However, he is dealing with some pretty powerful losses. He is angry at himself for not being able to fight the images off that overwhelm him during a dementor attack. But let us revisit, and pursue further, Hemingway's idea of the "sacred hurt." His theory is that life is a battlefield, and everyone is eventually wounded, either physically or spiritually. This sacred hurt can come at any time in your life, and it is the kind of thing that makes you stop and reevaluate your whole life. Things that before seemed possible no longer are, and you know it. What a person does from this point on is the measure of the man or the woman. There are several courses of action that will not work.

Once you have received that sacred hurt, you cannot run from it. You cannot escape it through drink or drugs. You cannot lie to yourself about it (that is the ultimate folly—how can you effectively lie to yourself when you know you are lying?), and you cannot forget it. There is really only one thing you can do—face it head on. Name the loss; confront it and acknowledge it. Know that it cannot be undone, not in this lifetime. Know that you have a right and a duty to put it behind you and soldier on as bravely as you can—not forgetting what has happened, but forgiving the past and yourself, and then moving on. Harry is somewhere in the middle of this process. He has experienced the sacred hurt—the loss of his parents. He knows the pain and suffering that the loss has caused him, but he has not yet fully accepted it and moved on.

He makes a good deal of progress toward this understanding with the help of Professor Lupin, who explains to Harry why the dementors have such power over him: "The dementors affect you worse than the others because there are horrors in your past that the others don't have....Dementors are among the foulest creatures that walk this earth. They infest the darkest, filthiest places, they glory in decay and despair, they drain peace, hope, and happiness out of the air around them...If it can, the dementor will feed on you long enough to reduce you to something like itself...soul-less and evil. You'll be left with nothing but the worst experiences of your life"(187). A dementor is despair. To be possessed by a dementor is to have lost all hope, all sense of love, all faith. It is the absence of God's grace; it is the province of evil. It is the madness that sometimes conquers people and makes them believe that their life is not worth living. Dementors spread evil and despair. Just as we can be possessed by this evil, we can also spread it. Just as smiles multiply, so does negativity. When we feel such despair overwhelming us, we must ensure that we do not act as dementors to other people and spread our misery. Instead, we must act to save ourselves, and to save each other from this hell, using the mightiest magic of all—love. Lupin reassures Harry that he is not a coward, not in the least. Again, we realize how grateful we are for his presence in this quest.

Lupin and Harry eventually discuss Sirius Black, and Lupin

tells us a little bit about Azkaban and Sirius: "The fortress is set on a tiny island, way out to sea, but they don't need walls and water to keep the prisoners in, not when they're all trapped inside their own heads, incapable of a single cheerful thought. Most of them go mad within weeks...Black must have found a way to fight them. I wouldn't have believed it possible...Dementors are supposed to drain a wizard of his powers if he is left with them too long"(188). There are several interesting ideas here. First of all—we make our own prisons. Overcome with guilt for past sins, unable to forgive ourselves and move on, unable to accept absolution and God's grace, we make our own prisons. Beyond that, we can be almost undone by terrible memories, losses of loved ones, or powerful disappointments. These too can overcome us, and almost paralyze us so that we cannot go forward. We can get "trapped inside our own heads," and that prison is stronger than steel. Secondly, if we are paying attention, we have our first strong hint that Sirius is good, maybe even powerfully good. For him to be able to escape Azkaban, he must be good. Evil does not defeat evil. Only good does. We have a lot to learn about Sirius. This might be a good moment to look at the etymology of his name—Sirius Black. Sirius is the name given to the brightest star in the constellation Canis Major. It is sometimes called the "dog star." The combination of the image of a star—a source of light, and the word "black", which suggests darkness might perhaps give us room to speculate about the complexity of human nature. We are all capable of acts of brightness and darkness. Sirius will certainly exhibit this complex nature as the quest moves on. Later on, we will understand the connection to the "dog" star.

Soon it is Christmas time, and Harry receives a very important present from Fred and George—the Marauder's Map. This is a magical map that shows "every detail of the Hogwarts castle and grounds. But the truly remarkable thing were the tiny ink dots moving around it, each labeled with a name in miniscule writing"(193). These dots tell the person studying the map where everyone is in Hogwarts. You can even watch them walking around by following their dot. This map will prove to be invaluable in the solution of the mystery at the end of this novel. Shortly after that, Harry finds a secret passage to Hogsmeade with help of this map, and aided by his father's invisibility cloak, heads out for this little town.

There, he secretly witnesses a conversation in The Three Broomsticks. Madam Rosmerta, who runs the pub, gives us another hint about Sirius' true nature: "Of all the people to go over to the Dark Side, Sirius Black was the last I'd have thought...I mean, I remember him when he was a boy at Hogwarts...If you'd told me then what he was going to become, I'd have said you'd had too much mead"(203). We further discover that James Potter and Sirius Black were the best of friends, and that James had trusted Sirius to be his Secret Keeper, a most sacred bond. A Secret Keeper is a person designated to keep a secret, bound by the Fidelius Charm. The secret is kept in their very soul. The only person capable of revealing the information that is thereby protected is the Secret Keeper, and he may reveal it by either speaking or writing the information down. If the Secret Keeper dies, then all the other people who know this protected information become Secret Keepers. It is a matter of trust. To designate someone as your Secret Keeper is tantamount to saying that you trust that person with your life.

Furthermore, we learn that Sirius is Harry's godfather. Once again, if we are paying attention, these revelations are gathering a kind of weight that should prepare us for what we are going to discover at the end of the novel. Hagrid, who is there having a drink with the other professors, says that he never would have believed that Sirius could be so evil as to betray his best friend, "but when a wizard goes over ter the Dark Side, there's nothin' and no one that matters to 'em anymore..."(207). So, we are invited to think about this idea. Is it possible that James and Lily Potter were such terrible judges of character? Did some terrible thing happen to Sirius that made him surrender all his goodness and go over to the Dark Side? We realize one thing—the dark side is the opposite of love. If no one and nothing matters to you anymore, you have lost all love. We also hear about Peter Pettigrew, whom Professor McGonagall describes as a hanger-on: "Hero-worshipped Black and Potter...Never quite in their league, talent-wise"(207).

Harry has just heard so much new information that he feels like his brain and his heart are ready to explode. He is filled with a hatred stronger than he has ever known, because at this point, he believes that Sirius was his parents' best friend, a trusted friend, and he betrayed them and helped Voldemort to kill them. J. K. Rowling suggests a link between hatred and poison: "A hatred such as he had never known before was coursing through Harry like poison"(213). This is a very powerful image. Hatred like that, coursing through you, can slowly poison your life. You cannot let it just fester in you, unaddressed. You have to get rid of it, one way or another. Harry is in the grip of such a poison right now.

One thing you can do is fight, and luckily, Harry begins to take Anti-Dementor lessons from Professor Lupin. He teaches Harry about the Dementor's most vicious weapon--the dementor's kiss: "It's what dementors do to those they wish to destroy utterly. I suppose there must be some kind of mouth under there, because they clamp their jaws upon the mouth of the victim and—suck out his soul... Much worse than (killing). You can exist without your soul, you know, as long as your brain and heart are still working. But you'll have no sense of self anymore, no memory, no...anything. There's no chance at all of recovery. You'll just exist. As an empty shell. And your soul

100

is gone forever...lost"(247). What a terribly sad description—almost overwhelming. Sadly enough, these words sound as though they might be a pretty good description of a drug addict, which, of course, makes drugs the equivalent of a dementor's kiss. It also reminds us of Samuel Taylor Coleridge's poem entitled "The Ancient Mariner," and the terrible fate of "Life in Death," which the speaker in the poem recognizes as much worse than death. Finally, it also sounds like a pretty good description of hell. Lupin tells Harry that if the Dementors can catch Sirius, this is his fate. When Harry says that he deserves it, Professor Lupin quietly asks Harry if he can really be sure that anyone deserves that. We get another hint that there may be more to Sirius' story than we have heard so far.

Meanwhile, Harry continues to feel the sting of Snape's disapproval, and we find out that there was bad blood between Severus Snape and James Potter, and that the sting of a childhood embarrassment rankles Snape still. Through all of this, Hermione is mysteriously appearing and disappearing, and the boys repeatedly notice that she seems to be in two places at the same time. They notice this peripherally, and she is always quick to tell them that they are deceived, but we later discover that at this time she is learning to work the Time Turner that will be so important in the final scenes. J. K. Rowling is playing with something like fire here, the manipulation of time, and she will be very careful to use it selectively and in a very limited way. We will talk more about this later. Nonetheless, one day, worn out and over-committed, Hermione blows up during Divination class, and Sibyll Trelawney essentially tells her to leave, calling her the most mundane student she has ever had the displeasure of trying to instruct. Since we know that Hermione is brilliant, we find ourselves suspecting that McGonagall is right to be suspicious of the "art of divination." Still, there is some truth to the idea that some skills, some knowledge cannot be acquired through reason and research. Although Trelawney sometimes drives us crazy with all her acting and her extravagant mannerisms, and we adore Hermione, Trelawney's supernatural gift does reveal itself on a couple of different occasions. No book could give Hermione that information, or that prescience. Hermione finds Trelawney exasperating, and so do we, but she certainly is interesting. However, most of us find ourselves maintaining a healthy skepticism about most of her prophecies.

In the course of Harry's defensive lessons with Lupin, he is trying to learn some very advanced magic. Lupin tells Harry that when this spell "works correctly, it conjures up a Patronus...which is a kind of anti-dementor—a guardian that acts as a shield between you and the dementor...The Patronus is a kind of positive force, a projection of the very things that the dementor feeds upon—hope, happiness, the desire to survive—but it cannot feel despair, as real humans can, so the dementors can't hurt it. But I must warn you, Harry, that the charm might be too advanced for you. Many qualified wizards have difficulty with it"(237). We notice the importance of the etymology of this word. The word patronus derives from the Latin word "pater" which means father. Now, in Harry's case, the word father works simultaneously on two levels, as it does for all of us, but perhaps it is even more poignant for Harry at this point in his life. p a t r o n u s

First of all, the strength of the word "father" refers back to James Potter, his earthly father who loved him so much that he gave his life for him. Beyond that, although J. K. Rowling never says this, the word hearkens back to his heavenly Father, in whose person Jesus gave His life for us two thousand years ago. J. K. Rowling is never preachy in this quest, and she never makes these links overt, but we, as scholars, have the opportunity to read between the lines. Certainly, it is not mandatory to do so; however, it may enrich your reading to pursue the imagery offered here. Beyond that, the etymology makes perfect sense for Harry—his patronus is a stag. We later find out that James Potter took the form of a stag when he transformed himself as an animagus. Suggested here is the universal idea of the protective relationship between parents and children. Parents do their best to protect their children from the forces of evil. There is the potential for much magic in the word "father." Many of us are lucky enough to know this first hand.

At first, Harry has a hard time conjuring up an image of

happiness powerful enough to summon a patronus. In the course of the novel, however, he experiences a moment of pure joy, as the Gryffindor team beats the Slytherin team after Harry's remarkable leap of faith which allows him to catch the golden Snitch: "Tangled together in a many-armed hug, the Gryffindor team sank, yelling hoarsely, back to earth. Wave upon wave of crimson supporters was pouring over the barriers onto the field. Hands were raining down on their backs... Words failed them...If only there had been a dementor around... As a sobbing Wood passed Harry the Cup, as he lifted it into the air, Harry felt he could have produced the world's best Patronus"(313). After this experience, Harry is finally able to conjure a Patronus, using this powerful memory of joyous rapture, love, and friendship. He has added an important ability to his arsenal of defensive skills. We might want to link this idea up with our earlier discussion of the debilitating effects of the poison of hatred. You cannot conjure up a Patronus if you are filled with hatred. It is a magical spell whose root is in joy and in love, not in cruelty and in evil.

In a bizarre moment at the end of the Divination class, Harry is alone with Professor Trelawney for a moment, and her eyes roll back into her head and she speaks in a voice that does not seem to be her own. Harry is frightened, and we don't blame him: "THE DARK LORD WILL RISE AGAIN WITH HIS SERVANT'S AID, GREATER AND MORE TERRIBLE THAN EVER HE WAS. TONIGHT...BEFORE MIDNIGHT...

THE SERVANT...WILL SET OUT...TO REJOIN...HIS MASTER"(324). We had almost written her off as a harmless quack, and then this! So, it is important to remember that every once in a while, coming from whatever you want to call the source, there can be a genuine prophecy. This seems to be one of them. Now, J. K. Rowling has everything in place for the exciting conclusion to the novel.

At this point, we are moving toward a major shift in the plot as Rowling brings our focus to an absolutely amazing final scene where many mysteries will be solved. It starts with our three young heroes going to comfort Hagrid, hoping against hope that the execution of Buckbeak might be reprieved. Eventually, it seems as if there is no hope, and Hagrid tells them to hurry and leave, for children should not witness something so horrible as this. As they are leaving his hut, huddled under Harry's invisibility cloak because they should not be out of the castle in the evening, suddenly Ron's rat, a tattered old thing named Scabbers, goes absolutely crazy. He is terrified of something; that much is certain, and then they see what it is—Crookshanks. Now, Hermione's cat has never liked Scabbers, but suddenly that antipathy is elevated to a whole new level, and Crookshanks attacks the rat. Not only that—seemingly out of nowhere, a gigantic, shaggy black dog comes bounding over to them, and he fastens his jaws on Ron's arm, the one protecting Scabbers, and drags him into an underground tunnel through a hole at the base of the Whomping Willow. As he is doing this, Harry and Hermione hear a dull thud, and they know that Ron's leg, which he had hooked around a root of the tree in order to stop his progress, has been broken.

Shocked, terrified, and bewildered, they know they must follow Ron, and they don't know how to open the passage. Hermione, frustrated and frightened, and worried about Ron, whispers a plea for help, and help is given. We are, after all, at Hogwarts. Suddenly, Crookshanks places his paw on a knot on the Whomping Willow, and it stops fighting them off. Instead, a passage opens—a passage that leads to the Shrieking Shack. Here, we sense a major transition in the plot, and we can feel ourselves getting closer and closer to some real answers. In a room in the shack, we suddenly come face to face with Sirius Black, who is an animagus that can disguise himself as a big black dog—the dog that they have seen prowling about the castle grounds with Crookshanks, the dog that just dragged Ron into the tunnel. Now, we remember the etymology of his name.

At this particular moment, Harry is full of hatred for Sirius, not knowing at all what is really going on here, but right from the beginning of the scene, we can see that Sirius means no harm to Harry, Ron, or Hermione. In fact, he is genuinely solicitous about Ron's injury. When Professor Lupin joins them in the room, it is clear that Lupin and Sirius know more than Harry, Ron, and Hermione about what is really going on. It is also clear that Lupin and Sirius have a past together, a past that Harry knows little or nothing about. At first, the two of them seem to be talking in riddles, and suddenly Lupin figures something out, and Sirius quietly nods. Harry's mind is whirling. Has he been betrayed by Lupin too, a man that he has trusted? New information now comes out quickly, bombarding us with realizations—Ron's rat is no rat at all. He is really Peter Pettigrew, who is definitely a rat, but not in the way we thought. Rather, he too is an animagus, who has now disguised himself as a rat (how appropriate) after betraying James and Lily Potter to Voldemort, and arranging for Sirius to take the blame for his betrayal. When Pettigrew is revealed in his human form, Sirius wants to kill him and can scarcely be restrained by Lupin.

By now, Hermione has figured out that Lupin is a werewolf, and she has alerted Harry and Ron to possible danger from him because of this. Lupin asks for a moment of quiet to explain himself. He tells them that when he was a small boy, he had been bitten by a wolf, and that ever since that time, he transforms, unwillingly, into a werewolf once a month, when there is a full moon. The only thing that can stave off this terrible transformation is a wolfsbane potion that has only recently been discovered and for which he depends on Severus Snape, who makes it for him. Before that, he depended on his friends to help him survive the dark hour of the soul, the hours of his uncontrollable transformations: "For the first time ever, I had friends, three great friends. Sirius Black...Peter Pettigrew...and, of course, your father, Harry—James Potter…they didn't desert me at all. Instead, they did something for me that would make my transformations not only bearable, but the best times of my life. They became animagi"(354). We realize that both James and Harry are great, loyal friends—life father, like son. Suddenly, Severus Snape is there in the room with them, having been hiding under Harry's invisibility cloak which he had found at the base of the tree where Harry dropped it. Sneeringly, he tells Lupin that he forgot to take his wolfsbane potion tonight, and an ominous chill shivers right through us.

Still smarting from a long held grudge, Snape tries to poison Harry's mind against Lupin, but Harry finally starts thinking, and his heart and his mind go to Lupin and Sirius: "Professor Lupin could have killed me about a hundred times this year…I've been alone with him loads of times, having defense lessons against dementors"(361). He disarms Snape, and then he listens to Sirius Black's story. The whole terribly sad truth comes out—how Sirius had encouraged Lily and James to make Peter Pettigrew their Secret Keeper, how Pettigrew, because of his enormous cowardice, had betrayed that trust, thereby causing James' and Lily's deaths. It is time to talk about this important character—Peter Pettigrew.

Long ago, he was a fellow Gryffindor, and a friend of James and Lily's. Somewhere along the line, when it seemed as if Voldemort was going to be triumphant, he became a double agent, secretly in the service of Voldemort although he maintained the illusion of friendship with his old buddies. What he seems to have been famous for is a general lack of talent and a deeply rooted cowardice. Even Professor McGonagall has told us that she never understood why Lupin, James, and Sirius let him hang around with them; she describes Pettigrew as a "hanger-on." However, he was secretly branded with the Dark Mark, and he swore his allegiance to Voldemort, having been promised power and wealth in the new order when he came to power. After the prophecy was made about Harry, James and Lily took him and went into hiding, in order to protect him. In an ill-fated attempt at misdirection, Sirius convinced James and Lily to name Pettigrew as their Secret Keeper. Pettigrew betrayed this sacred trust on Halloween night in 1981 when he told Voldemort where the Potters were hiding their son. Voldemort killed James and Lily on that night but was defeated when his own killing curse rebounded on him, killing his physical form. Realizing what had happened, Sirius, filled with rage and guilt, pursued Pettigrew. When he closed in, Pettigrew screamed that Sirius had betrayed the Potters. Using a blasting curse, he caused a huge explosion, one that killed twelve "Muggles." In the chaos that ensued, he faked his own death, cutting off his finger and leaving it behind. He then transformed himself into a rat, his animagus form, and fled, leaving Sirius to take the blame for the murder of these innocent people. This is the crime for which Sirius has spent twelve years in prison. We realize that Sirius is guilty of nothing other than bad judgment. He tells Harry: "Believe me, Harry. I never betrayed James and Lily. I would have died before I betrayed them"(372). And his words sound like the truth to Harry, and they are.

When Pettigrew transforms right before their eyes, Sirius tries to kill him, and Harry stops him. We are reminded of the code of honor of the Knights of the Round Table, and young Harry might well be one of those knights. That code included the following guidelines: always fight in just causes; defend women and children, and those too weak to defend themselves; consider the possibility of showing mercy to your adversary when his defeat is certain. Harry shows mercy. And maybe this is the most difficult part of the code. This decision on Harry's part has complex consequences—some good and some bad. Or, so it seems at this moment in the quest.

When Harry forbids both Black and Lupin to take matters into their own hands, "Black and Lupin both looked staggered"(375). Sirius reminds Harry that Pettigrew is the reason that Harry has no parents, and that he would have gladly looked on while Voldemort killed Harry too. Harry acknowledges that Pettigrew deserves to be punished, but something in his own soul forbids him to take his life in this manner. This is a marked difference from those who succumb to evil. As we have said before, there is no mercy in the heart of evil. This is part of what separates Harry from Voldemort and enables him to eventually win the battle. Harry understands, or is at least in the process of learning, the intangible magic, the magic far more powerful that any spell. Love , mercy, compassion, friendship, and honoring obligations. Harry possesses these attributes, and, while they do not always have obvious positive short-term effects, in the long run, they are what give him the power to defeat Voldemort. Harry understands something that Voldemort does not, or if he understands it, he does not give this idea enough weight: In killing someone, you violate your own soul. You can never be whole again. This does not apply to war— that is different. But at this particular moment, they are not in the condition of war. If anything, Peter Pettigrew could be considered a prisoner of war, and Harry knows that it would be wrong to kill him: "I'm not doing this for you. I'm doing it because—I don't reckon my dad would've wanted them to become killers—just for you"(376). Both Sirius and Lupin acquiesce to Harry's command, and we have the strong sense that Harry has taken his place among them as a man and a fellow warrior. Pettigrew acknowledges that this mercy is more than he deserves, and it is.

As they begin their ill-fated journey back to the castle, Sirius and Harry have a moment together, a moment where Sirius tells Harry, with some trepidation, that he is Harry's godfather, and that, if it all works out, he would like Harry to come and live with him during the summers. Harry is thrilled, and "Black's gaunt face broke into the first true smile Harry had seen upon it. The difference it made was startling, as though a person ten years younger were shining through the starved mask; for a moment, he was almost recognizable as the man who had laughed at Harry's parents' wedding"(379). This is the difference that love and forgiveness can make. We can only imagine how much guilt and suffering Sirius has been carrying around for all these years. And to be forgiven is to be lifted up, to have your heart made lighter. To love and be loved is a transformational thing. Remember, love is the most powerful magic of all.

As we all know, things go quickly wrong after this brief moment of happiness. As they start to cross the moor, the landscape is bathed in moonlight, and Lupin has not taken his wolfsbane. He transforms, unwillingly, and in the confusion, Pettigrew escapes. Lupin the werewolf injures Sirius, even though Sirius has transformed into a dog, trying to protect the three young warriors. Sirius is grievously injured, maybe almost dying. Dementors approach, and Harry tries to perform a patronus charm, without much success. Watch how cleverly J. K. Rowling limits what we know in this scene: "Facedown, too weak to move, sick and shaking, Harry opened his eyes…Something was driving the dementors back…It was circling around him and Black and Hermione…They were leaving…The air was warm again…Eyes blurred with sweat, Harry tried to make out what it was…It was as bright as a unicorn…Fighting to stay conscious…Harry saw, by its brightness somebody welcoming it back...someone who looked strangely familiar...but it couldn't be...(385).

When we read this passage, even if we know exactly what is going on here, we cannot help but feel our hearts race up hopefully. Harry is, at this particular moment in the narrative, a very good example of what we call an unreliable narrator. Not intentionally, but unreliable nevertheless. It could be argued, if you want to push it, every narrator is always to some extent an unreliable narrator, because their perception of the reality of the moment is, of necessity, formed by their own biases and experiences, by the person they have become. After acknowledging that this is a valid argument, and difficult to refute, let us clarify the term a little further. At this moment, Harry is not attempting to deceive us, as some unreliable narrators do, nor is he attempting to lie to himself. He really has not figured out what is going on, and most likely, neither have we. Certainly not the first time we read the scene, and this is, at least in part, because J. K. Rowling has not yet told us about the Time Turner, the wonderful gadget that allows the triumphant conclusion of this novel.

But we find out about it now. The next chapter is entitled "Hermione's Secret," and that is what the Time Turner is all about. Sirius is taken to a holding cell, Ron is in the hospital, Lupin is deep in the forest as a werewolf, and Snape wants Sirius hauled off back to Azkaban. Dumbledore lets him speak his piece, and then, rather summarily, dismisses him. Then, Dumbledore and Hermione have a pointed and somewhat elliptical conversation, and Harry feels completely bewildered. It is as if the two of them are speaking a different language for a moment. And they are. They are speaking the language of the manipulation of time. And that is what Harry and Hermione are about to engage in. J. K. Rowling manages to accomplish this manipulation very successfully and respectfully, and it works. Dumbledore tells them, very quietly, that he is just a man, not a god, and as such, he has no power to make other men see the truth, or to overrule the Ministry in its ignorant decision to imprison Sirius Black again for a crime he did not commit. He says, looking pointedly at Hermione, that what they need is more time: "Now, pay attention… Sirius is locked in Professor Flitwick's office on the seventh floor…If all goes well, you will be able to save more than one innocent life tonight. But remember this, both of you: you must not be seen. Miss Granger, you know the law—you know what is at stake…You—must—not—be—seen"(393). He is in deadly earnest, and she understands completely. Harry does not have a clue about what is going on, and neither do we, until Hermione explains.

She tells Harry that the tiny little hourglass hanging on a chain around her neck is a Time Turner, and that it allows them to go back in time. Three turns equals three hours back, and that is all Dumbledore said they should take. She knows how to do it, and she respects its power. After all, she has been using it all year as she attended an impossible number of classes. However, she cannot quite figure out what they should do with this extra time. What did Dumbledore mean? This is when Harry's intuition kicks in, as it so often does at critical moments. Suddenly, it hits him. They are to save not only Sirius, but also Buckbeak, who is to be executed tonight for attacking Draco Malfoy. In fact, Buckbeak will be the mode of transportation for Sirius' escape.

So, they go back three hours, back to Hagrid's cabin, where they were about to witness the execution of Buckbeak, an execution they think they already heard from a distance as they left his cabin, unwilling to see it. They were deceived and so were we. The narrative takes on a kind of metafictional quality here for a moment, as J. K. Rowling has Harry say: "This is the weirdest thing we've ever done"(398). We can almost feel J. K. Rowling grinning as she comments on her own story line here. She certainly seems to be having a little bit of fun with the whole thing. And just in case we have not understood the import of the moment, Hermione clarifies it for us: "Don't you understand? We're breaking one of the most important wizarding laws! Nobody's supposed to change time, nobody!"(398). If we let the word "wizarding" stand for the word "storytelling," we get an idea of what is going on here. J. K. Rowling is acknowledging to us that she is in tricky territory as a storyteller here, that she is playing with time, and she invites us to watch her do it, and to see the high respect and the distinct limitations she will observe. And it works.

This scene is a kind of aerial high wire act for a writer, making the manipulation of time believable. Using the Time Turner to turn back time for three hours, Harry and Hermione see themselves back at Hagrid's cabin and wait to make their move. While they are sitting together, Harry has a chance to talk to Hermione about the Patronus that saved him (or will save him) and Sirius. When she asks him, he is hesitant to explain, and now we know why. He believes that he has seen a really powerful wizard, and in his secret heart of hearts, he thinks it was his dad. What a beautiful misdirection on J. K. Rowling's part. She certainly engages our hearts with this one. Who among us has not yearned, with every fiber of our being, for the return of a loved one we have lost, particularly in a time of need. Hermione knows how much he is hurting, but she points out the obvious—James Potter is dead. And, unless J. K. Rowling wants to go into the realm of the supernatural, James Potter could not have conjured that Patronus. But a really powerful wizard did—Harry is right about that.

As the scene plays out, Harry watches as he and Sirius are attacked, lying by the side of the pond and almost dead, waiting for his dad to come and conjure the powerful Patronus that would save him. And then suddenly he understands—he is the "really powerful wizard" and the task is his: "And then it hit him—he understood. He hadn't seen his father—he had seen himself—Harry flung himself out from behind the bush and pulled out his wand. 'EXPECTO PATRONUM!' he yelled. And out of the end of his wand burst, not a shapeless cloud of mist, but a blinding, dazzling, silver animal...It looked like a horse... It wasn't a horse. It wasn't a unicorn either. It was a stag. It was shining brightly as the moon above...it was coming back to him... Slowly, it bowed its antlered head. And Harry realized"(411). Prongs. Astonished at the extent of his own powers, Harry figures it all out and explains it to Hermione. Harry would never have thought of himself as a "very powerful wizard." He is not guilty of that kind of hubris. Rather, he comes to the realization that he must have been the wizard that did this, only after he and Hermione have exhausted all other possible explanations. He has just conjured his first real patronus, and it is a stag—very much like the animal into which his father transformed when he, as an animagus, took his animal form—Prongs. This is not an accidental choice; in fact, it is brilliant. A stag is an important literary symbol with powerful associations that we should now explore.

First of all, a stag is a time-honored symbol of nobility and gentleness. It is also said to be a symbol for the conquest of death. In part, this comes from the regenerative power of the stag's horns. If they are broken off, the antlers will regrow—hence, the resurrection imagery. The stag has been used in many other pieces of quest literature, including the Arthurian cycle and the Chronicles of

Narnia, by C. S. Lewis. One of the most famous and perhaps earliest references to the stag comes from the Old Testament, the Song of Solomon: "Make haste, my beloved, and be like a gazelle or a young stag upon the mountain of spices"(8:14). There are many other lines where the stag represents the beloved. In this very sensual book of the Old Testament, the figure of the stag frequently comes leaping to his loved one. In the Judeo-Christian tradition, this imagery has been interpreted as the love of God for his beloved, the church. And we are God's church. By extension, then, the stag is a symbol of the intimate experience of divine love in the individual soul. It could be argued then, that the stag is a symbol for Jesus Christ, or at least for God among us. Finally, the stag is often cast in a role whereby he is said to be a protector of all animals, to have about him a quiet majesty and a restorative presence. So, how perfect is it that Harry's Patronus is a stag.

When Harry figures out that he is the really powerful wizard who conjured the stag Patronus while time is catching up, it is time for them to make their move to save both Sirius and Buckbeak. Harry and Hermione slip Buckbeak away and ride him up to Sirius' prison window, and with their help, Sirius escapes. All at once, Harry and Hermione are back in Ron's hospital room, and the two time images converge, the alternate universes collide, almost seamlessly, the three hours that the Time Turner gave them having expired. Harry finds out that Lupin has resigned his post; he knows that the parents of Hogwarts students are not going to want a werewolf instructing their children. However, before he goes, he returns the Marauder's Map to Harry. He had earlier confiscated it when Snape found Harry with it, saying that as the Defense Against the Dark Arts teacher, he should be the one to look at it. Actually, he had just been saving it for Harry. He also confirms for Harry that when James Potter transformed into his animal state as an animagus, he was a stag: "Yes, your father was always a stag when he transformed…you guessed right…that's why we called him Prongs"(424). This works very nicely with the etymology of the word patronus and father(pater), about which we have already spoken. Lupin departs, leaving Harry and Dumbledore together for the final wrap up—the wonderful scene that often comes at the end of the novel where Dumbledore usually helps Harry think his way through some things that he hasn't quite figured out yet.

At this moment, Harry is very low because he doesn't feel like he has accomplished enough. He wanted to clear Sirius' name and give him back his freedom, his unqualified freedom. He has questions too. He wonders about Sibyll Trelawney's predictions; her words are still haunting him. He tells Dumbledore about her prophecy: "her voice went all deep and her eyes rolled and she said…she said Voldemort's servant was going to set out to return to him before midnight… she said the servant would help him come back to power…was she making a real prediction?"(426). What an interesting and difficult question, and it is one to which there are no easy answers. It is worth noting that Trelawney's prediction was accurate. Voldemort's servant Pettigrew set out to return to Voldemort to help him come back to life. This once again supports the idea that destiny and free will shape the course of our lives. Pettigrew escaped not because of any divine power, but because of Harry's mercy. Harry has free will; he could have chosen to allow Sirius to kill Pettigrew. He did not, not because of the prophecy—he did not even understand what it meant—but because of who he is. There is a combination of things at work—things we cannot control and things we can.

We could call these things fate and free will. So, Harry asks Dumbledore if Trelawney was making a real prediction. Dumbledore recognizes that this is a question for which there is no easy answer. For the first part of his answer, Dumbledore acknowledges that now Sibyll has apparently made two real predictions, so we know there is another one floating out there. It will become very important in the fifth book in the series. Secondly, he addresses the question philosophically. Can any prediction ever be called real or true in and of itself? Or does a prediction require time and someone knowing it has been made to be called real: "Hasn't your experience with the Time Turner taught you anything, Harry? The consequences of our actions are always so complicated, so diverse, that predicting the future is a

120

very difficult business indeed"(426). In any given moment, an infinite number of possibilities exist. The future depends on our decisions. We are right at the heart of the primordial questions here—who am I, and why am I here? Is the course of my life determined by free will or fate? The answer is still the same complex answer we have articulated before. Life is a journey, a quest. The purpose of that quest is to find out who you are as a person, and why you are here. Both free will and circumstances beyond your control will contribute to shaping the course of your life. Frequently, a prophecy only becomes a prophecy if somebody knows it and honors it as having some validity, and if they do that—chances are that they will then set about trying to make that prophecy come true. We will return to this idea later in the quest.

The second thing that Dumbledore tells Harry is that he did a noble thing in sparing Pettigrew's life: "Pettigrew owes his life to you. You have sent Voldemort a deputy who is in your debt…When one wizard saves another wizard's life, it creates a certain bond between them…and I'm much mistaken if Voldemort wants his servant in the debt of Harry Potter…This is magic at its deepest, its most impenetrable, Harry. But trust me…the time may come when you will be very glad you saved Pettigrew's life"(427). Dumbledore further tells Harry that James Potter would have done the same thing. At this particular moment in time, Harry cannot quite bring himself to believe this. However, it is quite possible that Dumbledore is right. Sometimes, an act of kindness seems to go unrecognized, and certainly unrewarded. But acts of kindness never really disappear. They seem to set off resonances somewhere in the universe or in the secret universes of people's hearts. Sometimes they are acknowledged long after you have even forgotten any moment of patience or understanding that you ever gave that person.

Finally, Harry admits to Dumbledore his disappointment that he was the really powerful wizard who had conjured the stag patronus, and that he had half way hoped it might have been his father. And Dumbledore gives the most important insight of the whole novel: "You think the dead we loved ever truly leave us? You think that we don't recall them more clearly than ever in times of great trouble? Your father is alive in you, Harry, and shows himself most plainly when you have need of him. How else could you produce that particular Patronus? Prongs rode again last night...You know, Harry, in a way, you did see your father last night....You found him inside yourself"(428). I know the truth of this statement in my very bones. Several years ago, I lost my Mom after a long battle with cancer. I miss her every day, and I ask her to watch over me and guide me. There is not a day that goes by when I don't long to talk to her, just to have the pleasure of having a cup of coffee with her, just to hear her voice. But, I know that she is beside me and inside me, even as I type this sentence. In fact, it is in part because of her that I do type this sentence. One day, a long time ago, she said, 'Chrissy, you should write a book. You love to teach—so write, and teach!" I think I was just waiting for the right quest. And then, one day, it presented itself to me—in the eager faces of my students who said, "I would love to hear you talk about the Harry Potter books." And so, here I am, doing just that. This idea echoes in Dumbledore's statement that he will never be gone from Hogwarts as long as there are students there who remain loyal to him. Our memories of our loved ones keep them alive, keep them always among us, even after they have "gone on." Again, our loved ones never really leave us.

The novel closes with Harry at dinner in the great hall, eating with his friends and enjoying their company, knowing that a summer with the Dursleys is just around the corner. Hermione tells Ron and Harry that she has eagerly surrendered the Time Turner, that it was driving her crazy. We are reminded that there are limits—the time for the Time Turner is over. Soon, Harry finds himself back with the Dursleys, but he warns them, ever so delicately, that they had better not bully him too much. After all, he has a godfather, and "he's a convicted murderer, but he's broken out of wizard prison and he's on the run. He likes to keep in touch with me, though…keep up with my news…check if I'm happy…"(435). Vernon Dursley is not so simple that he cannot understand that implied threat, and Harry is delighted at the look of horror on his fat uncle's face. So concludes the wonderful third book in the series.

The primary contributions of this book include the following: we learn that things are not always what they seem to be, that we need to be careful about a rush to judgment. Harry was certain that Sirius was a horrible person, a man who had betrayed the trust of his parents. He was wrong about that. Sirius will become a very important presence in Harry's life going forward. We learn that an act of kindness is often repaid a hundred times over, and this is a theme that will continue. We realize that, at any given moment, an infinite number of possibilities exist in our courses of action, and that we should choose carefully. Contrary to what the Time Turner suggests, we cannot undo time. Once those angry words are spoken, they cannot be recalled. And finally, we learn, most powerfully of all, that our loved ones never leave us—that their love gives us courage, protection, and strength, even in our darkest hours. Once again, the most powerful magic of all is love.

Harry Potter and The Goblet of Fire

The fourth novel opens with a glimpse back in time, and we learn about the "Riddle House," to which the residents of Little Hangleton, a small and unimportant village, have given a wide berth, because "half a century ago, something strange and horrible had happened there…the story had been picked over so many times, and had been embroidered in so many places, that nobody was quite sure what the truth was anymore"(1). This little statement asks us to contemplate the elusive quality of truth, and the power of narrative. When we tell a story, we embroider the details, not necessarily out of any desire to deceive, but rather just because that is the nature of storytelling. We shape the stories with our words; there is no other way it can be. So, by extension, language determines the "reality principle." We cannot ever completely agree on "reality" because no two people see the world in exactly the same way. We do search for consensus on the "reality principle," by finding as many touch points as we can agree on. This search necessarily involves compromise. Arguably, by extension, an agreed upon "reality principle" moves farther and farther away from any individual person's view of "reality" as there are more commonalities agreed upon. There may be a Truth out there, but we tell "truths" to each other. Plato versus Aristotle. Plato believed in a

125

Note: is that is truth reality? (handwritten margin note)

capital T truth. Aristotle said that truth is relative to the truth teller. We enter the modern world, which tends to be Aristotelian rather than Platonic in our concept of truth. It is amazing, however, that these concepts were being debated by the greatest minds of their time, back in 400 B.C.

Nonetheless, we hear about a terrible violence that occurred in the house fifty years ago. The Riddle family was found dead, mysteriously dead, perhaps even murdered, although no coroner could ever be certain. No marks were found upon the victims. Since that time, the house has been tended by Frank Bryce, the old gardener, who continues his duty to the household out of some sense of obligation to his old master, or perhaps out of a desire not to have to mingle with the gossipy residents of the village. He does not know that Voldemort and Wormtail are in hiding in this house, and Frank inadvertently hears them planning the murder of a boy named Harry Potter. When he bravely confronts Voldemort and threatens to report him to the police, Voldemort instantly kills him. Miles away, Harry Potter's scar begins to burn.

After this sinister opening, we find ourselves back at the Dursley residence, where Harry is hoping that the summer vacation ends soon. He feels sad that things did not work out for him to live with Sirius, his godfather who is living in exile. But once again, the Weasleys come to the rescue, asking Aunt Petunia if they might have permission to take Harry to the Quidditch World Cup with them. There follows a very funny scene in which the Weasleys try to arrive at the Dursley residence via floo powder, find the chimney blocked since it is not a real fireplace, and blow their sealed up fireplace open so that they can get into the house.   We can actually feel J. K. Rowling having fun with her magical world in scenes like these, imagining the consequences of the magical world and the Muggle world crashing together—even in the Dursley's living room.

Back at the Burrow, we have the distinct impression of excitement as the Weasleys work out the logistics of transporting themselves to the site for the World Cup competition. In passing, we hear some concern expressed for a witch named Bertha Jorkins who has been missing for over a month now.   Mr. and Mrs. Weasley are concerned about her disappearance, but it doesn't really register with us as a major concern. Later we discover that Voldemort has captured and tortured her, trying to get some information from her about how best to trap Harry.   At this time, however, we simply register a slightly unsettled feeling, a kind of uneasiness about her unexplained disappearance.

The Weasleys, along with Harry and Hermione, travel by portkey to the lovely deserted moor which will be used for the competition. As Mr. Weasley says, precautions have been taken so that the gathering of the magical community is not too noticeable: "The trouble is, about a hundred thousand wizards turn up at the World Cup, and of course, we just haven't got a magical site big enough to accommodate them all. There are places Muggles can't penetrate, but imagine trying to pack a hundred thousand wizards into Diagon Alley or platform nine and three-quarters. So, we had to find a nice deserted moor, and set up as many anti-Muggle precautions as possible"(69). So, this is a large arena, as big or bigger than many major university stadiums in our country. And this will be a big event.

When they arrive at the campsite, they meet the site manager, a Muggle named Mr. Roberts. He takes one look at the wizards, inexpertly dressed as Muggles, and regards them as foreigners: "You foreign?...People from all over. Loads of foreigners. And not just foreigners. Weirdos, you know? There's a bloke walking 'round in a kilt and a poncho"(77). Whenever Mr. Roberts gets to noticing too much detail, one of the wizards carefully wipes his memory clean, using the Obliviate charm, and very quickly, a look of dreamy unconcern washes over his features. Clever.

There is a great deal of fun for us as we encounter the Weasley's magical tent, hear about the ban on flying carpets, and meet Ludo Bagman and the Diggory men. Suddenly, it is time for the Weasleys to take their seats for the first match, and, surprisingly, they have been given very desirable seats. It is here that we run into the Malfoys, and we meet Draco's mother Narcissa for the first time: "His mother was blonde too, tall and slim, she would have been nice-looking if she hadn't been wearing a look that suggested there was a nasty smell under her nose"(101). Interesting observation—her arrogance makes her unattractive. Lucius Malfoy, Draco's hate-filled father, sneeringly asks how the Weasleys came to have such expensive seats, and Arthur Weasley wisely ignores him. Immediately thereafter, the mascots for the Bulgarian team take the field, and we meet the wizarding equivalent of a cross between the Dallas Cowboy cheerleaders and the mythical Sirens.

Veela. Veela are women, "the most beautiful women Harry had ever seen…except that they weren't—they couldn't be—human. This puzzled Harry for a moment…but then the music started, and Harry stopped worrying about them not being human—in fact, he stopped worrying about anything at all. The veela had started to dance, and Harry's mind had gone completely and blissfully blank…And as the veela danced faster and faster, wild, half-formed thoughts started chasing through Harry's dazed mind. He wanted to do something very impressive, right now. Jumping from the box into the stadium seemed a good idea"(103). We can witness almost the same behavior from men attending an NFL game when the professional cheerleaders start their seductive dancing. Furthermore, we can compare this behavior to the Sirens of ancient mythology. At this particular moment, Harry and Ron would gladly crash on the rocks, like Ulysses of old. However, the veela stop, just in the nick of time. Hermione mocks them for being so silly; perhaps she has forgotten how smitten she was with the illusion of manliness that Gilderoy Lockhart had so carefully crafted. Then, the Irish mascots take the field, and Leprechaun gold seems to fall from the sky. Deceived again, the wizards eagerly gather the "gold" up, but remember, real gold never falls from the sky, not even in the wizarding world.

The match is exciting, and the twins seem to have won a big bet from Mr. Bagman, and Harry happily goes to bed, exhausted at the end of a wonderful day. However, part way through the night, Harry is awakened, and something is very wrong. Outside the tent, he hears terrible noises—screams and explosions. They hurriedly dress and step outside the tent to see a terrifying sight—the Roberts family (the Muggles who operate the campsite) are suspended in mid-air, unable to defend themselves. Mrs. Roberts is being made to spin around, upside down, showing her underwear. This is sick and cruel, and the Weasley family is quick to identify it as such. Sadly, there are some wizards that are laughing at the abuse. The wizard world is obviously not unlike our own. Everyone is running from the campsite, and Draco sneeringly warns Harry and Ron that they had better protect Hermione, that the Muggles are under attack. In their flight, Harry drops his wand, and almost at the same moment, notices Winky, Mr. Crouch's house elf, running oddly. He files this observation away, luckily, but at the moment, all he notices is that he does not have his wand, and without it, he feels vulnerable. Suddenly, a voice calls out a very scary word, "Morsmordre," and the Dark Mark is conjured in the sky. This strange word is really a repetition of the Latin word for death, which is appropriate for Voldemort, of course.

A chill runs through us. The Dark Mark is Voldemort's calling card. He and his faithful followers, the Death Eaters, post it in the sky whenever they kill. It hasn't been seen for thirteen years, but it is in the sky tonight. Lord Voldemort is once again gaining power. Bill and Arthur Weasley point out that it is impossible to know who placed the dark mark on display. And problematic. Bill explains that, at least at some level, the Death Eaters must be worried about the possibility of Voldemort coming back to power: "I bet they'd be even more frightened than the rest of us to see him come back. They denied they'd ever been involved with him when he lost his powers, and went back to their daily lives…I don't reckon he'd be over pleased with them, do you?"(143).

They all arrive back at the Burrow, and Molly Weasley is so relieved to see that they are safely back. Anyone who is a parent can identify with Molly at this moment. She confesses that she had been worried sick, and even more so because she had parted from the twins in anger. This episode reminds me so much of my Mom, who always said that we should never go to bed or part from each other angrily.

It may seem silly, but I have tried to make this practice a part of my code of honor for my life. Molly Weasley is the quintessential Mom in this quest narrative. That does not imply that she is incapable of defending herself or fighting to protect her loved ones. Quite the contrary. She is a formidable warrior in her own rite, and we will see a clear demonstration of that in the final stages of the quest.

Soon after the disastrous conclusion to the World Cup, we hear the name of the obnoxious reporter, Rita Skeeter. Her very name is appropriate—it sounds like the word mosquito, and that is perfect for her. She is always annoying, buzzing around, bothering people, trying to suck their lifeblood or their privacy out of them. Anyone in the profession of journalism is embarrassed by her behavior in this novel. She is the quintessence of everything we despise in unethical reporters. Shortly after meeting her, it is time to be off to Hogwarts, and the school year begins under the shadow of the possibility of the Dark Lord having regained his powers. When we get to Hogwarts, we meet the new Defense against the Dark Arts teacher, Mad-Eye Moody. He is a retired Auror, a dark wizard catcher, and he has accounted for the apprehension of many of the inmates at Azkaban.

Harry and Ron overhear Draco talking about another wizarding school, Durmstrang, one that seems to be more comfortable with the Dark Arts than Dumbledore or the staff at Hogwarts is. Ron says that he wishes that Lucius Malfoy had sent Draco to Durmstrang so they wouldn't have to deal with him, and says that it is too bad that Narcissa loves her son. We could hardly imagine how important this little bit of information about Narcissa will be later on in the quest.

As the students are enjoying the start of term feast, Dumbledore announces that this year, the Tri-Wizard Tournament will be held at Hogwarts. The tournament has been in existence for 700 years, but it has not been held in about 100 years, since it had become too dangerous—the death toll was too high. But this year, Hogwarts will host it, with the competitors from Durmstrang and Beauxbatons due to arrive soon. We cannot help but think that this is no accident— that the forces of history are coming together for a significant battle. The tournament has not been held for 100 years, and now, it is going to be held, right when Harry Potter is at Hogwarts. Once again, we feel the presence of almost a divine providence or a plan. When there is a need for a hero, one will arise.

At this point in the narrative, the young students get their first Defense against the Dark Arts class with Mad-Eye Moody, and he is obviously serious about giving them real, practical information about how to battle the powers of darkness. He tells them: "I'm not supposed to show you what illegal Dark curses look like until you're in the sixth year. You're not supposed to be old enough to deal with it till then. But Professor Dumbledore's got a higher opinion of your nerves, he reckons you can cope, and I say, the sooner you know

3 unforgivable curses

what you're up against, the better. How are you supposed to defend yourself against something you've never seen?"(212). So begins our lesson about the three unforgivable curses, and we are at the heart of powerful dark magic right now.

The first of the unforgivable curses is the "Imperius Curse." Using a spider to demonstrate it, Professor Moody shows that this illegal curse takes away the victim's free will. That right there should make us stop dead in our tracks. Free will is sacred. It is a God given right and a God given responsibility. To take away someone's free will is an act of hubris that is truly unforgivable. Every person has the right to direct the course of his or her own life in as much as it is possible. Any curse that overrides free will is against God's law. It is that simple. Moody tells the students that the curse can be fought, but "it takes real strength of character, and not everyone's got it. Better avoid being hit with it if you can. CONSTANT VIGILANCE!"(213). The second of the unforgivable curses is then demonstrated, much to poor Neville's chagrin. He has some first-hand knowledge of this curse, for it was the curse that caused his parents to lose their minds and become lost to him forever. The Cruciatus Curse causes someone such unbearable pain that they are lost in it. The word cruciatus, of course, derives from the word crucify. To perform this curse on anyone is unforgivable, as it should be.

All of this has been leading up to the final unforgivable

134

curse—the last and the worst. This is the curse that killed James and Lily Potter, and yet, it is also the curse that Harry Potter mysteriously survived. "Avada Kedavra." During an interview at the Edinburgh Book Festival in 2004, J. K. Rowling said that the etymology for these words derives loosely from the Aramaic words "let the thing be destroyed." Other readers have pointed out that the words are similar to the Japanese words for "demand your life." Even English gives us a possible hint—the words look very much like "evade the cadaver," or a demand for life to leave the body. Professor Moody tells his class that there is no known countercurse, and there is no blocking it: "Only one known person has ever survived it, and he's sitting right in front of me"(216). Although all of his classmates are, at that moment, staring at Harry, all he can do is think of is the moment of death for his parents—a flash of green light, and the rush of speeding death. His heart is heavy with his sense of loss, and it takes a great deal of effort for him to pull himself back to listen to Moody's words of warning: "Avada Kedavra's a curse that needs a powerful bit of magic behind it—you could all get your wands out now and point them at me and say the words, and I doubt I'd get so much as a nosebleed...Now, if there's no countercurse, why am I showing you? Because you've got to know. You've got to appreciate what the worst is. You don't want to find yourself in a situation where you're facing it. CONSTANT VIGILANCE!"(217).

There are some interesting ideas here. First of all, to kill someone is an unforgivable act. We are right back to the Fifth Commandment: Thou shall not kill. It is the unforgivable act of hubris—to take someone else's life. Secondly, in order to make this unforgivable curse work, you must hate. You must HATE. Saying the words is not enough. Your heart and soul must be filled with hatred. Thirdly, Professor Moody says that these young people need to know that this kind of evil is out there. Sadly, there are people who have given themselves over to evil and whose hearts and minds are filled with hatred. And we need to know that this kind of evil exists. As Professor Moody explains, there is no point in pretending otherwise. At the end of the lesson, both Harry and Neville are badly shaken. Moody comforts Neville, and Harry swallows his pain quietly and bravely. He has faced this kind of evil before.

During the next lesson, Professor Moody demonstrates the possibility of fighting the Imperius Curse, using Harry, of course. At first, Harry surrenders to the commands issuing from Moody. He kind of liked the feeling of having no thoughts of his own: "It was the most wonderful feeling. Harry felt a floating sensation as every thought and worry in his head was wiped gently away, leaving nothing but a vague, untraceable happiness. He stood there feeling immensely relaxed, only dimly aware of everyone watching him"(231). This feeling is another Siren song. This temporary bliss and lack of responsibility make it tempting to give in to another's control or to the control of a drug, but we must fight such temptation. If we have a strong moral compass and a desire to live our lives fully, not some sort of half-life where we are alive physically by not really mentally, then we must listen to the little voice saying no, the voice telling us to stay true to ourselves. And suddenly, Harry realizes this, and then a wonderful thing happens—his free will and self-determination kick in and he says, "No!" With all of his inner strength, he begins to fight the commands issuing from Professor Moody. His independent spirit and sense of responsibility for his own actions would not allow otherwise. We all have this same ability and this same responsibility. There is a little voice in the back of our heads that speaks up—we can call it our conscience if we like. And it has the power to say "No!" to anyone who is trying to force us to do his will. Where does this power come from? From within. From having a good strong sense of what is right and what is wrong. From having a sense of who you are as a person, what you stand for, what you believe in. And any one of us can develop this very powerful kind of countering skill. Once again, we are struck with the notion that we are all, at least at some level, Harry Potter, and his quest is very much the archetype for our own in many ways. The magic he is capable of is magic that we are capable of as well.

Soon afterwards, the competitors from Durmstrang and Beauxbatons arrive, and the Tri-Wizard Tournament excitement heats up. Professor Dumbledore announces that there will be three tasks in the course of the competition and "they will test the champions in many different ways…their magical prowess—their daring—their powers of deduction—and, of course, their ability to cope with danger"(255). Each of the wizarding schools will be allowed to enter one champion, and these competitors are being chosen by an interesting impartial judge—the Goblet of Fire. It is a large, roughly hewn wooden cup. How interesting. We cannot help but feel a connection to the Holy Grail, which of course, represents God's grace among us. The Grail is frequently thought to have been a large, roughly hewn chalice as well. We probably should not push this connection too far here, but it certainly is interesting. Dumbledore goes on to warn the young people that once they have chosen to enter the tournament, if they are selected by the Goblet of Fire, they must see their mission through to the end: "Once a champion has been selected by the Goblet of Fire, he or she is obliged to see the tournament through to the end. The placing of your name in the goblet constitutes a binding, magical contract. There can be no change of heart once you have become a champion"(256). He further announces that there is an age restriction—no one under sixteen may submit his or her name to the Goblet.

In a way, we are all champions, and the Tri-Wizard tournament is life. We will be facing many tasks in our lifetime, and they will test our daring, our will to live, our deductive powers, and our endurance.

Again, we are all on a quest, chosen as champions the moment we are born. Just as the champions must "see the tournament through to the end," we cannot give up on life, no matter how difficult the challenges are.

Now, of course, comes the puzzling moment when the Goblet of Fire announces that four champions will be competing this year. Cedric Diggory will represent Hogwarts, Victor Krum will represent Durmstrang, and Fleur Delacour will represent Beauxbatons. However, suddenly, a fourth name is announced: Harry Potter! And this should not have been able to happen because Harry is technically too young to compete. Besides that, it gives Hogwarts two entries in the competition and the representatives of the other schools are furious. The home school has been given an unfair advantage. And although Harry had secretly dreamed of being able to compete, now that it is a reality, he finds himself frightened and alone. The worst of it is that many of his schoolmates have turned on him, most painfully, even Ron. And, filled with self-doubt and puzzled about how his name came out of that Goblet, since he never put it in, he must begin the challenge of the tournament. The omniscient narrator comments about Harry's sense of foreboding: "It is a strange thing, but when you are dreading something, and would give anything to slow down time, it has a disobliging habit of speeding up...Harry's feeling of barely controlled panic was with him wherever he went"(317). Notice that with this comment, we are subtly asked to recall Sibyll Trelawney's most recent pronouncement to Harry—that the thing he is dreading is coming, even more quickly than he would like. When we make this link, we realize, one again, how such a vague prophecy could be applied to anyone, or to anything. There are many times in life where we find ourselves approaching some task we must do with trepidation, and these obligations or tasks seem to march steadily toward us, as inexorably as time itself. Such is the nature of the human condition.

One further thought—if the Tri-Wizard Tournament could be said to be a metaphor for life, and Dumbledore and other professors have agreed that many of the obstacles in store for the champions are too dangerous or difficult for younger witches and wizards to face, there is another direct link to real life. Some of life's challenges are believed by many to be too much for children to handle, and there is certainly some truth to that. However, there really is no age restriction for much of what happens in life, is there? Bad things happen, and many times they happen to good, innocent people who are too young to face them. But these people have no choice but to deal with what life throws at them. Harry is the perfect example. He was too young to be stripped of his parents, but he was, and he is now forced to deal with it. Sadly, this happens to children in our world every day. And Harry has been strong and wise beyond his years. He is just a young boy, but he has done it. How appropriate that he has now been forced into the Tri-Wizard Tournament as well. He had dreamed of entering, just as many young people dream of doing things at their age that they cannot and should not do, but now that he actually has to do it, he is scared, just as many of us are when we find ourselves in adult situations we had only envisioned before.

As they approach the first task, which is supposed to be a secret until the moment it is publicly revealed, Harry finds out from Hagrid that they will be facing dragons. He is convinced that Victor and Fleur probably already know, so, in the interest of fair play, he takes it upon himself to tell Cedric Diggory. When Harry does this, Cedric is surprised and grateful. In that moment, there begins a friendship between them that is very powerful. That is not to say that they are no longer rivals—they are. However, they are rivals who respect each other, and who will compete fairly, as best they can. At some point along here, there is an important event we do not witness, and Professor Moody must have dropped his guard, his "constant vigilance." The Moody who advises Harry on how to attack the tasks of the tournament is an impostor, as you well know if you have finished the book. We will speak more about that later. However, the impostor Moody tells Harry that cheating has always been a part of the tournament, and that he should play to his strengths. Although Harry must be puzzled by the conflicting messages here, as are we, he understands one thing. He does have a strength that he is sure of, and that is flying. So, he has Hermione teach him how to do a summoning charm successfully. This ability will stand him in good stead when he faces his dragon.

Now comes the exciting scene of Harry and the Norwegian Ridgeback, and clearly, Harry is in great danger. However, he flies well, completes the task, and wins the respect of the tournament observers. Most importantly of all, he wins Ron's respect and honest admiration. When Ron and Harry are joyfully reconciled, and Ron acknowledges that Harry could never have wished this danger on himself, Harry's heart is filled with joy: "Harry helped himself to food; he had almost forgotten what it was like to feel properly hungry, and sat down with Ron and Hermione. He couldn't believe how happy he felt; he had Ron back on his side, he'd gotten through the first task, and he wouldn't have to face the second one for three months"(365). We are subtly reminded of one of the most important lessons of the Potter quest. In the course of our lives, there will be many dangers and difficult moments that we need to struggle through, but there will also come "seasons of grace," and when they come, we need to try to slow our engines down and appreciate them. Once again, we are reminded of the imagery from "The Open Boat." Another wave is surely coming at our frail little craft, so when we find ourselves in calm seas, we ought to smile, lift our face to the sun, and drink the good feeling in.

At this point in the story, Rowling cleverly introduces another kind of stress—dating members of the opposite sex! It is Christmas time, and all of the students will be attending the Yule Ball. As such, the boys must ask the girls to go to the dance with them, and more terrifying than that, they must dance with each other. They must actually move together in some sort of respectable semblance of a ballroom dance. Here, Rowling gives us a glimpse of the universal experience of teenage angst. She lets us see that no one is exempt—the whole experience is equally unsettling for young men and young women. Most teens, in a moment of candor, would agree. People who have survived those perils can look back at them and smile. We all know that the other sex can be terrifying. In fact, it is one of the tasks or challenges that all of us face in the course of our personal quests. Negotiating the perils of dating is no easy accomplishment, and it requires courage and persistence. It often also requires the ability to shake off disappointments and keep going. It is definitely not for the faint of heart. Both Ron and Harry, brilliant and brave though they are, handle the entire situation very awkwardly, making a whole series of mistakes with which almost any reader can readily identify. Perhaps the most important lesson that comes out of the whole episode is this—don't pretend to feel something that you don't. Furthermore, if you are attracted to someone, speak up. Be honest. Dare to take a chance on love. If you do not, you may live your life without love, which, quite honestly, is not really living at all. In his brilliant poem entitled "The Wasteland," T. S. Eliot refers to love as "the awful daring of a moment's surrender...by this, and this only, we have existed"(Eliot line #). We take a leap of faith when we dare to fall in love, and we make ourselves vulnerable—that much is certain. We may fall and get hurt, but unless we love, we will never fully live. Voldemort is an extreme example of that decision, but he is certainly someone who made that decision. And, Hermione has something to say about this whole idea too. After attending the Yule Ball with Victor Krum, when she would rather have gone with Ron, she gives him a good talking to right at the end of the night. She says: "Well, if you don't like it, you know what the solution is, don't you?...Next time there's a ball, ask me before somebody else does, and not as a last resort!"(432). William Shakespeare deals with this same theme in almost all of his festive comedies.

In many of these plays, young would-be lovers engage in adapting disguises, putting on masks (either real or symbolic), and pretending to be someone that they are not. Although these deceptions result in a good deal of laughter on our part, they eventually go too far. Almost always, the deceptions or disguises must be dropped before the joyful resolution can be found at the end of the play. Three of Shakespeare's comedies that pursue this idea are Twelfth Night, As You Like It, and Much Ado about Nothing. In all of these plays, young people are only happy when they drop

144

their masks, admit their deception, and take a chance on declaring their love honestly. It's a dangerous moment, because hiding behind a mask seems comfortable and safe. Telling the truth and honestly admitting that you are in love with someone puts you in a very vulnerable position. Still, it is the only path to love. And really, there is some wisdom in that too. Lovers should be humble, because love is a humbling experience. Really, in essence, you are saying to the person that you love, "My life is in your hands." That's a very powerful moment in a person's life.

Back in our story, Cedric Diggory returns Harry's earlier favor. An act of kindness is often remembered, and both Cedric and Harry are fair, decent people who are trying to play fair. Both Harry and Cedric have been given a golden egg, and it is supposedly a clue to the next task they will face, but Harry cannot make heads or tails of it. Cedric suggests that Harry take it up to the prefects' bathroom and take a bath with it. Strange advice—that's for sure. But wisdom and knowledge can come in unexpected ways, so Harry files away this strange little piece of information, and he will act on it, in time.

Meanwhile, we are again irritated by the annoying reporter, Rita Skeeter. She has taken it upon herself to attack poor Hagrid, who is not very clever with words. Hagrid is overwhelmed and frightened by her meanness, but Dumbledore tells him that he should consider the source of the attack, and just put it out of his mind: "Really, Hagrid, if you are holding out for universal popularity, I'm afraid you will be in this cabin for a very long time...Not a week has passed since I became headmaster of this school when I haven't had at least one owl complaining about the way I run it"(454). There is an important lesson here for all of us. There is that old saying—you can please some of the people all of the time, all of the people some of the time, but never all of the people all of the time. True.

But there is another way we can express this idea—and it helps to slow down and figure this out. When you receive praise from someone, ask yourself if that person matters to you. Is it someone you respect, love, and trust? If yes, then treasure those words of praise. If not, then file it away, or consider that the praise may not be sincere. At any rate, it is not worth any more of your thought or time. Conversely, when someone criticizes you, put yourself through the same analysis. Does this person matter to you? Is it someone you love, admire, and trust? If so, then you need to think about what they have said. If not, then you can throw the words away with the rest of the garbage of the day. It is a very liberating thought when you come to understand the wisdom of it.

Back to our story. Eventually, Harry takes his egg up to the prefects' bathroom, where Moaning Myrtle can be found. They, of course, have a long-standing relationship by now, and she is glad to see Harry and to teasingly guide him into figuring out what the egg's secret is. With his head underwater, Harry can hear the message of the egg, and he figures out that he will have to deal with merpeople, and to rescue someone that he cares very much about from them. He is very apprehensive about this task because he does not consider himself to be a very good swimmer, and he cannot imagine how he is going to breathe underwater. Good point, Harry. That is a problem.

We get our first substantial hint that Moody might not be Moody right after that. But we only see it if we go back through the story. The Marauder's Map shows that Mr. Bartie Crouch was in Snape's office. Now, we know from the end of the story that Bartie Crouch Jr. is masquerading as Moody at this point in the novel, through the continued application of polyjuice potion. He asks Harry if he can borrow the Marauder's Map for a while, and Harry, thinking that he is really speaking to Mad-Eye Moody, the famous auror, gladly gives it to him. What Crouch is really doing is trying to keep others, namely Harry, from finding out that he is not who he appears to be. Nonetheless, Ron and Hermione are summoned away, and Harry approaches the second task with a heavy heart, not having figured out how he will breathe underwater. Dobby arrives in the nick of time with gillyweed, and Harry runs to the lake. This help from Dobby is the first of many acts of kindness on his part. Dobby never forgets Harry's earlier act of kindness and respect, and he will reward Harry for it many times. It will become really important later on. Once again, we realize that

147

no act of kindness is really forgotten. The gillyweed that Dobby gives to Harry is an herb or "weed" that gives him "gills" like a fish, thereby allowing him to breathe underwater.

Harry swims through the cold, brackish water for what seems like an eternity, until he finally comes upon a strange looking underwater village. He sees something that makes his blood run cold: "Ron was tied between Hermione and Cho Chang. There was also a girl who looked no older than eight, whose clouds of silvery hair made Harry feel sure that she was Fleur Delacour's sister. All four of them appeared to be in a very deep sleep"(498). The merpeople object when Harry tries to free more than the one person assigned to him, and he must fight them with every bit of his strength to do what he believes is the right thing. Eventually, Cedric and Victor show up, freeing Cho and Hermione, but Harry must struggle to the surface with Ron and Fleur's sister, and he is almost overcome by the cold and the weight: "He was drawing breath with extreme difficulty. He kicked his legs so hard and fast it felt as though his muscles were screaming in protest; his very brain felt waterlogged, he couldn't breathe, he needed oxygen, he had to keep going, he could not stop—And then he felt his head break the surface of the lake…All around him, wild, green-haired heads were emerging out of the water with him but they were smiling at him"(503).

Although Harry loses the race, the judges appreciate his

"moral fiber." Subtly, once again, we are taught an important lesson. When all is said and done, the only real judge that matters is your own conscience. Do what you honestly think is the right thing in a given circumstance, and do it to the best of your ability. The rest will take care of itself. This whole event speaks powerfully about Harry's character. He does not care about his personal glory, but rather about helping those he loves or those too weak to defend themselves. Just as he sacrificed the win in this contest so that Fleur's sister would live, he later sacrifices himself for the rest of the world. Once again, winning isn't everything. Or, perhaps more accurately, you can lose the contest and win respect and dignity. There are many ways to measure winning.

Under the cover of his animagus disguise Padfoot, Sirius arrives to talk to Harry about the nearness of evil. He is concerned about the mysterious disappearance of Bartie Crouch, who is somebody he knows quite a bit about. It is time for us to learn about him. Sirius tells Harry that Bartie Crouch Sr. was the one who gave the order for him to be sent to Azkaban, without a fair trial. Sirius also gives us some important background material that we now need. There was a time when Crouch was an up and coming man in the Ministry of Magic, powerful and power-hungry. In the difficult times when Voldemort was on the rise, with Muggles dying and terror widespread, Crouch became "as ruthless and cruel as many on the Dark Side"(527). This remark reminds us of something Friedrich Nietzsche once said: "He who fights with monsters might take care lest he thereby become a monster. And if you gaze too long into the abyss, the abyss gazes also into you." There is an ominous aspect to this warning that the story of Bartie Crouch will bear out. When his own son became involved with the Death Eaters, Crouch sentenced him to Azkaban, without a fair trial and with no fatherly compassion at all. According to Sirius, he did not want anything to tarnish his reputation as a worthy candidate for the position of Minister of Magic. He put his own career goal ahead of the duties of love and loyalty to his family. As a result, he lost everything, as we shall see. Sirius tells us that the young man died in Azkaban, shortly after he arrived. This is not at all what happened, but Sirius believes it to be a true account of the events. Again, we will be surprised with a series of revelations right at the end of the novel.

There is something heart-rending about a split between a father and a son. Certainly, the relationship is fraught with agendas and expectations, but underneath all of the tension, there is usually powerful love. When a father condemns or kills his own son, he has committed a crime against nature from which he can probably never recover. He has, in effect, killed part of himself, and it is only a matter of time until that bitter harvest makes itself known to him. It is one of the oldest patterns in literature. We can go back to the story of Laius and Oedipus, which comes to us from ancient Greek mythology.

When Laius hears the terrible prophecy, that his wife would bear him a son, and that the son would kill the father and marry the mother, he immediately takes steps that will make certain that the prophecy comes true, however unintended those consequences are. When his wife gives birth to a son, he tells one of his servants to take the baby away, under the cover of darkness, out into the wilderness, and kill him. In doing this, he is essentially saying that his own life is worth more than that of his son, and with this act of hubris, he puts the wheels in motion that will result in the prophecy coming true. Once again, we see an illustration of the idea that a prophecy has no weight at all unless someone knows it. Then, we start making that prophecy real. We will explore this idea fully in the sixth book. Nonetheless, for our purposes here, let it be noted that a father killing a son, or a son killing a father most often results in nothing but disaster. Either way, the man has killed a part of himself, and he cannot recover from this act of violence.

Soon after this moment in the narrative, we see the elusive Mr. Crouch stumbling out of the forbidden forest, and he is a broken man, mumbling half sentences and clearly terrified. He says to Harry: "Don't leave me!...I...escaped...must warn...must tell...see Dumbledore...my fault...all my fault...Bertha....dead...all my fault... my son...my fault...tell Dumbledore...Harry Potter...the Dark Lord... stronger...Harry Potter"(556). Harry is understandably bewildered and frightened by his words, but he recognizes the urgency in them. He leaves Victor guarding Crouch and runs back for Dumbledore. However, when he returns, Victor has been stunned, and Crouch is gone. The man who pretends to be Professor Moody is quickly on the scene, and says he cannot imagine what happened to Crouch. Harry notices that Moody looks even worse than usual, and that he seems to be drinking from his ever-present hip flask even more than he usually does. We are getting closer to the truth, when deceptions will come undone, and we find out who this false Professor Moody really is. Meanwhile, the third and most dangerous task looms larger and larger in Harry's mind.

Suddenly, Harry's scar starts burning more and more frequently and intensely, and he knows that this is some kind of warning. Beyond that, he has a vision of Voldemort scolding Wormtail. He does what he knows he should do—he seeks an audience with Professor Dumbledore. As he waits alone in his office, Harry sees the beautiful, shallow stone basin we will come to know as the Pensieve. He sort of tumbles into it, and into a series of flashbacks which culminate in the trial of Bartie Crouch Jr. and the words his father speaks as he condemns him to Azkaban: When Harry emerges, shaken, from the vision, Dumbledore explains the purpose of the Pensieve: "I sometimes find, and I am sure you know the feeling, that I simply have too many thoughts and memories crammed into my mind…At these times…I use the Pensieve. One simply siphons the excess thoughts from one's mind, pours them into the basin, and examines them at one's leisure. It becomes easier to spot patterns and links, you understand, when they are in this form"(597). What a wonderful invention. Perhaps the closest most of us can come to it is our unconscious mind, which works in much the same way. Nonetheless, it is a clever invention for the plotting of the narrative, for it is time for us to get to the bottom of Bartie Crouch's personal tragedy, which we are able to do through Dumbledore's memories.

Professor Dumbledore tells us what happened to Neville's parents, that they were tortured by servants of the Dark Lord, and that they are alive, but insane. So, Neville has lost his parents just as effectively as Harry has lost his: "It was Voldemort. Harry thought, staring up at the canopy of his bed in the darkness, it all came back to Voldemort… He was the one who had torn these families apart, who had ruined these lives"(607). He recognizes that, in many ways, Neville's loss is even more painful than his own. Neville's parents are physically alive, but mentally broken. They are completely beyond his reach, and even though he can stand in their presence, they do not know him at all. If you think about it, that kind of loss is something that many people experience with loved ones who no longer recognize them because of a powerful mental illness. How incredibly painful that experience is. Harry will look at Neville with even more understanding from this time forward. The fact that Harry can think in these terms show us, once again, that he is great of heart and wise beyond his years.

Then it is time for the third and final task of the Triwizard Tournament—the deadly maze. As the competitors walk on to the quidditch field, they find that it is completely unrecognizable. It has been transformed in a complex maze, made of gigantic hedges that tower over the young competitors. Professor McGonagall announces that anyone who believes that he or she is in trouble should simply send up a flare, and they will be rescued. The Triwizard Cup is at the center of the maze; they are to make their way to it, and there will be tasks and challenges along the way. Harry reviews all the charms and spells that he knows, and he actually feels pretty confident entering the maze. This final task really doesn't sound too bad at all, but it turns into a deadly nightmare.

We will not discuss all of the tasks that they encounter here. Suffice it to say that the challenges increase in their level of danger and darkness. At one terrible moment, Victor Krum does an unthinkable and uncharacteristic thing—he uses one of the unforgivable curses on Cedric. Harry has already heard Fleur's screams coming from somewhere deep in the maze, and works a "Stupefy!" curse on Victor to free Cedric from the cruciatus curse. Harry and Cedric suspect that Victor is under an Imperius curse himself, because although he is a tough competitor, he is also a very ethical young man, and he would not harm Fleur or Cedric in a competitive event. Their suspicions are correct. We later discover that Bartie Crouch Jr. had planned for Harry to win easily because he would eliminate all of Harry's opponents. Again, a man who is evil does not recognize the power of love, the power of loyalty and friendship and sportsmanship. Harry and Cedric work together, and that is something they had not counted on. Voldemort and his Death Eaters keep making the same mistake over and over. It is the kind of mistake that a person who has decided to live a life without love or obligation would make.

Having worked together for a moment, Harry and Cedric then remember that they are opponents and split up. Suddenly, Harry comes face to face with a sphinx: "It had the body of an over-large lion; great clawed paws and a long yellowish tail ending in a brown tuft. Its head, however, was that of a woman. She turned her long, almond-shaped eyes upon Harry as he approached...Then she spoke, in a deep, hoarse voice"(628). She tells Harry that the quickest way to the center of the maze is through her, but he must answer a riddle in order to pass. *reference to mythology*

Here we are in familiar territory. In one of the most famous plays of antiquity, Oedipus Rex, we hear the story of the most famous sphinx of all. Oedipus, who thinks he is a stranger arriving at Thebes for the first time, must answer a riddle in order to open the city gates and free the city from the plague that has a strange hold on it. He is, of course, deceived. He is no stranger to Thebes; in fact, it is his birthplace, and the terrible prophecy he ran from he has already, in part, fulfilled. He had been told that he would kill his father and marry his own mother. Believing old Polybus and Merope of Corinth to be his birth parents, he ran from them, vowing never to return to Corinth, the city he thinks is his birthplace. However, he is very wrong about almost everything that matters. He is, in fact, the son of Laius and Jocasta of Thebes. By the time he gets to Thebes, he has already killed his father in a moment of great rage at a famous crossroads, and in solving the riddle of the sphinx, he will be awarded the kingship of Thebes and the hand of his own mother in marriage. The riddle of this ancient sphinx is the most famous riddle in literary history. She asks Oedipus the following question: "What goes on four legs in the morning, two legs in the afternoon, and three legs in the evening?" Oedipus answers correctly—a man, who crawls as an infant, walks upright as a man, and uses a cane in the evening of his life. When he answers the riddle correctly, he enters into a danger he cannot foresee or understand. The same is true for Harry at this moment in his quest.

Harry's sphinx asks him a tangled riddle about a creature of night that deceives and is creepy and ends in the suffix "er" and you certainly wouldn't want to kiss him, and Harry answers correctly, a spider. Cedric has also solved the riddle, and he and Harry reach the center of the maze at almost the same moment, although Cedric is a couple of steps closer to the Cup than Harry. Then, a most wonderful moment of good sportsmanship happens, but it has deadly consequences. Still, we must not forget to honor the fact that both Harry and Cedric prove themselves to be men of honor and integrity. They admit to each other any advantage or secret information that had come their way and speak frankly of their respect for each other. In fact, Harry tells Cedric to grab the cup—he doesn't really want it. However, Cedric will not hear of it. So, they compromise, and decide to grab the cup together. From the moment that Cedric touches the Tri-Wizard Cup, he enters a vortex of a nightmare intended only for Harry.

The cup, we find out, was a portkey created by Bartie Crouch Jr. in order to bring Harry to Voldemort, and so both Harry and Cedric land in a graveyard where Voldemort immediately has Cedric killed. Then, in an absolutely barbaric scene, Wormtail mixes his flesh, Harry's blood, and the bone of Tom Riddle's father in a hellish cauldron, from which the weak half-life of Voldemort is strengthened, and the nightmare is complete: "The thin man stepped out of the cauldron, staring at Harry…and Harry stared back into the face that had haunted his nightmares for three years. Whiter than a skull, with wide, livid scarlet eyes and a nose that was as flat as a snake's with slits for nostrils…Lord Voldemort had risen again"(643). There follows a hellish scene in which Voldemort brags of his evil alliance with the powers of darkness, with hell itself. He brags of killing his father, and he explains why he has taken Harry's blood: "His mother died in the attempt to save him—and unwittingly provided him with a protection I admit I had not foreseen...I could not touch the boy...His mother left upon him the traces of her sacrifice...This is old magic, I should have remembered it, I was foolish to overlook it...but no matter. I can touch him now"(652). What an interesting speech, and there is something very important here. Even Voldemort realizes that love is "old magic," the most powerful magic of all. And it is a magic that every single one of us can access. Of course Voldemort did not foresee it, because evil cannot feel or recognize love. He has no idea how powerful that old magic is. Voldemort claims that he understands now that this old magic, Lily Potter's love for her son, resulted in his temporary destruction, but he has no real idea of the extent of the power of such old magic, of the love that surrounds and defines Harry. Time and time again this love will stymie Voldemort and empower Harry to elude and eventually destroy him.

Voldemort boasts that he has gone further than any man alive in his attempt to conquer death, to achieve earthly immortality. Schooled as we are in the classics, and in our faith, our blood runs cold when we hear his words. This is a powerful expression of the greatest sin of all—the sin that the ancient Greeks called hubris. To think that you can make yourself a god, can by force of will achieve immortality,

hubris

that your life is more important than anyone else's, and that you have a right to kill other people so that you might live is hubris. It is a deadly sin, and it will be punished. However, as Voldemort stands there, renewed in strength, surrounded by his faithful Death Eaters, we feel desperately frightened for Harry.

Filled with his characteristic arrogance, Voldemort tells Wormtail to untie Harry so that they might duel. He firmly believes that he will defeat this young man, and Harry knows he is face to face with mortal evil: "He had never learned anything that could possibly fit him for this. He knew he was facing the thing against which Moody had always warned...the unblockable Avada Kedavra curse—and Voldemort was right—his mother was not here to die for him this time...He was quite unprotected"(660). But that's where Harry is wrong. We are never alone, and the strength of character and integrity of our souls are awesome powers. The love of the people who have shaped us in the course of our lives is ever at our sides. And Voldemort is shocked to find that he is not facing a weak young man, but rather a mighty warrior, a warrior empowered by the old magic of love. Unable to love, scornful of love, it is Voldemort who stands alone, not Harry. As Voldemort screams the unforgivable curse, Harry shouts "Expelliarmus!" with all his might.

"Expelliarmus" is a defensive move, seeking to "expel" the weapon from your opponent's hand. It is not a charm that requires hatred or a commitment to evil; rather, it is a move whose sole purpose is to disarm your opponent. We would not ordinarily expect it to be a powerful enough move to handle the unforgivable curse Voldemort has spoken, but it is. A jet of light bursts from the end of each of their wands, and the light itself locks in a battle. Harry concentrates with all the force of his mind on holding his wand and keeping the connections, and suddenly, a beautiful sound surrounds him: "And then an unearthly and beautiful sound filled the air…it was coming from every thread of the light-spun web vibrating around Harry and Voldemort. It was a sound Harry recognized, though he had heard it only once before in his life: phoenix song"(664). We remember that the phoenix is the symbol for resurrection. He arises from the ashes of his own former life, renewed and beautiful and young and strong. Remember—help will always be given if you ask. Remember—you are never alone. You are surrounded by the love of those you have loved, strengthened by their love, lifted up as if on eagle's wings.

And then, in one of the most haunting and eerily beautiful scenes of the quest, we discover the magic of a spell called Priori Incantatem. Cedric Diggory's image emerges from the tip of Voldemort's wand, and it urges Harry to hang on. Several moments later, Harry's wish to see his parents again comes true, as their spirits emerge and speak to him: "Harry, his arms shaking madly now, looked back in to the ghostly face of his mother. 'Your father's coming…' she said quietly. 'Hold on for your father...It will be all right...hold on...' And then he came...first his head, then his body...tall and untidy-haired like Harry, the smoky shadowy form of James Potter blossomed from the end of Voldemort's wand, fell to the ground, and straightened like his wife. He walked close to Harry, looking down at him"(667). Harry is almost overcome with longing to be with them, but he has learned that we must live in the present, knowing that if we do, the future will take care of itself.

Or, another way of expressing this idea is that we must live in this earthly reality, no matter how tempting it might be to dwell on our dreams or impossibilities. As we found out through the Mirror of Erised in the first book, Harry wants nothing more than to be with his parents, and having their images around him and talking to him is pretty close. However, Harry knows by now that "it does not do to dwell on dreams and forget to live." He has heeded Dumbledore's advice and knows that we must live in the present. We will be with our loved ones again, in time. At this moment, Harry is surrounded by their love, but he still has work to do in this life. Their presence gives him strength, and they give him a moment to escape. Harry honors Cedric's request to return his body to his father, and in an exciting conclusion, under the wings of their protection, Harry runs back to the portkey. James Potter tells Harry to be ready to run, and "Harry... didn't think he could have held on for another minute anyway—he pulled his wand upward with an almighty wrench, and the golden thread broke; the cage of light vanished, the phoenix song died—but the shadowy figures of Voldemort's victims did not disappear—they were closing in upon Voldemort, shielding Harry from his gaze—And Harry ran as he had never run in his life"(668). He grabs Cedric's body and the Triwizard Cup, and after speeding through a vortex of wind and color, he arrives back to the relative safety of Hogwarts.

The terrible scene of Harry's arrival back at Hogwarts absolutely hurts to read. Cedric Diggory is dead. He was a fine young man, a person of great personal integrity and intelligence, a warrior, and a son. Sadly, there will be many other casualties before this war is done. J. K. Rowling never entirely lets us forget that this is a war, and there will be losses. The loss of Cedric is excruciatingly painful, and as readers, we mourn him. Suddenly, Harry is back in Mad-Eye Moody's office, and the deceptions start to come undone. Exhausted, broken-hearted, and weak, Harry is bewildered and confused as Moody seems to be disintegrating right before his eyes. J. K. Rowling has us experience Harry's confusion as the fake Moody expresses his allegiance to the Dark Lord. We realize, as does Harry, that this cannot be Mad-Eye Moody, the famous Auror. It makes no sense at all. The man who is masquerading as Moody says: "The Dark Lord and I...have much in common. Both of us, for instance, had very disappointing fathers...very disappointing indeed. Both of us suffered the indignity,

Harry, of being named after those fathers. And both of us had the pleasure...the very great pleasure...of killing our fathers to ensure the continued rise of the Dark Order!"(678). We realize immediately that we are in the presence of evil incarnate. Patricide is perhaps the greatest sin of all—to kill one's own father.

Going back to our three primordial questions—who is my father, why am I here, and is my life directed by free will or fate—we realize that, by extension, to kill one's father is to kill one's very self. There is no way a person can survive that kind of action with his soul intact. This discussion is a good introduction to the idea of horcruxes, which we will come back to in time. As Harry sits there, too weak, confused, and exhausted to fight or even understand what is going on, Dumbledore comes into the room. There are many times in the quest narrative when Dumbledore acts like a surrogate father for Harry, and this is certainly one of them.

Soon, it is revealed that Bartie Crouch Jr. has been masquerading as Mad-Eye Moody for a very long time now. It was his intention to ease Harry's way through the tournament so that he will get to the champion's cup, which is really a portkey to the graveyard where Voldemort is waiting for him. This complicated scenario is about to be revealed when Professor McGonagall tells Dumbledore that Harry has been through too much this evening, and that he should go to the hospital wing and rest. Dumbledore is adamant that

Harry should stay and see this thing out, and his reason is an important one: "Understanding is the first step to acceptance, and only with acceptance can there be recovery. He needs to know who has put him through the ordeal that he has suffered tonight, and why"(680). We see, once again, that Dumbledore never speaks condescendingly to Harry. He respects him as an adult, as a young warrior who has to know what he is up against. Soon afterwards, the real Mad-Eye Moody is discovered and released, and we hear Bartie Crouch Jr.'s demonic confession about killing his father to revenge himself on him for his absolute lack of fatherly love and understanding. We also hear that Voldemort had killed Bertha Jorkins, the Ministry Witch whose disappearance was troubling people at the beginning of the novel, after he had tortured her for information about the TriWizard Tournament, information that he hoped would help him kill Harry.

There is, as we have discussed earlier, perhaps no interpersonal relationship more fraught with wonder and peril than that between a father and a son. Bartie Crouch Sr. most certainly loved his son, but in his son's most terrible hour of need, he denied him a father's love and compassion. Bartie Crouch Sr. was absolutely in a very difficult, if not impossible, position. However, we need to be careful not to oversimplify this particular difficulty. There is no question that Bartie Crouch, Jr. had become a very evil young man. He performed the Cruciatus curse on the Longbottoms, in effect destroying them. He

164

tortured and murdered people eagerly, and was fully committed to the Dark Lord. Certainly, Bartie Crouch Sr. could not have looked the other way. His son had committed grievous crimes and deserved punishment. He was a danger to society, and something had to be done. But we find ourselves wondering—at what point did the whole relationship get so lost? Perhaps if Barty Crouch Jr. had known genuine fatherly love from the beginning, he never would have become a Death Eater. Once again, we realize how very complex is the relationship between father and son. The Bible gives us perhaps the most famous example of the healing power of a father's love.

One of the most famous parables in the Bible is the parable of the Prodigal Son. We all know it. That profligate son deserved punishment; his father would have been within his rights to disown him and let him suffer the bitter fruits of his harvest. Instead, he kills the fatted calf and welcomes him home, forgiving his sin, and giving him another chance. We see a model for the love of our heavenly Father in his actions. Now, there is no way Bartie Crouch Sr. could have ignored the depth of his son's evil, but he certainly could have handled the whole arrest and trial with more compassion. However, at the crucial moment, Bartie Crouch Sr. denied a father's love or understanding to his son. There is even the suggestion that he did so in order not to hurt his chances at getting the position of Minister of Magic, and his treatment of his son bore a terrible fruit. His sin of hubris sets terrible wheels in motion, culminating in his son apparently losing his very soul.

Conversely, James Potter died trying to protect his son; he gave his very life for Harry. And, his act of love gave rise to the wonderful young man we see in Harry Potter. Perhaps it is not that simple. Certainly, it is a complex relationship. Fathers have such high hopes and expectations for their sons. They want their sons to be even better and smarter and stronger and more successful than they themselves have been. These hopes are born of a fierce love, but sometimes the burden weighs too heavily on the sons. Still, one thing is certain. If the son knows he is loved, knows it in his very heart and soul, with the kind of love that St. Paul is talking about, (see our discussion at the end of the first book) a lot of problems will work themselves out.

We are now near the end of the novel, and it is time for the truth to be told, and for all of our questions to be answered. Sirius, Harry's other surrogate father, shows up, worried about Harry's safety and health. Fawkes, the beautiful phoenix, comes and lands on Harry's knee. It is as if, in Dumbledore, Sirius, and Fawkes, we have Harry surrounded symbolically by God's love, in the three person Trinity of Father, Son, and Holy Spirit. Sirius worries that Harry has been through too much, and once again, Dumbledore shows his respect for Harry. He tells him, "If I thought I could help you...by putting you into an enchanted sleep and allowing you to postpone the moment when you would have to think about what happened tonight, I would do it. But I know better. Numbing the pain for a while will make it worse when you finally feel it. You have shown bravery beyond anything I could have expected of you. I ask you to demonstrate your courage one more time. I ask you to tell us what happened"(695).

This approach is the same one that is suggested in the Hemingway canon—when you have suffered that sacred hurt, you have to face it, to name it. You can't run from it, drink from it, lie to yourself about it, or pretend it didn't happen. You must face it. You must call it what it is, and only then can the healing begin. In a way, it is like confessing a sin. Only when you purge yourself of it can you move on. And that is exactly what Harry does, and as he tells the story of what happened in the graveyard, exhausted though he is, he feels as if some of the poison is leaving his body. Once again, the important theme of confronting the truth emerges in the quest.

As Harry narrates the sequence of events, we get an explanation of what happened between the two wands during the duel. Dumbledore tells us what happened: "Priori Incantatem... Harry's wand and Voldemort's wand share cores. Each of them contains a feather from the tail of the same phoenix. This phoenix, in fact...They will not work properly against each other...If, however, the owners of the wands force the wands to do battle...a very rare effect will take place. One of the wands will force the other to regurgitate spells it has performed—in reverse. The most recent first...and then those which preceded it"(697). So, Harry confesses that this is exactly what happened, and that he saw Cedric, and his mother and father. When Sirius asks if that means that Cedric came back to life, Dumbledore answers quickly that there is no earthly magic that can accomplish that. We are reminded, subtly and frequently, that we are only men and women, and our powers do not extend to that of the heavens. These novels are a quiet little act of faith, in fact, a leap of faith. J. K. Rowling never lectures us, but she quietly indicates, in many different ways, that she believes in a life after this one. However, she also reminds us that that life is beyond the province of our knowledge right now. We must live in the here and now, doing the best we can. The time to come will take care of itself. Once again, Dumbledore expresses his gratitude and respect for what Harry has accomplished: "You have shown bravery beyond anything I could have expected of you tonight, Harry. You have shown bravery equal to those who died fighting Voldemort at the height of his powers. You have shouldered a grown wizard's burden and found yourself equal to it"(699). Harry is a young warrior, a young man, and a great wizard. He has most definitely come of age.

It is interesting to note that the wands that fought against each other had the same phoenix feather core. This brings us back to an important theme in these novels. It is not a person's abilities that give us the measure of the man or the woman. It is the choices that they make. What matters is the choices the person makes. Choices, not blood. Choices. *choices vs. abilities*

Or, as Dumbledore says it at the end of this novel, when he is scolding Cornelius Fudge for his cowardice: "You fail to recognize that it matters not what someone is born, but what they grow to be... The only one against whom I intend to work is Lord Voldemort. If you are against him, then we remain, Cornelius, on the same side"(709). We hear an echo of Jesus' words to his disciples here: "For he that is not against us is for us"(Mark 9:40). Dumbledore, pursuing this idea through to its logical conclusion, then absolutely demands that Sirius Black and Severus Snape set aside their differences and reconcile: "You will shake hands. You are on the same side now. Time is short, and unless the few of us who know the truth stand united, there is no hope for any of us"(712). These powerful words will resonate throughout the rest of the quest narrative, as the battle heats up, and we would do well to remember Dumbledore's unequivocal faith in Severus Snape.

It might be interesting to take a moment at this point to talk about Cornelius Fudge. He is, as we have said before, rather Machiavellian in his leadership and management. He is a man who loves having power and who guards his power jealously. He is intimidated by Dumbledore, a man of integrity and vision. Fudge's

169

name has interesting and complex etymological significance. His first name, Cornelius, is from an old Roman clan, but it has an appropriately stuffy sound for our character. The word Cornelius comes from the Latin word "cornu" for horn, and Cornelius Fudge does like to toot his own horn, so that might be in play. As to his last name—our first thought might be that fudge is chocolate, and chocolate has been shown to be a good thing to use to fight against despair, which the Dark Lord is associated with, so that might be a good thing. However, let us not forget that the word fudge has another meaning. People are said to "fudge," using the word as a verb, when they lie or cheat, or intentionally intend to deceive. We say that someone is fudging on their taxes, or fudging the truth just a little. Perhaps this connotation is more relevant for our Minister of Magic. He does all he can, on several occasions until he is deposed, to invalidate Harry's testimony about what happened in the cemetery. He continues to try to discredit Dumbledore, because he does not want it to be true that the Dark Lord has returned to power on his watch. His love of power and reluctance to rise to a challenge completely cloud his vision. All of his "fudging" will catch up with him in the end, and eventually he will realize that he should have been more courageous. In the end, he will not be a bad man, but he is certainly a disappointing man. Through his character, we get a subtle commentary from J. K. Rowling about the disappointing nature of many politicians. When Dumbledore says that Fudge should approach and try to enlist the help of the giants in the coming battle, Fudge replies: "If the magical community got wind that I had approached the giants—people hate them—end of my career"(708). Sadly, Fudge is a very believable representation of a politician. Too often they put reelection and public opinion above doing the right thing. Harry is, by contrast, a genuinely good leader because he respects others, and he always tries to do what is right, not what is politically expedient. Do what is popular or do what is right: The best leaders and the best people always choose the latter.

In the closing scene, at the end of the year banquet, we see a subdued and solemn mood, and once again, Dumbledore speaks to this theme of uniting against a common enemy, of setting aside petty differences as they approach this inevitable battle: "I say to you all, once again—in the light of Lord Voldemort's return, we are only as strong as we are united, as weak as we are divided. Lord Voldemort's gift for spreading discord and enmity is very great. We can fight it only by showing an equally strong bond of friendship and trust. Differences of habit and language are nothing at all if our aims are identical and our hearts are open"(723). Sadly, what he is hoping for here seems hopelessly naïve. If such a consensus were possible, it certainly would not hold for long—maybe only until the common enemy is faced and fought. And so, the novel ends on this cautionary note. There have been moments in human history when a common enemy unites people of different habits and language. Unfortunately, these moments of a united vision and purpose are rather ephemeral. When that moment has passed, the divisions and petty differences seem to reassert themselves very quickly.

We Americans know a little bit about this because of September 11, 2001. Right after the attacks, we were not Democrats or Republicans, but Americans. People put out their flags and a fervent patriotism was reborn. We put our safety and the goal of ending terrorism above all ideological bickering and worked together. For a while. Now, we have slipped back into insults and bickering. We focus now not on our common goals but on our differences. We have not destroyed terrorism; the threat is as strong as ever. Nonetheless, our sense of unity has ended. Perhaps that feeling of being united is the silver lining that comes with a shared tragedy. And, every now and then, perhaps we get a glimpse of what is possible—maybe not in this world, but maybe in the next one.

In closing, the fourth novel contributes several significant ideas to the overall quest. First of all, we have a strong affirmation of the importance of friendship—not just among our three major characters and their companions on the quest, but also between people and other creatures. The act of kindness that Harry did for Dobby at the end of the second book apparently resonates very powerfully with Dobby, and we see that he will be a constant and true friend to Harry.

In time, he will even give his life to save Harry. We see the young people becoming men and women, starting to think about dating, with all the thrills and disappointments that experience entails. We witness the corrosive power of evil in the person of Bartie Crouch Jr., and we see that hatred between family members can absolutely tear a family apart. We learn, once again, that the quest is ongoing—that we will complete one set of challenges only to be faced with another. That is the nature of the human condition. However, we also learn, with Harry, to appreciate the moments of calm, the "seasons of grace" when they come, and to use them to let our strength refill for the next test, which will most assuredly come, in time.

Seasons of grace

Harry Potter and The Order of the Phoenix

This fifth novel in the series opens with a very powerful scene, the Dementor attack on Dudley Dursley and Harry Potter. The attack proves the clear and present danger of the evil of Voldemort's followers who are making their presence felt, more boldly that ever, even in the neighborhoods of Muggles. As Harry sees his cousin's life force ebbing away, he summons his strength, his joy, and his faith in the goodness of mankind, and produces a Patronus charm which charges the Dementors and sends them swooping away into the darkness. But not before Dudley is badly hurt, almost mortally hurt. Harry is immediately threatened by the Ministry of Magic because he has summoned a Patronus charm in an area inhabited by Muggles and in the presence of a Muggle. Blah blah blah. This novel is J. K. Rowling's not too subtle attack on the mentality of the bureaucracy that gets drunk on its own power and loses sight of what it is supposed to be doing—protecting the people whom it supposedly represents. We can all think of our own examples of this happening in our world.

Nevertheless, very soon after this near disaster, an advance guard arrives at the Dursley residence to get Harry back into their protection. Harry is thrilled to see real friends, trusted fellow warriors, and to meet some of the members of the Order of the Phoenix. They escort Harry through the night sky over London to Number Twelve Grimmauld Place, the headquarters for the Order of the Phoenix, those who are committed to fighting Lord Voldemort and his Death Eaters, the powers of darkness. The word Grimmauld is etymologically, "grim old," and it is a grim, old place, for it is the Black family residence, and they were allied with Lord Voldemort. That is to say, everyone in the Black family, except for Sirius, who is now the heir of the place and who has donated it to the Order of the Phoenix so that they can use it as their headquarters. We know enough about phoenixes by now to understand the symbolic connection suggested to goodness and faith, even to the imagery of resurrection and life. At Number Twelve Grimmauld Place, Harry is quickly reunited with the Weasley family and with Hermione, and the fifth novel is off to a running start.

The adults are soon in the midst of a very heated discussion about how much Harry should be told about what has been going on in their world during the summer. This time, Sirius sounds very much like Dumbledore, saying that Harry is not a child and needs to know the truth. Molly Weasley is afraid of telling Harry too much, taking away his innocence, frightening him. We can understand where Molly is coming from—she is trying to preserve Harry's innocence, or his right to be a child. But Sirius and Lupin are being much more realistic. However unfair it seems to be, Harry lost his innocence long before he "should have," and must face reality. This is the same idea that we discussed in the fourth book with the Triwizard Tournament. Sometimes, life throws you things that you may be "too young" and "unprepared" for, but you must face the obstacles head on and do the best you can. This has certainly been true for Harry. Although they understand Molly's concern, Lupin and Sirius argue that Harry lost his innocence long ago, arguably the night his parents died to protect him. Lupin says: "Personally…I think it better that Harry gets the facts—not all the facts, Molly, but the general picture—from us, rather than a garbled version from…others"(89).

The facts are that the Ministry of Magic is suggesting that Dumbledore and Harry concocted the whole story about Voldemort killing Cedric Diggory in the graveyard and having returned to corporal form and strength. Harry and Dumbledore supposedly have done this because they are glory seekers, and they want the adulation of the masses. It has even been subtly suggested that Harry may have killed Cedric himself, and the story Harry and Dumbledore told is simply their effort to cover up that terrible truth. Cornelius Fudge is in charge of the Ministry at this time, and this is another demonstration of his unethical behavior. He is clearly threatened by Dumbledore, and has convinced himself that Dumbledore has his eye on becoming the Minister of Magic. So, the Ministry, under Fudge's leadership, has decided to discredit Dumbledore in every way they possibly can, and with him, Harry. After all, they say, there is no sign of the Dark Lord's presence right now. Under this cloud of mistrust, Harry must stand trial for conjuring a Patronus illegally. Harry finds himself in serious trouble for conjuring a Patronus to defend Dudley from an attack by the Dementors. This seems curious because we remember that the Ministry was rather understanding about Harry using magic to launch Aunt Marge into the London twilight in the third book. The reason for the different reaction is this: In the third book, Harry was supposedly in imminent danger from an escaped maniacal killer, Sirius Black. At this time in the quest, the Ministry has convinced itself that Lord Voldemort is not a threat. Rather, they see Harry as a threat to stability. Therefore, Fudge sees no benefit in protecting Harry, and he is more than willing to have his henchmen punish Harry for his "illegal" use of magic.

Although as Lupin tells Harry, the law is on his side, and that even under-age wizards are allowed to use magic in life-threatening situations, it will be the Ministry's contention that no such circumstances existed. In keeping with their subterfuge, the Ministry officials secretly reschedule the trial, hoping to make Harry and Dumbledore miss it. This will supposedly prove that they are liars. Still, Arthur Weasley gets word of their machinations and manages to get Harry to the courtroom in time. There, Harry faces the Wizengamot, the high court of the wizard world, and Arthur Weasley is not allowed to accompany him. Harry thinks he will be completely alone in this trial until Dumbledore strides in, announcing himself as witness for the defense. Although the Ministry tries to discredit the testimony given by Mrs. Figg, the little old lady who lives across the street from the Dursleys and secretly keeps an eye on Harry, there is enough evidence to convince the majority of the court that Harry was truly in danger and was therefore within his rights. It is at the trial that we get our first glimpse of the woman who will be Harry's foe throughout this novel, Dolores Umbridge.

The etymology of her name is significant on several levels. Her first name, Dolores, comes from the Latin word "dolor" which means sorrow or suffering. And her surname suggests our word "umbrage," which means offense or affront. How appropriate, for she will cause Harry, and many of the other children she is in charge of, much pain and suffering, and she is an affront to anybody in the teaching profession. Our first description of her could not be less flattering: "He thought she looked just like a large, pale toad. She was rather squat with a broad, flabby face, as little neck as Uncle Vernon, and a very wide, slack mouth. Her eyes were large, round, and slightly bulging. Even the little black bow perched on top of her short curly hair put him in mind of a large fly she was about to catch on a long sticky tongue"(146). To make matters worse, she speaks in a rather simpering, girlish voice, a voice that cannot disguise her commitment to evil, brutality, and self-aggrandizement. She is a portly little, self-righteous beast of a woman who is, in every way, a danger to children.

When the trial is over, and Harry is exonerated, Dumbledore strides away, without a word to Harry, as mysteriously as he had appeared. Harry is understandably bewildered by this behavior on Dumbledore's part, and we share his astonishment. Nonetheless, Harry will be allowed to return to Hogwarts, and for the moment, his fears are quieted. When he returns to Grimmauld Place, he hears astonishing news—both Ron and Hermione have been chosen as prefects for the Gryffindor House, and he has not! Although Harry is secretly disappointed and maybe even a little embarrassed about not having been chosen, he expresses his happiness and support for his friends. Still, it is at this point in the novel that Harry acknowledges a secret malaise—a kind of spiritual darkness which he will battle with throughout much of this novel.

In the classic heroic quest narrative, the young hero frequently experiences a dark hour of the soul, a time when it all just seems like it is too much, like he can't go on. He sometimes even feels sorry for himself, languishing in self-pity. It is not an attractive phase for a young hero, but, in many ways, it makes him all the more real and believable to us. Harry will, unfortunately, spend a lot of time in this novel feeling just a little bit sorry for himself. Sometimes, you find yourself as a reader wanting to just shake him and say, "Snap out of it." However, if we are going to be entirely honest, there are many times when we probably need to say that to ourselves as well.

Nonetheless, this is not to say that he does not have good reason to feel a little sorry for himself. The Ministry has convinced many people that he is a liar, a glory seeker, and maybe even a secret murderer. Dumbledore is, for some strange reason, avoiding him. He has been bypassed for the position of prefect. Ron, Hermione, and even Draco have all been honored by having been chosen for this honor. He sees suspicion and mistrust from just about everybody at school, Percy advises Ron to stop hanging around with Harry, and he feels worn out by it all. The only person, besides Ron and Hermione, who consistently expresses belief and support for him is Luna Lovegood, and most people think she is as loony as her name suggests. She is a peculiar yet delightful character in this novel, and even though she is a little loony, we ought to at least pay a little more attention to her surname, right from the beginning. She is connected to two very powerful words—love and good. In fact, it's hard to think of two more important or highly honored words than those two. Her first name suggests a connection to the moon. Although it is tempting to wonder if this connection suggests that she is changeable or fickle, we know she is not. Perhaps a better connection might be to Diana, the goddess of the moon, who is a symbol for a woman who is chaste, pure, or innocent. Luna Lovegood is certainly that. She has a charming innocence that quite steals our hearts, and she is steadfast in her friendship to Harry.

When they arrive at school for the new year, the Sorting Hat sings a peculiar new song, one that warns about the dangers of discord and fear: "Oh, know the perils, read the signs, the warning history shows, for our Hogwarts is in danger, from external, deadly foes. And we must unite inside her or we'll crumble from within"(207). With these words of warning, we are reminded of Dumbledore's closing remarks from the previous year. Still, a chill runs through Harry as he sees the toad-like witch he met at his trial sitting on the dais as the new Defense against the Dark Arts teacher. When Dumbledore is addressing the students, she rudely interrupts him and makes a speech about her intention to prune away any practices at the school that she feels ought to be prohibited. That kind of rhetoric sends a small shiver down our spines. Clearly, she is there to spy on Dumbledore and to undermine his authority at the school, which is the goal of the Ministry. Harry is right to be afraid of her; she is the quintessence of everything that could be evil in a teacher.

Any teacher who reads this novel probably cringes as we watch this woman in action in her classroom. She allows no student to offer any interpretation that she does not support, she openly mocks and belittles her students, and she threatens them with physical harm. Even worse than that, she is not afraid to use it, and she does so with a smug, self-righteous little smirk that brings a whole new slant to the kinds of evil that are portrayed in the Potter quest. She uses her position of authority to abuse the trust of her students and terrify them into obeying her. When Hermione asks her if they are not going to be actually taught to perform defensive skills, she says that there is no reason for this and that they are in no danger. When Harry insists that she is wrong, she loses her temper, sends him to Professor McGonagall, accuses him of calling her a liar, and assigns him a detention. Although Minerva McGonagall clearly sympathizes with Harry, she tells him that he has to learn to keep his head down, and that he must serve the detention.

What follows here is a series of chapters where Harry must return to her over a series of several days to serve the most barbarous detention we could have ever dreamed of. He is made to write lines with a special pen: "He let out a gasp of pain…He looked back at the parchment, placed the quill upon it once more, wrote 'I must not tell lies,' and felt the searing pain on the back of his hand for a second time; once again, the words had been cut into his skin, once again they healed over seconds later. And on it went. Again and again Harry wrote the words on the parchment in what he soon came to realize was not ink, but his own blood"(267). As he suffers and bleeds, she smiles. It is hard to imagine any teacher more loathsome than this woman. She does not deserve to be called a teacher. She is a sadist, the most despicable kind ever, one who would take pleasure in the suffering of children. Days later, when Ron notices the bloody scars on Harry's hand, Harry refuses to tell McGonagall, not wanting to give Umbridge the satisfaction of knowing that she got to him. On the fifth day of his torture, she "looked back at him, a smile stretching her wide, slack mouth. 'Yes, it hurts, doesn't it?' she said softly"(275). As she touches his hand to make sure that the words are scarred into his skin, Harry feels his scar burn very intensely. He wonders if it is a coincidence. We think not, and we suspect that we are in the presence of one who gladly serves the Dark Lord.

Still, Harry's malaise begins in earnest at about this point in the novel: "Harry was exhausted. He also felt an odd, sick, empty feeling in his stomach that had nothing to do with tiredness...He knew that half the people inside Hogwarts thought him strange, even mad; he knew that the Daily Prophet had been making snide allusions to him for months"(300). At this moment when Harry is filled with doubt and sadness, Sirius' head appears in the fire, using a secret method of communication that is still available to him, and he tries to reassure Harry and encourage him to hang on. He says that Umbridge is there at the school to try to discredit Dumbledore and usurp his authority, but he does not think she is a Death Eater. He tells Harry that Fudge is paranoid about Dumbledore, and that Fudge thinks Albus Dumbledore wants the position of Minister of Magic, so he is considering having him arrested on some trumped-up charge to get him out of the way. He further suggests that Fudge is afraid that Dumbledore may be raising a secret army. Perhaps it is here that the idea for Harry's group of young warriors initially emerges.

Soon, Dolores Umbridge announces a new title for herself: She is now the "High Inquisitor" for Hogwarts, and it is her task to root out any practices that the Ministry does not support. The very word "inquisitor" sends a chill down our spines, and we think of the brutality of the Spanish Inquisition, which supposedly was rooting out heresy but was actually terrorizing thousands good and innocent people. Under the auspices of Ferdinand and Isabella, who sought to banish the Moors from Spain, terror reigned. In the Harry Potter saga, Dolores Umbridge is supposedly seeking to purge the teaching staff of those teachers whose methods are too open-minded and accepting for her taste. The ugly prejudice against those who are not pure blood witches and wizards again begins to raise its monstrous head. There is no arguing with the High Inquisitor in the Spanish Inquisition; the very term in synonymous with the word tyrant. Therefore, it is particularly frightening that Dolores Umbridge proudly calls herself this, and with an absolutely chilling demeanor, Umbridge starts to evaluate and threaten all of the other teachers. Armed with her smug, condescending smile, her simpering voice, and her ever-present clipboard, she begins terrorizing the staff. Her first victims are, of course, those less able to defend themselves, including Sibyll Trelawney. She quickly reduces

Sibyll to a quivering mass of stuttering and tears, and it is clear that she takes pleasure in this kind of abuse. When she scolds Hermione for asking if they are going to learn any practical skills in class this year, Umbridge calls her questions "pointless interruptions." Umbridge says that they do not need to learn any practical skills; studying theory will be enough because there is no serious threat anyhow. At that point, Hermione decides that it is time for them to take matters into their own hands: "She's an awful woman....Awful. You know, I was just saying to Ron when you came in...we've got to do something about her...I was thinking that—maybe the time's come when we should just—learn Defense Against the Dark Arts ourselves"(325). So begins what will become one of the best parts of this novel—Dumbledore's Army.

We really cannot say enough about Hermione at this point. She realizes that the students are going to have to take matters into their own hands and learn to defend themselves. At this point in the novel, Harry is still feeling a little sorry for himself, and he does not seem inclined to reach out to anyone. Hermione insists that he pull himself together and teach those who are willing to learn. She brings together a small group of students who are ready and eager to learn how to defend themselves. They are Gryffindors, Hufflepuffs, and Ravenclaws. Their first meeting takes place in the Hog's Head Inn, and after they get organized, they meet about once a week in the Room of Requirement, the magical room that appears when you need it to do so, if asked properly. When Dolores Umbridge finds out about it, she bans all student-organized activities, and they have to go underground. Hermione cleverly works out a system of summoning the members of Dumbledore's Army by putting an enchantment on fake galleon coins that can tell them when to show up for a meeting. When Hermione summons these students who might be interested in learning real defensive skills for the first time, there is a distinct tension in the air.

Many of them have listened to the rhetoric from the Ministry, and they are therefore suspicious of Harry. Harry is defensive and prickly with them: "'If you've come to hear exactly what it looks like when Voldemort murders someone I can't help you,' Harry said. His temper, always so close to the surface these days, was rising again. He did not take his eyes from Zacharias Smith's aggressive face, determined not to look at Cho. 'I don't want to talk about Cedric Diggory, all right? So if that's what you're here for, you might as well clear out'"(341). Harry almost blows an opportunity to get this thing going because of his defensiveness, but Hermione speaks quickly, smoothing over his angry words, saying further that Harry can produce a corporeal Patronus. And that changes everything. Hermione brilliantly gets the students to sign a document declaring their intention to become a part of Dumbledore's Army, and further promising not to talk about their secret society to those not involved and committed to it. She even puts a jinx on the signing paper, so that if someone talks, the rest will be able to figure out who the guilty party is. In spite of all of these precautions, Umbridge finds out about their secret meetings, and declares them illegal.

At this point in the novel, with his scar burning more frequently and intensely, something starts to happen to Harry, something that he is embarrassed about. The connection between his mind and Voldemort's seems to be intensifying; in fact, sometimes Harry sees things through Voldemort's eyes. Harry explains: "I'm just getting flashes of what mood he's in...Dumbledore said something like this was happening last year...He said that when Voldemort was near me, or when he was feeling hatred, I could tell. Well, now I'm feeling it when he's pleased too"(382). It embarrasses Harry to admit, even to Ron, that this is happening. We can hardly blame him for feeling uncomfortable with this experience. In his secret heart of hearts, old doubts start to surface. He wonders about this link between himself and Voldemort? He hopes that he is not secretly attracted to evil.

Dobby is now working, as a freed house elf, in the Hogwarts kitchen, and he makes a visit to Harry, asking if there is anything he can do for him. Harry, figuring that Dobby probably knows the castle as well as anyone could by now, says: "I need to find a place where twenty-eight people can practice Defense Against the Dark

Arts without being discovered by any of the teachers. Especially...
Professor Umbridge"(386). Dobby is pleased to be consulted and
treated with respect, and he knows the perfect place, the wonderful
"Room of Requirement," which Dobby explains is a room that reveals
its presence only when somebody has a real need of it. He tells Harry
that many people have stumbled upon it accidentally, but never been
able to find it again, in spite of the fact that it is always there, waiting
to be called into service. He teaches Harry the trick for calling it up,
and it becomes the splendid meeting place for their secret, and illegal,
meetings. Once again, Harry's kindness to Dobby long ago has paid
big dividends.

When they have their next meeting, Hermione announces
that they ought to elect a leader, and Cho says that obviously Harry
is the leader. However, Hermione stipulates that they should do this
formally, so as to make it official and to bestow upon the leader real
authority. She is always practical. It is agreed that Harry will lead
them, and it is Ginny who comes up with the name: Dumbledore's
Army. Not Potter's Army—Dumbledore's. Harry whole-heartedly
approves of this choice. He considers himself a fellow warrior with his
classmates. He definitely has had more experience in hand to hand
combat with real and powerful evil, but he does not want the group
named for him. He is, as he says, often, "Dumbledore's man, through
and through."

This is a good moment to point out that Harry is not guilty of the hubris that is such a powerful component of Voldemort's flawed psyche. Harry humbly recognizes that even though he is the most skilled fighter of this group of students, he is nowhere near godlike, nowhere near invincible. He recognizes that Dumbledore is a much more powerful wizard than he is, and he wants only to be a good foot soldier in the quest for doing the right thing to protect the innocent who cannot defend themselves. Immediately after agreeing on the name and the mission, Harry and his classmates start working on learning some real defense against the dark arts magic. Harry teaches them his favorite move, the disarming charm of "Expelliarmus!" Notice that it is a true defensive skill. It is not aggressive; rather, it seeks to defuse and disarm a dangerous enemy. Very quickly, the students are genuinely working with each other, teaching each other, and Harry experiences the joy of being a successful teacher. Being with Dumbledore's Army gives Harry some rare moments of happiness in this novel.

Knowing that Umbridge is spying on them, and intercepting their messages, Hermione cleverly designs magical galleons that each of the members of the DA can carry around in their pockets. We should take a closer look at them, just for a moment. They look like ordinary galleons, but the numbers will change to reflect the time and the date of the next meeting. Harry looks at Hermione oddly, telling

hubris

her that the galleons remind him a little bit of the Dark Mark which is burned into the Death Eaters' forearms. Hermione admits: "That is where I got the idea...but you'll notice I decided to engrave the date on bits of metal rather than on our members' skin"(399). J. K. Rowling makes an interesting point here—the same technology can be used for good or for evil. We can all think of a lot of examples of that simple but powerful truth. It gets back to a core idea of the quest narrative—it is not our abilities that make us who we are, it is our choices.

In the meanwhile, the quidditch season heats up, and Ron is going to be the Gryffindor goalie. He is very nervous about his abilities, and when he gets nervous he makes mistakes, an experience with which many of us can identify. Draco Malfoy knows this and has the Slytherin fans sing a mocking song: "Weasley cannot save a thing. He cannot block a single ring. That's why Slytherins all sing; Weasley is our king"(407). Draco is the quintessential class bully, who thinks he makes himself more important by belittling others. He is utterly tiresome. When Harry catches the snitch, and the Gryffindors win, Draco makes sarcastic remarks about the Weasley family, and Harry punches him. For this action, Dolores Umbridge announces that Harry is banned for life from ever playing quidditch again. She is trying to break him, and she is completely unscrupulous. Here, she strikes at something that she knows is important to Harry, something that gives him joy. Of course, she wants to take any kind of happiness away from him. She wants to break his spirit and make him beg her for mercy, but this is something that Harry will never do.

In the background of the novel, there is a quiet little struggle going on—a struggle for the loyalty and help of other powerful forces, namely the goblins and the giants. Neither of these groups is exactly human, and neither of them trusts witches and wizards. There is bad blood between them. Still, they may come into play when the battle heats up, and both Dumbledore and his agents and Voldemort and the Death Eaters are trying to create an alliance with these powerful groups. When Hagrid returns to the castle after a prolonged and mysterious absence, he admits to Harry and Ron that he had been trying to enlist the help of the giants at Dumbledore's request. He is bruised and battered, so it is pretty clear that negotiating with giants is not a task for the faint of heart. These allegiances will become more and more important as the quest presses on.

Suddenly, Harry feels like his own mind is under attack. In the middle of the night, he is awakened by a terrible nightmare. He sees Arthur Weasley being attacked by a terrible snake, and it feels to Harry as if he is the snake: "His body felt smooth, powerful, and flexible. He was gliding between shining metal bars, across dark, cold stone…He was turning his head…Harry put out his tongue…He tasted the man's scent on the air…He reared high from the floor and struck once, twice, three times, plunging his fangs deeply into the man's flesh"(463). He

191

awakens from this nightmare screaming, telling Ron that his dad has been attacked by a huge snake, unable to bring himself to tell Ron the more terrible truth. How awful a moment this is for Harry, to feel himself lose control of his own mind. As bizarre as his story is, Professor McGonagall immediately believes him, and she takes steps to get help to Arthur Weasley, thereby saving his life. If Harry had not experienced this vision and acted upon it immediately, Arthur would have died. So, this incursion by Voldemort into Harry's mind has a good result, but that is small comfort to Harry at this time.

We spoke earlier of the idea that this novel is Harry's dark hour of the soul. This is a perfect time to go further into that. The term comes from an autobiographical novel that F. Scott Fitzgerald wrote called The Crack Up. He describes this emotional darkness as a constant feeling of numbness or a desolation of the spirit, when it feels like the whole world is peacefully sleeping and only you are awake, your heart helpless thrumming away, your mind pounding with images and disappointments, and a feeling of loss overwhelms you. You descend into a kind of hopelessness from which you do not expect to ever emerge. That is a pretty good description of what Harry is feeling right now. He is overwhelmed with shame: "Was this why Dumbledore would no longer meet Harry's eyes? Did he expect to see Voldemort staring out of them...He felt dirty, contaminated, as though he were carrying some deadly germ...He had not merely seen the snake, he had been the snake, he knew it now"(492).

This possession of a portion of Harry's mind is perhaps one of the most interesting and most terrifying ideas in this novel. When Harry realizes what is going on, he feels very sorry for himself, and he frequently indulges in bouts of self-pity that the reader can find tiresome, even if we kind of understand where they are coming from. Again, we want him to snap out of it. Our frustration is aptly expressed by an old headmaster, Phineas Nigellus, speaking from his portrait: "You know...this is precisely why I loathed being a teacher! Young people are so infernally convinced that they are absolutely right about everything. Has it not occurred to you, my poor puffed-up popinjay, that there might be an excellent reason why the headmaster of Hogwarts is not confiding every tiny detail of his plans to you?"(496). Now the truth of the matter is that Dumbledore will not look at Harry right now, not because he is afraid of seeing Voldemort looking out through Harry's eyes, but because he does not want to give Voldemort even more motivation to possess Harry. If Voldemort believes that he can use this method to get to Dumbledore, things will get worse and worse for Harry until he learns to shut his mind to Voldemort's attacks, and that is something Harry does not know how to do yet. However, the scolding from Phineas Nigellus is not enough to snap Harry out of his depression, and in his defense, who could blame him?

The idea of mind control is a very interesting feature in this book—interesting and dangerous. Dumbledore becomes suspicious that Voldemort will try to use this mental connection for his own benefit, and he instructs Harry to start taking Occlumency lessons from Severus Snape. The word "occlumency" comes from the word "occlude," which derives from Latin and means to conceal and the word "mens" which is Latin for mind.

This is exactly what the occlumency lessons are supposed to teach Harry—to conceal his mind from Voldemort's incursions. Snape is rough on Harry; he always is, but he gives us a good introduction into what he will be attempting to teach Harry: "The mind is not a book, to be opened at will and examined at leisure…The mind is a complex and many-layered thing, Potter…The evidence suggests that at times, when your mind is most relaxed and vulnerable…you are sharing the Dark Lord's thought and emotions. The headmaster…wishes me to teach you how to close your mind to the Dark Lord"(531). Snape goes on to explain that it is their most egregious fear that if Voldemort gets to be very good at entering Harry's mind, he might be able to control his actions. This is an absolutely terrifying thought to consider. The thought of this kind of Satanic possession should cause our blood to run cold. To take away a person's free will at this most fundamental level is the most vicious sin imaginable, an expression of that demonic hubris that marks Voldemort throughout the quest.

Snape tells Harry that, in order to do this, he must empty

himself of emotion. It is interesting to note that, before they do battle, Snape has to get rid of several of his own thoughts, bad memories, and weaknesses into a nearby Pensieve. He does not allow Harry the same courtesy. Snape conducts several occlumency lessons over a series of nights, and Harry comes to dread them. In between the lessons, Harry continues to experience this weird psychic connection with Voldemort, and each episode seems to take a lot out of him, leaving him screaming, collapsed on the floor, and weakened as though by a seizure. It is very clear that it is increasingly important for Harry to master the skill of occlumency, but it continues to elude him. That is not to say that he does not have great force of mind—he does. In fact, he is able to break into Snape's memories, and he gets a glimpse of Severus Snape as a young man.

In the course of this memory, he sees his father threatening to take off Snape's pants in public. In other words, apparently James Potter at the age of fifteen or sixteen, was a first class bully. This vision changes things for Harry. He realizes that his father was no saint, and James tumbles off his pedestal for Harry from that moment on. He was not a god; he was just a man, and he had flaws and a certain meanness that is very unattractive. The fact that Harry has had some personal experience with two other bullies—Draco Malfoy and Dudley Dursley—makes this realization hit him all the harder. His father definitely had not been a spotless hero. In fact, "judging from what he had just seen, his father had been every bit as arrogant as Snape had always told him"(650). However, Snape is humiliated by Harry having seen this terrible memory, and he throws Harry out of his office, telling him that the lessons are over. Perhaps at that point, Harry has already learned as much as Snape can teach him. Unfortunately, Voldemort can teach him more.

In the meantime, Dolores Umbridge continues her reign of terror in the school. She dismisses Sybill Trelawney, fires Hagrid, gets Dumbledore to temporarily resign his post rather than be arrested, and attacks Minerva McGonagall, who is injured so grievously she must be hospitalized. Having eliminated anyone who seems to be a threat of any kind, she arrogantly tries to move into Dumbledore's office, which locks itself against her. How appropriate. It is as if it would only allow the true headmaster access. It would only show loyalty to the person who really deserves it. Undaunted, she takes up residence in a new office and promptly proclaims herself the new headmistress of Hogwarts. Firenze, the outlaw centaur, replaces Trelawney as the professor of Divination. Tucked in his first lesson to Harry and his fellow students is an interesting bit of wisdom—we cannot know the future. It really is that simple. It is not for us to know—we are not privileged to know the great plan, and we are fools if we think we are. When the students want a typical Trelawney lesson from Firenze, he scoffs at their folly: "Trivial hurts, tiny human accidents...these are of no more significance than the scurrying of ants to the wide universe, and are unaffected by planetary movements…I, however, am here to explain the wisdom of centaurs, which is impersonal and impartial"(603). In the final analysis, Firenze tells his young students that nothing is certain, that even centaurs, careful and impartial as they are, often misread the signs, if in fact they are signs at all. The bottom line is—there may well be a plan, but we cannot know it. This may be why Dante commits the false prophets to the eighth circle of hell in his famous book, The Inferno. We ought not claim to know the future. We cannot know it, not really. We come back to Isaiah: "As high as the skies are above the earth, so high above our ways the ways of the Lord." We have said this to each other before.

Now, J. K. Rowling has one last move to make before the brilliant final scene at the Ministry of Magic. Hermione cleverly tricks Dolores Umbridge into following them into the forest, where Hermione claims to have Dumbledore's secret weapon concealed. When Umbridge arrogantly attacks a centaur, she is seized and imprisoned by a group of his fellow centaurs and carried off into the forest, for humiliations that we imagine with some delight. Once again, Voldemort and his henchmen repeatedly consider themselves superior to almost all other humans, and certainly better than all non-humans. On the other hand, Harry and his friends treat them with the respect they deserve. House elves, centaurs, goblins, giants, and phoenixes all prove to be a huge help as Harry's battle progresses. They fight for Harry and his cause because from Harry they receive respect and kindness, whereas from Voldemort they receive condescension and cruelty. The centaurs' taking of Umbridge is one more example of kindness reciprocated and condescension punished. Charity to non-humans is an underestimated, but powerful act, in the course of the Potter quest, and Harry's continual commitment to kindness is repaid again and again as the quest progresses.

And then it begins—the unbelievably big scene at the Ministry of Magic that concludes this novel. Using his ability to invade Harry's mind, Voldemort has deceived Harry, knowing full well that he will not be able to refuse the bait. Voldemort has given Harry the image of Sirius being in trouble at the Department of Ministries. Harry, frightened that Sirius might be killed, summons his friends to help him rescue Sirius. The best of Dumbledore's Army—Harry, Ron, Hermione, Ginny, Neville, and Luna—assemble, ride thestrals into London and enter the Ministry of Magic. It is worth noting that, once upon a time, Harry would not have selected these five as the best warriors. He has no doubts about Ron and Hermione, but he has definite doubts about the abilities of the others. Harry sees Ginny as too young, Luna as too much of a dreamer, and Neville as a well-intentioned but largely ineffective young man. He is wrong on all counts, and he has completely underestimated the great heart that each of these young warriors brings to the fight. Eventually, all the important antagonists assemble for this battle—the Death Eaters and the members of The Order of the Phoenix. The result is a colossal battle, once again with deadly consequences. We are always aware that the quest involves battles and will lead to a final war, and there will be losses. Significant and painful losses. This scene at the Ministry is pure genius, and it stands up to multiple readings, revealing just a little bit more each time you read it.

The first thing we notice is the mysterious veil that covers the pointed archway. Harry is drawn to this veil; it almost pulls him in and he is loath to resist: "Still the veil swayed gently, as though somebody had just passed through it…He had the strangest feeling that there was someone standing right behind the veil on the other side of the archway"(773). It is very interesting to note that Harry is mysteriously drawn to this veil; it has almost a physical and emotional tug for him. This thin and transparent veil is the barrier between this world and the next, and it has almost a hypnotically attractive quality for Harry. Perhaps this idea suggests that, at least at some level, all souls long to rest beyond the burdens of this world, and maybe Harry even more than others, even though we fear death because it is essentially an unknown. This is the very stuff of Hamlet's famous "To be or not to be" soliloquy. He says that if dying is like sleeping, it doesn't sound too bad to him, but we do not know what lies beyond the veil. The idea of death

Hamlet

both tempts us and puzzles us: "'Tis a consummation devoutly to be wished. To die, to sleep, to sleep, perchance to dream—aye, there's the rub. For in that sleep of death what dreams may come when we have shuffled off this mortal coil must give us pause"(3.1.64-68). Hamlet says that sometimes death is a temptation, because it would clearly be a cessation of hostilities with the burdens of life. Like Hamlet, Harry certainly notices this mysterious veil, and in some ways, it looks very lovely to him, rustling in the light unseen breeze, with almost of hint of voices just beyond it: "The gently rippling veil intrigued him; he felt a very strong inclination to climb up on the dais and walk through it…. He had just heard something. There were faint whispering, murmuring noises coming from the other side of the veil"(774). Therefore, the fact that Harry feels such a strong attraction for the veil can be interpreted symbolically to mean that death has a powerful attraction for him, understandably so. He has lost his mother and father to death. He longs to be reunited with them, and sometimes this longing almost overwhelms him. Hermione seems to instinctively understand this; she urgently pulls Harry away from the veil, frightened that it has such an attraction for him, knowing that he must not step through it. Not now, and not yet.

The Death Eaters who serve Voldemort have been lying in wait for Harry in the chamber where the prophecies are kept, and an enormous battle ensues. This veil we have just described is the very one that Sirius falls through when Bellatrix Lestrange kills him: "It seemed to take Sirius an age to fall. His body curved in a graceful arc as he sank backward through the ragged veil hanging from the arch...he fell through the ancient doorway and disappeared behind the veil, which fluttered for a moment as though in a high wind and then fell back into place"(806). Harry tries to charge after him, hoping to pull him back, but Lupin hangs on tightly, and tells Harry that Sirius is beyond his reach now. Once again, we are reminded that there is a boundary between this world and the next, and once we have crossed it, there is no coming back. Harry cries out in anguish, having lost his godfather, whom he had come to love, almost like a combination of father and brother. However, while those who die may be physically out of reach for us, they are certainly not far from us. They are with us and within us, and they exist in their own rite, just beyond the veil, just beyond the realm of our earthly existence. Harry does not realize this yet, but he will come to understand this before the end of the novel.

Voldemort's purpose in summoning Harry to the Ministry was to get him to retrieve the prophecy made so long ago by Sibyll Trelawney. Voldemort believes that he knows what it says, but he must hear it for himself. In the course of the battle, Neville drops the crystal vial holding the words of the prophecy, releasing a weird apparition that speaks but cannot be heard because of the noise of the battle all around them. Harry and Neville, the two boys about whom the prophecy could have been spoken, are together at the moment that it breaks. They "stared at the place where it had broken…a pearly-white figure with hugely magnified eyes rose into the air, unnoticed by any but them. Harry could see its mouth moving, but in all the crashes and screams and yells surrounding them, not one word of the prophecy could he hear"(805). This imagery is absolutely appropriate for J. K. Rowling's message about prophecies—they do not exist, they have no validity until someone hears them. So, at this moment, the prophecy is drowned out by the noise of the battle, and that is as it should be. For all intents and purposes, it does not exist because it cannot be heard. We are reminded that we ought to concern ourselves with the present, not the future. The future is not within the province of our knowledge. We need to live in the present, and do the best we can with the given moment. We can plan for the future, but we ought not seek to know it.

future

Another interesting idea emerges when Harry comes face to face with Bellatrix Lestrange, the Satanic Death Eater who has just killed his godfather. Harry, in his rage, tries to use the cruciatus curse on her, but he cannot produce the unforgivable curse. Certainly, at that moment, Harry hates Bellatrix, but he has such a purity of soul, a wholeness, that makes him incapable of causing such immense pain to another person. Here, Harry's wholeness prevents him from achieving the revenge he so desires, but later in the quest, when we reach the final climactic battle, his goodness and wholeness prove to be his biggest assets. Perhaps wholeness is the best word to use at this moment because it calls to mind the notion of horcruxes, which we will talk about at some length in the last two novels. And Harry is too whole to really speak the words of an unforgivable curse. So, Harry speaks the words, but without real and nihilistic hatred in his heart. He cries out seeking revenge, but not destruction. Instead, Bellatrix gives him a lesson about hatred: "Never used an Unforgivable Curse before, have you, boy?...You need to mean them, Potter! You need to really want to cause pain—to enjoy it—righteous anger won't hurt me for long"(810). These are absolutely chilling words. You need to hate, you need to want to hurt someone, and you need to enjoy watching them suffer. To understand that someone could actually be in that kind of mindset makes our blood run cold. We are at the heart of darkness, the essence of evil, the horror. It is very clear that she and Voldemort are truly kindred spirits.

And it is only a moment before Voldemort shows up, hoping to finish Harry off. However, Dumbledore is suddenly there, and he does battle with Voldemort. Dumbledore calls him Tom Riddle, using the familiar term to express his contempt for him, refusing to recognize him as "Lord Voldemort." For a moment, it seems that Voldemort has the upper hand, and once again, Dumbledore tries to teach him, and to reach his soul, giving him a chance to understand

and repent. Voldemort says that there is nothing worse than death, and Dumbledore replies, "You are quite wrong…Indeed, your failure to understand that there are things much worse than death has always been your greatest weakness"(814). In his final move of their battle, one which he firmly believes will result in his victory, Voldemort enters Harry's body, and Harry, filled with that kind of hatred, and simultaneously being exhausted and broken hearted about Sirius' death, simply longs for his own death. To Harry, it feels as if his scar has burst open: "He knew he was dead; it was pain beyond imagining, pain past endurance"(815). Harry suddenly understands, with the portion of his mind that he can still control, that Voldemort has fused himself to Harry, and Harry is in a torment that cannot even be expressed in words. However, using every last bit of his mighty magic, Dumbledore is able to exorcise the demon, and Harry is released from this hell: "And as Harry's heart filled with emotion, the creature's coils loosened, the pain was gone, Harry was lying facedown on the floor, his glasses gone, shivering"(816). Suddenly, the atrium is full of people, and many of them have seen Voldemort with their own eyes. There can be no denying now that what Harry and Dumbledore had said is true. Among those who have now seen this terrible truth with their own eyes is Cornelius Fudge, the Minister of Magic. Instead of humbly acknowledging his mistake and gratefully thanking Dumbledore for holding back Voldemort, he starts spluttering and objecting to the destruction of the fountain and the use of an "illegal portkey." His response might almost be comical if it weren't so very annoying. Dumbledore puts him in his place very quietly: "You will give the order to remove Dolores Umbridge from Hogwarts…You will tell your Aurors to stop searching for my Care of Magical Creatures teacher so that he can return to work. I will give you…half an hour of my time tonight, in which I think we shall be more than able to cover the important points of what has happened here. After that, I shall need to return to my school"(818). Cornelius Fudge looks rumpled and defeated. Those of us who have suffered a run in with a pompous little bureaucrat at some point in our life cannot restrain a small chuckle of delight.

Now we come to the final scene in the novel where Dumbledore again explains to Harry what he hasn't quite figured out, and once again, we hear several important ideas. This closing scene between Harry and Dumbledore is probably the most powerful scene in the book. It absolutely stands up to multiple readings, as great scenes always do, and it reveals more every time we read it. This scene can even make us a little uncomfortable, because we can recognize ourselves in Harry in a very powerful way. We have all known the experience of feeling overwhelmed, when you feel like you have been treated unfairly, and you are just worn out. It is understandable at those times to feel frustrated, angry, and depressed. Often it seems as if things are just never going to get any better, and we can wallow in self-pity. Safely back in Dumbledore's office, Harry says that he almost wishes he had died, because he is so heartsick about having been used by Voldemort and having contributed to Sirius' death by summoning him to the Ministry. Dumbledore tells Harry that there is no shame in feeling pain and sorrow, that in fact it is his greatest strength. It is what makes him a man. To be sorry is the essence of humility, and that is our greatest strength. J. K. Rowling could very well be drawing on Scripture in this brilliant passage. This set of lines from the Second letter of St. Paul to the Corinthians can give us some insight into understanding this idea: "He said to me, 'My grace is sufficient for you, for my power is made perfect in weakness.' I will all the more gladly boast of my weaknesses, that the power of Christ may rest upon me. For the sake of Christ, then, I am content with weaknesses, insults, hardships, persecutions, and calamities, for when I am weak, then I am strong"(2 Corinthians 8-10). This is a complicated and thought-provoking idea. However, we can start with true humility. Many of the most brilliant scholars that have ever lived have said that their most brilliant realization is that we should have a genuine humility in the face of the complexities of life. There is so much we cannot know. We cannot know what life is waiting beyond the veil, but occasionally, we can hear whispers that suggest that there is another life waiting for us. We can go back to St. Paul for a supporting passage: "For while we live we are always being given up to death for Jesus' sake...so death is at work in us, but life in you...so we do not lose heart...Though our outer nature is wasting away, our inner nature is being renewed every day. For this slight momentary affliction is preparing for us an eternal weight of glory beyond all comparison"(2 Corinthians 4.7-5.4). St. Paul reminds us that this body is not meant to last, but our souls are. This earthly incarnation is preparing us for the "eternal weight of glory beyond all comparison," for our life when we have crossed beyond the veil. Once again, there are some things that we are not meant to know in this life; we must soldier on, and "walk by faith."

In this final scene, Dumbledore finally explains to Harry his reasons for trying to avoid him during the school year, and he also acknowledges that in doing so, he made a mistake: "Harry, I owe you an explanation...An explanation of an old man's mistakes. For I see now that what I have done, and not done, with regard to you, bears all the hallmarks of the failings of age. Youth cannot know how age thinks and feels. But old men are guilty if they forget what it was to be young...and I seem to have forgotten lately"(826). In essence, Dumbledore confesses that he has come to love Harry like a son, the son he never had. He suspected that Voldemort would use his ability to enter Harry's mind in order to spy on him, and he therefore tried to distance himself from Harry. He explains the terrible truth of what happened at the Ministry to Harry: "Voldemort's aim in possessing you, as he demonstrated tonight, would not have been my destruction. It would have been yours. He hoped, when he possessed you briefly a short while ago, that I would sacrifice you in the hope of killing him"(828). Harry lets his words wash over him, but his primary emotion at this time is a kind of spiritual numbness. All he can think about is that Sirius is dead, and he had inadvertently contributed to that happening by going to the Ministry, believing the images that Voldemort had planted in his mind.

In spite of the fact that Harry is only half listening, Dumbledore pours his heart out. He tells Harry that Voldemort cleverly counted on Dumbledore developing powerful feelings for Harry: "I cared about you too much…I cared more for your happiness than your knowing the truth, more for your peace of mind than my plan, more for your life than the lives that might be lost if the plan failed. In other words, I acted exactly as Voldemort expects we fools in love to act"(838). Once again, we hear echoes of Biblical imagery. Dumbledore's next revelation calls to mind the story of Herod trying to kill the Christ Child: "Voldemort tried to kill you when you were a child because of a prophecy made shortly before your birth. He knew the prophecy had been made, though he did not know its full contents. He set out to kill you when you were still a baby, believing he was fulfilling the terms of the prophecy"(839). Ever since that attempt backfired, he has been seeking the knowledge of how to kill Harry. That is why he wanted his henchmen to retrieve the prophecy, the one that broke during the

208

battle. In spite of the fact that neither Harry nor Neville could hear the words, we now hear them, because the person to whom the prophecy was spoken is standing right in front of us—Dumbledore.

And he tells us what was said, so long ago, using his Pensieve to summon the memory. We witness Sibyll Trelawney speak the words of prophecy: "THE ONE WITH THE POWER TO VANQUISH THE DARK LORD APPROACHES...BORN TO THOSE WHO HAVE THRICE DEFIED HIM, BORN AS THE SEVENTH MONTH DIES...AND THE DARK LORD WILL MARK HIM AS HIS EQUAL, BUT HE WILL HAVE POWER THE DARK LORD KNOWS NOT...AND EITHER MUST DIE AT THE HAND OF THE OTHER FOR NEITHER CAN LIVE WHILE THE OTHER SURVIVES"(841). Dumbledore explains to Harry that the prophecy was vague enough to refer to either Harry or Neville, but when Voldemort marked Harry with his lightning scar, he had essentially chosen his adversary. Dumbledore tells Harry that Voldemort knew that it could be dangerous to try to kill Harry. After all, he had already tried several times and failed. He thought, this time, that he knew enough, but he did not fully understand that Harry had the most powerful magic of all. When he says this, Harry splutters indignantly that he has no such power.

And then, Dumbledore explains: "There is a room in the Department of Mysteries...that is kept locked at all times. It contains a force that is at once more wonderful and more terrible than death, than human intelligence, than forces of nature. It is also, perhaps, the most mysterious of the many subjects for study that reside there. It is the power held within that room that you possess in such quantities and which Voldemort has not at all. That power took you to Sirius tonight. That power also saved you from possession by Voldemort, because he could not bear to reside in a body so full of the force he detests. In the end, it mattered not that you could not close your mind. It was your heart that saved you"(844). Once again, J. K. Rowling is telling us about the mightiest magic of all, and it is a magic that we are all capable of. It must never be underestimated or taken for granted. That is one of the most powerful lessons of the Potter quest.

Harry is broken hearted at having lost Sirius—that is only human, and he suffers and he hurts. We understand, and many of us know this very heartsickness, know it in our bones. However, we must be of good courage, and soldier on, or walk by faith. You cannot have love without pain. If you love someone, truly love someone, you make yourself vulnerable to that powerful hurt that Harry knows and that many of us have experienced. For when you lose someone you love, it hurts, almost beyond all telling. But that is the price of love, and a life without love is not worth living.

At the end of the novel, Harry consults Nearly Headless Nick about the idea that maybe Sirius could become a ghost, and he could still see him. Nick tells Harry, in an almost wistful tone, that Sirius will not come back, that he will have "gone on." Lonely and hurting, comfort comes to Harry from a source he might not have expected, Luna Lovegood. Standing outside the end of term feast, he sees her searching, rather half-heartedly for some of her lost possessions. He finally hears her story, about how she lost her Mom, but she reminds Harry that she knows she will see her Mom again. Luna refers to the veil that had so captivated Harry, and which she now reveals had the same powerful attraction for her: "Oh, come on. You heard them, just behind the veil, didn't you?...In that room with the archway. They were just lurking out of sight, that's all. You heard them"(863). Our loved ones are not lost to us. They are present in our hearts, and we can talk to them when we need to feel their presence. It is as if they are just in another room, waiting for us, and we will be united with them, in the fullness of time. *lost loved ones*

As we have said before, prophecies acquire power if someone knows they have been spoken, and many people, on both sides of this conflict, know that these words have been spoken. However, our young hero continues to have power that the Dark Lord does not understand or recognize. We all have that mighty power within us, and it is the most powerful magic of all.

Harry Potter and the Half-Blood Prince

Everything that J. K. Rowling has done in the first five novels of this wonderful series has been to prepare us for the two last novels, which are the best of all. The Wall Street Journal has this to say about her art: "With each book she has revealed progressively more of her brilliantly clever parallel world...It is only as we proceed—and ideas seeming thrown casually into the mix ripen into great significance—that it becomes clear that it's a world she has seen in its fantastic complexity all along. We enthusiasts, we happy millions, can only marvel at her skill at sustaining innumerable narrative skeins and wrapping them ever more tightly together—in the process keeping us...rapt." That is it exactly! J. K. Rowling has told us herself that she planned for almost five years before she wrote the first novel, with a storyboard mapping out the major events along the way. All the planning pays off, and these last two novels are the reward for any reader who has followed the quest narrative thus far.

She opens the novel with a scene where the Prime Minister of England has an audience with the outgoing Minister of Magic, Cornelius Fudge, who has been sacked, as he says, and the new Minister, Rufus Scrimgeour, who looks rather like an old lion. It is interesting to examine the etymology of his name. Rufus derives from the Latin word for red, and his surname Scrimgeour is Scottish in origin, meaning skirmish. Its root goes back to the French word "escrimeur" for swordsman. This makes sense for this character, who has shaggy, reddish hair, and who has been the head of the Aurors, and is therefore a man skilled in combat. The three men discuss the hurricanes, the terrible storms, and the feeling of depression that seems to have a stranglehold on England, and the wizards tell the Prime Minister that these events are the result of the work of dementors, who breed fear and desperation wherever they go. J. K. Rowling is cleverly suggesting that the parallel worlds overlap all of the time. Caught up in the magic of her storytelling, we may well find ourselves reading the morning papers with an eye as to how she would use the events that are recorded there.

However, the most important idea in the opening comes in chapter two, where Narcissa Malfoy and Bellatrix Lestrange, who are sisters, come to visit Severus Snape, each of them with their own agendas. This may be a good moment to talk about the interesting etymology behind Bellatrix's name. First of all, the word "bella" is from the French and Latin word for beautiful, and Bellatrix is physically attractive. However, in Latin, the word bella is also the plural for bellum, which means war. That right there is an interesting and appropriate combination for this mentally unbalanced character. Furthermore, Bellatrix is the name of the third brightest star in the constellation of

Orion, the hunter. It is frequently known as the "Amazon star." Since Bellatrix is a gifted warrior and duelist, this also seems appropriate. Although her surname at birth is Black, when she marries Rodolphus Lestrange, she completes her etymology perfectly, since that name comes from the French word "l'estrange," meaning "the strange one." And she certainly is this. Her sister Narcissa takes her name from the well-known character in Greek mythology of the same name, the character that was beautiful but very vain, and lost his life because he was so in love with his own appearance. Narcissa is certainly very vain, but she is not a Death Eater, like her vicious sister. She does, however, profess to believe that pure bloods are superior and ought not intermarry with those of lesser blood status. Both of these sisters have broken off all communication with their sister Andromeda, who married a Muggle, Ted Tonks. Since that time, Bellatrix has made it her personal goal to purge her family's bloodline of this impurity, this embarrassment. She has a personal vendetta against the Tonks family, a vendetta that will come to its fullest statement in the Battle of Hogwarts.

In this cleverly written chapter, Snape's loyalty is in question—from Narcissa, from Bellatrix, and from the reader. There are many lines that could be read to support various interpretations. It is particularly interesting, after you have finished the seventh book, to go back to this chapter with an eye to this cleverly written ambiguity. Still, the most important thing happens right at the end of the chapter. Narcissa asks Snape if he will make the Unbreakable Vow with her, vowing to protect her son Draco. At this point, Draco has been chosen by Voldemort to kill Dumbledore, supposedly to prove his loyalty to him, but actually more as a punishment to the Malfoy family for angering Voldemort. Narcissa is worried that he will not be able to do it, or perhaps may die in the attempt. She therefore binds Severus with an unbreakable vow, who surprises Bellatrix by agreeing to her terms: "Will you, Severus, watch over my son, Draco, as he attempts to fulfill the Dark Lord's wishes…And will you, to the best of your ability, protect him from harm…And, should it prove necessary…will you carry out the deed that the Dark Lord has ordered Draco to perform?"(36). Bellatrix, who has doubted Severus' loyalty, is very impressed when Snape agrees to take this vow, and his doing so makes her believe that he is truly a faithful servant of the Dark Lord. When Severus gives his consent to these terms, a blaze of fire, in the form of a snake, encircles their bound hands. We learn, much later in the novel, that when someone makes an unbreakable vow, he quite literally cannot break it. The price for doing so is death. We will look back to this scene when we reach the end of the novel, and guess that, at some point, Dumbledore and Snape had already planned that this would happen.

There is a significant difference between Narcissa and Bellatrix in this scene. Narcissa wants to protect her son, even if it is against the wishes of the Dark Lord, while Bellatrix proudly states that if she had children, she would gladly sacrifice them to do Voldemort's bidding: "You should be proud…If I had sons, I would be glad to give them up to the service of the Dark Lord"(35). It is important to remember, however, that she does not have sons. She has no children. We cannot help but remember Lady Macbeth, who also apparently had no children, and who proudly proclaims: "I have given suck, and know how tender tis to love the babe that milks me. I would, while it was smiling in my face, have plucked my nipple from its boneless gums and dashed the brains out had I so sworn as you have done to this"(Macbeth 1.7.54-58). What a difference between these two sisters, both of whom have pledged their allegiance to evil. However, as Bellatrix has never given birth to a child, she clearly does not understand, and even more importantly, underestimates, the love that Narcissa has for Draco. This love that Narcissa has for her son becomes absolutely crucial in the final scenes of the Potter quest. We are reminded, once again, that love is the mightiest magic of all.

Immediately thereafter, Dumbledore comes to personally fetch Harry from the Dursley residence. This is the first time he has ever done that. Our interest and sense of danger are certainly elevated, although Dumbledore gives no sign of worry himself. Rather, he scolds Petunia for having been, at best, neglectful and cruel to Harry, and tells her that her obligation will only last one more year, for when Harry turns seventeen, he comes of age in the magical world and she will no longer be able to protect Harry, even unwillingly. Then, he grabs Harry's hand and they leave to "pursue that flighty temptress, adventure"(57).

Their first stop is a Muggle house where Horace Slughorn, a former professor and head of the house of Slytherin, has been hiding out. He is a cowardly man, hence the surname "slug," but he has a big ego, and he likes to "collect" the rising stars in the world of magic. Needless to say, he can't quite resist the opportunity to work with the young Harry Potter, the brightest star in the world of magic at this time. So, Dumbledore dangles Harry as bait in front of Slughorn, and he bites, agreeing to return to Hogwarts and teach Potions for the year. His name has several interesting connections. First of all, Horace is a famous Roman poet from the first century B. C. His well-known phrase, "Carpe diem," is often quoted. It means seize the day, and it is the battle cry of all Epicureans, from that time to this. It means that we should enjoy the pleasures of life that are available to us. Since Horace Slughorn is known to like good food and drink, perhaps a little too much, this etymological connection is certainly in play. His surname, Slughorn is supposedly from an old Scottish term which means war-cry or battle cry. This meaning certainly works, because Horace is an accomplished warrior, and in the Battle of Hogwarts, he duels with the

Dark Lord himself, although he has two very accomplished duelists on his side at the time. However, the word Slughorn may actually be simply a connection to his rather sluggish appearance and demeanor. He is not a very brave man; this is for sure. It is important for Dumbledore to lure Slughorn back to Hogwarts, because Slughorn knows things about Tom Riddle's past that Dumbledore needs to know. In this early chapter, we get our first glimpse of Dumbledore's damaged hand, which will become more apparent and more important as the novel moves toward its breathtaking conclusion.

It is at this point in the novel, when Harry reaches the relative safety of the Burrow, that he finally tells Ron and Hermione what the prophecy had said, and he does this at the urging of Dumbledore, who tells Harry that the two of them are sacred friends to Harry. He suggests that they are going to be involved in Harry's battle against Voldemort and that they therefore have a right to know all they can about what they are up against. So, Harry tells them everything he knows, but no one else. He tells them in a rather matter of fact manner, although in his heart, he feels very uneasy about what it all means. However, in the process of telling them, he feels a burden lifting from his heart: "A warmth was spreading through him that had nothing to do with the sunlight; a tight obstruction in his chest seemed to be dissolving. He knew that Ron and Hermione were more shocked than they were letting on, but the mere fact that they were still there,

218

on either side of him, speaking bracing words of comfort…was worth more than he could ever tell them"(99). They will be his most important companions and fellow warriors in these last stages of the quest, and Dumbledore is correct—they have a right to know. There is an important lesson for all of us here, and that lesson is one of the most important ones of the whole Potter quest. We are reminded of the importance, of the sacredness, of friendship and of love. Dumbledore tells Harry that although it is wise not to have told everyone about the prophecy, he should tell Ron and Hermione: "A wise decision, on the whole…Although I think you ought to relax it in favor of your friends, Mr. Ronald Weasley and Miss Hermione Granger…I think they ought to know. You do them a disservice by not confiding something this important to them…You need your friends, Harry. As you so rightly said, Sirius would not have wanted you to shut yourself away"(78). As Dumbledore repeatedly states, Harry's power over Voldemort is his love, and if he keeps secrets from his friends that he can fully trust, he diminishes in part that which is his greatest power. Although each of us is, in the final analysis alone, we have the opportunity to have companions on the quest that is our life, and that opportunity is sacred. We can refer back to the Nietzsche and Schopenhauer allusion we discussed earlier here. We are each of us in our own boats from the moment of our birth, but occasionally, we can reach out and touch another person in a flash of understanding, an epiphany. This gives us

219

a glimpse of the great mystery that lies behind the veil, the universal oneness underlying the nature of the human condition.

We pick up an alarming bit of news just before the young students head back to Hogwarts for the year. The wand maker, Ollivander, the old gentleman who gave Harry his wand, has disappeared, and no one has any idea what this is all about. However, we remember what happened at the end of The Goblet of Fire, and an alarm bell goes off in the back of our heads. That novel concludes with the amazing duel in the graveyard, where Harry's wand and Voldemort's wand locked in a mighty battle, and Voldemort was defeated. If Ollivander has disappeared, we wonder if it might have something to do with that defeat. The very thought of Voldemort having taken poor old Ollivander makes us shiver with apprehension. Soon afterwards, when they are at Madam Malkin's, Harry notices something horrible: Draco Malfoy has been branded with the Dark Mark, and has apparently taken his father's place as a Death Eater. We remember the opening scene with Narcissa and Severus, and our blood runs cold.

At the start of term feast, Dumbledore's injured hand is very noticeable: "Dumbledore's right hand was as blackened and dead-looking as it had been on the night he had come to fetch Harry from the Dursleys"(166). This injury does not seem to be a normal injury; enough time has gone by that it should have begun to heal, and Hermione whispers: "It looks as if it's died...but there are some injuries you can't cure...old curses...and there are poisons without antidotes"(166). We are getting an introduction to something that will be a major theme of this novel—that there is a point of no return. It is possible for a person to be so physically ill that he cannot become better. Many of us have watched a loved one be overcome by a life-threatening illness that they can no longer defeat. There is no medicine that can protect them any longer. So too, it is possible for someone to do so much damage to his own soul that he cannot find his way back to absolution. He can lock himself in his own personal hell and be beyond the reach of the power of love to heal or redeem. We will come back to this idea in our discussion of horcruxes. Dumbledore's damaged hand resulted from his encounter with dark magic, but his physical injury is the full extent of his suffering and damage. The physical injury will cost him his earthly life; it is like a cancer working on his body. However, it cannot touch his soul because he, like Harry, has a pureness of heart and a wholeness of soul that is so good, and so committed to good, that evil cannot corrupt him, no matter how hard it tries.

Severus Snape finally has the position he has coveted from the beginning of the quest. He is the new Defense Against the Dark Arts professor. In his opening lecture, he tells his students that the "Dark Arts...are many, varied, ever-changing, and eternal. Fighting them is like fighting a many-headed monster, which, each time a neck is severed, sprouts a head even fiercer and cleverer than before. You are fighting that which is unfixed, mutating, indestructible"(177). There is a great deal of wisdom in these lines. How interesting to say that the forces of evil are both eternal and ever changing. Can they be both? Yes. Unfortunately, when you think about it, these words give us a very apt description of much of the evil we are facing in our world today. It also should put us on alert that there will be no final resolution at the end of the Potter quest. J. K. Rowling is far too wise to suggest that such a resolution is possible. In our own personal quest, in the course of our life here on earth, all any of us can do is battle the monsters we have to face, with no illusions that our battle will be the "be all" or the "end all." Again, there may well be a larger plan or vision, but it is not in the province of our knowledge. We do the best we can. As St. Paul says, "we walk by faith." Furthermore, as Hermione points out, Snape sounds a lot like Harry—and St. Paul. She says, "When you were telling us what it's like to face Voldemort. You said it wasn't just memorizing a bunch of spells, you said it was just you and your brains and your guts—well, wasn't that what Snape was saying? That it really comes down to being brave and quick-thinking"(181). We do the best we can and keep our hearts centered on goodness. We walk by faith.

When Harry reports to Potions class, which Horace Slughorn is teaching, he does not have a book, and quite by accident (although we suspect there are no accidents) he uses an old potion book that belonged to someone who called himself "the half-blood prince." Harry starts to follow the instructions that are hand written in the margins of this old potions book, and he starts to shine—to become, in fact, the best potions student that Slughorn has seen in a long time. Hermione is angry with Harry for following these notes; in fact, she regards it as a kind of cheating. Poor Hermione. Although she is right, she is just a little bit jealous of Harry's new status as the best pupil in the class. She is not used to NOT being the shining star, and she comes by her academic excellence through good old-fashioned hard work. So, we understand her resentment, even as we chuckle a little bit as her exasperation mounts. Still, Harry continues to excel at Potions in a way that he has never done before. From the notes written in the margin of his borrowed potions book, he learns that if someone has been poisoned, rather than calculating complicated antidotes, he can "just shove a bezoar down their throats." This little bit of wisdom will save Ron's life when he accidentally drinks a poisoned wine that was intended for Dumbledore, as a result of another one of Draco's clumsy attempts to fulfill his promise to Voldemort. We will come back to Harry and Potions class a little later in our discussion.

Throughout the novel, Dumbledore persists in a series of private lessons for Harry, most of which involve trips into the Pensieve as Harry learns all about Voldemort's past. When Harry

Choices vs. abilities

asks Dumbledore if this is really necessary, Dumbledore tells Harry that what happened to Voldemort in his youth has everything to do with the prophecy. There is a powerful message here—the child is father to the man, as Wordsworth said. However, we come back to the important theme of choices. Despite Voldemort's unhappy childhood and the mistakes he made, he still could have chosen to start fresh at Hogwarts. Dumbledore clearly tried to guide him in that direction, knowing that as a child, Tom Riddle had experienced many sadnesses and losses that contributed to his suspicious nature. As Dumbledore explains the significance of what they are about to witness, Harry becomes an attentive student. Once again, he notices many similarities between himself and the young Tom Riddle. Both of them are orphans, although Tom Riddle's father deserted his family whereas James Potter died trying to protect his. Furthermore, we learn that Merope, Tom's mother, was a witch who had won her husband by using a love potion, and that she eventually lost him. She ended up alone, poor, homeless, unloved, and pregnant. When Harry expresses anger at her lack of courage and heart, Dumbledore cautions patience and understanding: "Merope Riddle chose death in spite of a son who needed her, but do not judge her too harshly, Harry. She was greatly weakened by long suffering and she never had your mother's courage"(262). Just as an interesting footnote here—Merope is the name of the adoptive mother of Oedipus, in the ancient Greek myth of

Oedipus Rex. She and her husband chose not to tell their adopted son the truth, that they were his adoptive parents, not his birth parents, and with this lie, arguably could be said to have contributed to the tragic spin of events that followed. When Oedipus ran away, trying to avoid the desperate prophecy he had heard, Merope never saw her adopted son again, and died, never knowing what had happened to the boy she loved. Perhaps this old story was echoing in J. K. Rowling's mind when she named this sad character.

Through the Pensieve, we then witness the scene where Albus Dumbledore came to the orphanage where Tom Riddle was living, offering to take him to Hogwarts. The woman who runs the orphanage seems only too happy to let Tom go, saying that he frightens the other children, and he seems very odd, having no sympathy or human feeling. With these words of caution echoing in the back of his head, Dumbledore extends his invitation to young Tom, and tries to guide him toward the idea of using his powers for good, not evil: "At Hogwarts...we teach you not only to use magic, but to control it. You have—inadvertently, I am sure—been using your powers in a way that is neither taught nor tolerated at our school. You are not the first, nor will you be the last, to allow your magic to run away with you"(273). Once again, we are given a subtle reminder that there will be no absolute closure at the end of this particular quest. There cannot be. One journey closes, but billions more are still ongoing. Each of us will "go on," in time, but the largest quest goes on and on. The message from the end of the fifth book in the series echoes in the back of our minds. Dumbledore tells Harry there that in life we must fight, and fight again for only then can evil be kept at bay, even though it can never be completely eradicated. We must stand up for what is right when it is our turn to do battle. In time, the battle will be in other people's hands.

In the course of this memory scene, Dumbledore helps us realize some of the important qualities in Voldemort's personality, even when he is still a child that are warning signs for us. Dumbledore says this about Tom Riddle: "He wished to be different, separate, notorious. He shed his name, as you know, within a few short years of that conversation and created the mask of 'Lord Voldemort' behind which he has been hidden for so long...I trust that you also noticed that Tom Riddle was already highly self-sufficient, secretive, and apparently, friendless...You will hear many of his Death Eaters claiming that they are in his confidence, that they alone are close to him, even understand him. They are deluded. Lord Voldemort has never had a friend, nor do I believe that he has ever wanted one"(277). Voldemort has chosen, even at this young age, not to love anyone. In so doing, he has turned his back on the best and most sacred experience a human being can ever have. Truthfully, he has also turned his back on the mightiest magic of all, the transcendent power of love. That is arguably the definition of evil—an absolute lack of love or any human understanding. Tom Riddle's determination not to trust anyone or to have any true friends in his life contrasts powerfully with Harry, who time and time again relies on his friends for his very life. Dumbledore also points out that Tom Riddle steals things and marks them with great value, marks them as souvenirs of his conquests. We are getting our first glimpse into what we will later call horcruxes.

With Harry hiding under his invisibility cloak, we witness a scene between Snape and Draco Malfoy, who seems to look more and more ill with each passing day. It is as if the alliance he has made with evil is taking a physical toll on him. Again, we are confused about Snape's loyalty, because he reminds Malfoy that he has made an unbreakable vow, promising to protect him, and he scolds Malfoy for being too aggressive and careless about his attempts to fulfill his promise to the Dark Lord. When Malfoy says that he does not care if he gets caught, Snape is furious: "Where do you think I would have been all these years, if I had not known how to act? Now listen to me! You are being incautious, wandering around at night, getting yourself caught"324). Draco's answer, that he thinks that Snape is trying to steal his glory, lets us know that this young man is in trouble, in way over his head, and is feeling desperately alone. We will eventually learn that he is frightened for his family as well. We could even begin to feel just a little bit sorry for him. Maybe. We continue to be as puzzled as ever as to where the loyalties of Severus Snape lie. This conversation with Draco seems to place him firmly in the camp of the powers of darkness, but at the Burrow over Christmas time, Remus Lupin gives strong testimony on Snape's behalf: "Do not forget that during the year I taught at Hogwarts, Severus made the Wolfsbane Potion for me every month, made it perfectly, so that I did not have to suffer as I usually do at the full moon…he could have wreaked much worse damage on me by tampering with the potion. He kept me healthy. I must be grateful"(333). And whenever Harry questions Albus Dumbledore about Snape, there is no equivocation on Dumbledore's part. He always tells Harry that he trusts Snape with his life, which is exactly what he will do at the end of this novel.

Professor Dumbledore continues his series of "lessons" with Harry. When Harry asks him what this is all about, Dumbledore is evasive. He says only that he believes that it is time that he "took a greater hand" in Harry's education, but he refuses to specify what exactly their goal is. Certainly, he wants to teach Harry about Voldemort's past, which means that they continue to travel back in time via the Pensieve. We see that Voldemort's affinity for souvenirs is becoming an important factor, and we watch him acquire the cup that had once belonged to Helga Hufflepuff, and the locket and ring that he deemed should have been his. All of these objects had once belonged to one of the four founders of Hogwarts, a place that was very powerful in Tom Riddle's life, a fact that will be very important in the final book. We find out that Voldemort has acquired all of these "sacred" objects by killing the proper owner, thus making them the appropriate objects to serve as horcruxes, in time.

We witness a scene where Tom Riddle, who at this time already calls himself Lord Voldemort, applies for a teaching position at Hogwarts. By now, he has been in communion with evil for so long that his good looks have all but disappeared, as well as his soul. He mocks Albus Dumbledore, who seems to be trying one last time to save him: "Nothing I have seen in the world has supported your famous pronouncements that love is more powerful than my kind of magic, Dumbledore"(444). Dumbledore tells Voldemort that there is no way he would ever hire him for a teaching position at Hogwarts: "Let us speak openly. Why have you come here tonight, surrounded by henchmen, to request a job we both know you do not want…you do not want to teach any more than you wanted to when you were eighteen. What is it you're after, Tom? Why not try an open request for once?"(445). Even at this late date, we see Dumbledore trying to break through Voldemort's evil and his deceit. However, his attempts fall on deaf ears, and Voldemort sneers at him and storms out of his office. We feel like Dumbledore has failed in his last attempt to break through to Voldemort. HORCRUXES

Dumbledore is now convinced that Voldemort has been

making horcruxes out of the "sacred" objects that he has been accumulating, but before he explains to Harry exactly what they are, he needs one last piece of evidence. Dumbledore suspects that Horace Slughorn is the person who, perhaps inadvertently, taught Voldemort how to make a horcrux. Slughorn refuses to admit this; clearly, he is ashamed of having done so, but Dumbledore needs to know just how far Voldemort might have gone with this process. Slughorn is so ashamed of having been a part of this that he has gone so far as to alter the memory that Dumbledore holds in his Pensieve. Dumbledore shows Harry the garbled or altered memory and then tells Harry that it is his task to get Slughorn to surrender the true memory, and that is not going to be an easy thing to do. However, he suspects that if Slughorn will tell the truth to anybody, it might be Harry. It should not surprise us that the mightiest magic of all is involved in the moment of surrender when Slughorn finally agrees to give Harry the unadulterated memory. Harry reminds Slughorn that he liked Lily Potter very much, and that Lily died to save Harry.

Slughorn, having drunk too much wine with Hagrid after Aragog's "funeral," knows exactly what Harry is after, and is reluctant to surrender the truth. Harry tells Horace that he is the man that must kill Voldemort: "I am the Chosen One. I have to kill him. I need that memory…You don't want to get rid of the wizard who killed Lily Evans?…Be brave like my mother, Professor"(490). There are many times during the Potter Quest when many characters are very brave, and this is Slughorn's moment. As a prelude to surrendering it, tells Harry that he is ashamed of what Harry will see: "I am not proud...I am ashamed of what—of what that memory shows...I think I may have done great damage that day"(490). Harry, priestlike, gives him absolution: "You'd cancel out anything you did by giving me the memory...It would be a very brave and noble thing to do"(490). We see how much he has come of age, and it is interesting to note that he can even speak in a rather matter-of-fact manner about the idea that he must be the one to kill Voldemort eventually. Then we witness the terrifying memory, which will lead us to horcruxes, and to the horror to which we have been journeying all along.

Harry takes the important memory from Slughorn to Dumbledore, and together, they tumble into the past via the Pensieve, into the real memory of that ominous night so long ago. Once again, as Harry watches Tom Riddle, he is struck with the realization that there are many similarities between them. However, Harry has chosen to fight for love and goodness; Voldemort has chosen to fight for hatred and evil. The important theme of choices echoes very powerfully here. In this fateful memory, the young Tom Riddle asks Professor Slughorn to tell him about Horcruxes. The etymology of the word is simple—the crux, the heart of horror. Slughorn, although uncomfortable, explains what they are: "A Horcrux is the word used for an object in which a person has concealed part of their soul…you split your soul, you see…and hide part of it in an object outside the body. Then, even if one's body is attacked or destroyed, one cannot die, for part of the soul remains earthbound and undamaged. But of course, existence in such a form…few would want it, Tom, very few. Death would be preferable"(497). Undaunted, Riddle presses him for more information, to find out how to do this very thing. Slughorn tells him, and he has regretted that he was the one who gave him that information ever since: "The soul is supposed to remain intact and whole. Splitting it is an act of violation, it is against nature…By an act of evil—the supreme act of evil. By committing murder. Killing rips the soul apart"(498). Instead of being horrified, the young Tom Riddle is excited. He wants to know how far a really brilliant dark wizard could push this process—could he create as many as seven Horcruxes? The fact that he asks this question indicates that Tom Riddle contemplates, with no hesitation at all, the necessity of killing seven people.

There is significance to the number seven as it is used here. First of all, the word "seven" comes from a Hebrew word "shen-ban" which means complete, or full. This usage derives from the Biblical story of creation, where God created the world in six days and rested on the seventh, the day of fullness or completion. Beyond that, the number seven is the most commonly used number in Scripture—in both the Old Testament and the New Testament. Jesus told his

232

disciples that they must forgive their brothers seven times seven times seven times, and this is thought to mean, an infinite number of times. So, perhaps it is no accident that Tom Riddle, with his deadly hubris, has chosen to split his soul into seven pieces, acting almost as an anti-Christ figure. In fact, in the Old Testament, God calls himself, "I am who am." This term is almost the exact opposite of what we have heard many of the characters calls Voldemort—"He who must not be named." We understand, as a result of this secret memory scene, that a Horcrux is the "crux of horror," and it requires an act of horror to create one. We learn, with Dumbledore's guidance, that the diary was the first Horcrux, one that Harry had destroyed five years ago by stabbing it with a basilisk fang, down in the chamber of secrets.

When they emerge from the terrible memory, Dumbledore and Harry have a portentous discussion about the task that lies ahead. Harry is horrified when he realizes that Voldemort has made seven Horcruxes, and that they could be anywhere and anything. Dumbledore answers: "I am glad to see you appreciate the magnitude of the problem…But firstly, no, Harry, not seven Horcruxes: six. The seventh part of his soul, however maimed, resides inside his regenerated body…That seventh piece of soul will be the last that anybody wishing to kill Voldemort must attack—the piece that lives in his body"(503). Together, they work out that two of the Horcruxes have already been destroyed—the diary, and Marvolo's ring, the destruction of which Dumbledore accomplished last summer, but which has cost him his hand, and which will, in time cost him his life. It is as if a cancer is already at work within his body, and he is running out of time to teach Harry what he needs to know to go forth on the quest when he must finally pass him the torch. He reminds Harry that Voldemort likes to collect souvenirs of his triumphs, and that he would seek out objects that have a strong symbolic significance to him: "I will hazard a guess that, having secured objects from Hufflepuff and Slytherin, he set out to track down objects owned by Gryffindor or Ravenclaw. Four objects from the four founders would, I am sure, have exerted a powerful pull over Voldemort's imagination"(505). One final guess from Dumbledore, and it will have to stand Harry in good stead when the time comes for him to go on alone, is that the final Horcrux could well be the snake Nagini, which is always in Voldemort's company.

As this very ominous scene closes, Harry and Dumbledore come back, once again, to one of the most important ideas of the quest. Harry asks Dumbledore if all six of the Horcruxes are destroyed, could Voldemort be killed? Dumbledore says that this is exactly what he believes to be true, for then he will be an ordinarily mortal man, although lacking the power of the wholeness of soul. Still, he will be a man with prodigious skill in deadly combat and a keen but unscrupulous intellect. When Harry expresses the thought that he cannot match wits and skills with a wizard like Voldemort, Dumbledore corrects him, saying that Harry has a power that Voldemort has never understood, and has always underestimated. Harry knows that Dumbledore is referring to love, and Harry expresses his doubts that love is enough to make any significant difference. Dumbledore says, once again, that love is the mightiest magic of all: "You are protected, in short, by your ability to love…In spite of all the temptation you have endured, all the suffering, you remain pure of heart, just as pure as you were at the age of eleven…You have flitted into Lord Voldemort's mind without damage to yourself, but he cannot possess you without enduring mortal agony…I do not think he understands why, Harry, but then, he was in such a hurry to mutilate his own soul, he never paused to understand the incomparable power of a soul that is untarnished and whole"(511). The message at the very heart of the Potter quest is reiterated—that love is the mightiest magic of all, and it is the very same thing that St. Paul tells us in that letter to the Corinthians. It is something that Voldemort has turned his back on, and this decision to do so will bring him down.

There is one other very important message at this point in the novel, and it has to do with understanding the nature of a prophecy. Harry is struggling with this idea of free will vs. fate. He is almost feeling sorry for himself that he has been marked or fated for this task for which he has so many doubts about his own skill. With

free will
vs. fate

some exasperation, Dumbledore tells Harry that he is setting too much store in the prophecy, and that, in fact, the prophecy has no value until we decide to give it some: "If Voldemort had never heard of the prophecy, would it have been fulfilled? Would it have meant anything? Of course not! Do you think every prophecy in the Hall of Prophecy has been fulfilled?...If Voldemort had never murdered your father, would he have imparted in you a furious desire for revenge? Of course not! If he had not forced your mother to die for you, would he have given you a magical protection he could not penetrate? Of course not, Harry! Don't you see? Voldemort himself created his worst enemy, just as tyrants everywhere do! Have you any idea how much tyrants fear the people they oppress? All of them realize that, one day, amongst their many victims, there is sure to be one who rises against them and strikes back...He heard the prophecy and leapt into action, with the result that he not only handpicked the man most likely to finish him, he handed him uniquely deadly weapons"(510). The prophecy, in essence, does not exist unless we know it and decide to believe it. We can put this idea another way—perhaps this makes it stronger: If we do not know it, it does not exist. It is a dangerous sin to ask to know the future. That is not our province. We can think back to the ancient Greek story of Oedipus Rex. If Laius had not sent to the oracle at Delphi in an attempt to know that which is beyond the appropriate province of his knowledge, he would not have heard the terrible prophecy. Having heard it, he unwittingly but immediately takes steps to make it come true. The same is true with Voldemort. Having heard the prophecy, he sets out to kill the Potter family. In killing James and Lily, he sets wheels in motion that will lead to the creation of a brave young man who will have the courage, motivation, and heart to destroy him.

Harry finally gets it. The prophecy does not mean that he has to kill Voldemort. However, knowing the prophecy caused Voldemort to "mark Harry as his equal." Harry can choose to walk away, to turn his back on the prophecy, but to do so would be an act of cowardice, and Harry is not made of that: "He understood at last what Dumbledore had been trying to tell him. It was, he thought, the difference between being dragged into the arena to face a battle to the death and walking into the arena with your head held high. Some people, perhaps, would say that there was little to choose between the two ways, but Dumbledore knew—and so do I, thought Harry…that there was all the difference in the world"(512).

However, immediately after this moment of brilliant insight and understanding on Harry's part, he makes a mistake. J. K. Rowling is again following the pattern of inflation—deflation in her narrative style. This stylistic decision is a good choice, because it mirrors life. We have moments of recognition and clarity, when it seems like we finally see what must be done. Almost right after that moment, something goes wrong, and our feelings of certainty and rightness slip away, as ephemeral as a morning mist. When we catch our balance again, we can soldier on, calling back our determination with an effort of will, but no one feels good and certain for very long. It just doesn't hold. At any rate, Harry makes a terrible mistake almost immediately after this important conversation with Dumbledore. He comes across Draco Malfoy, up in Moaning Myrtle's bathroom, and Draco is sobbing: "No one can help me...I can't do it...I can't...It won't work...unless I do it soon...he says he'll kill me..."(522). We see that this young man is almost breaking under the weight of what he has promised to do, and we suspect that there is still some goodness in him that is fighting against the hellish bargain he has made. Perhaps, he could still be saved. And, as we will discover, this is exactly what Dumbledore hopes to be true. Still, when Draco sees Harry staring at him, he starts to call out the cruciatus curse on him, and Harry, without really planning it, yells "SECTUMSEMPRA," which is a curse he has seen in the Half Blood Prince's potion book, and which he does not know anything about. This is a mistake on Harry's part, roughly the equivalent of breaking the old lawyer maxim: Never ask a question to which you do not know the answer. And it has disastrous results. Draco's face and chest are slashed open, and he almost bleeds to death. In fact, he might have done just that had Snape not entered almost immediately and stemmed the bleeding. However, Snape now knows that Harry has his book, and Harry feels ashamed and frightened at what he had almost done. Because Harry is a good person, he is overwhelmed with shame about having hurt Draco like this. In his anger, he had lashed out, spoken words whose power he did not know. When Snape saves Draco, he also saves Harry, because Harry might never be able to forgive himself for this ignorant action, this moment of uncontrolled anger that almost cost Draco his life. Even Harry has noticed that Draco is an unwilling participant in this hellish bargain, although he still doesn't like him. Harry learns something about the danger of speaking words whose meaning and power you do not know.

Almost immediately after this scene, it is time for Dumbledore's last lesson with Harry, and he sets some ominous conditions in place before they leave on this final journey together. He makes Harry promise that he will obey any command he gives that night, at once and without question, including that Harry must abandon him if he gives the order. As Dumbledore warns Harry that the night's activities may be very dangerous, Harry indicates that he just does not care. He has just found out that it was Snape who told Voldemort about the prophecy that Sibyll Trelawney had spoken. Dumbledore tells Harry, as he has many times before that he trusts Snape completely. He further tells Harry that Snape deeply regrets what he had done: "Professor Snape made a terrible mistake. He was still in Lord Voldemort's employ on the night he heard the first half of Professor Trelawney's prophecy. Naturally, he hastened to tell his master what he had heard, for it concerned his master most deeply. But he did not know…which boy Voldemort would hunt from then onward…You have no idea of the remorse Professor Snape felt when he realized how Lord Voldemort had interpreted the prophecy, Harry. I believe it to be the greatest regret of his life"(549). Snape loved Lily Evans, and it nearly killed him to realize that he had played a role in her death. His great love for Lily will help to save Harry's life at the end of the Potter quest. Again, we realize the mighty power of love.

And yet, a dark foreboding sweeps over us as we begin this journey with Harry and Dumbledore. We understand that they are searching for a Horcrux, and that Dumbledore believes he has figured out where one is hidden. We are journeying to a sea swept cave, and it has the feeling somehow of being on the edge of the very earth itself: "A towering cliff stood behind them, a sheer drop, black and faceless…It was a bleak, harsh view, the sea and the rock unrelieved by any tree or sweep of grass or sand"(555). Dumbledore admits to Harry that Tom Riddle brought two children from his orphanage to this forbidding spot in order to torture them. As they approach the cave together, having made payment for passage with some of Dumbledore's blood, the aura of evil and dark magic intensifies: "The darkness was somehow denser than normal darkness"(560). It is as if the evil that was done here long ago has left scars on the very earth, maybe in the very air of the place. Together, they finally reach the stone basin in which Dumbledore believes the Horcrux is hidden, and he makes Harry force him to drink off the strange emerald green potion that covers it from sight. Harry volunteers to be the one to drink the terrible potion, but Dumbledore will not hear of it. He says that he must be the one to drink it "Because I am much older, much cleverer, and much less valuable"(570). Poor Harry, remembering his promise, forces Dumbledore to drink this poison, and, as he does so, he cries out in agony: "Dumbledore drank like a child dying of thirst, but when he had finished, he yelled again as though his insides were on fire. 'No more, please, no more...I want to die! I want to die! Make it stop, make it stop, I want to die...KILL ME!"(573). In his agony, Dumbledore probably relives the greatest regrets of his own life—his hubris, his involvement with Grindelwald, his accidental contribution to his sister Ariana's death. He experiences remorse at such a powerful level that it quite literally brings him to his knees.

We are reminded, as we hear his weeping, of Jesus Christ's suffering in Gethsemane. Jesus, being the Son of God, knew what terrible suffering lie ahead of him. On the eve of his death, he went to the Garden of Gethsemane, where he asked his heavenly Father if there was some other way: "Abba, Father, all things are possible to thee; remove this cup from me; yet not what I will, but what you will be done"(Mark 14:36). Jesus has told us so many times that

Jesus ✝ 241

Gethsemane

we must take up our cross and follow him. We will each of us have our own Garden of Gethsemane someday, and we must trust that we walk by faith, in the shadow of the wings of the Holy Spirit. This scene presents us with a vivid portrait of Dumbledore's Gethsemane. We cannot even imagine the intensity of his pain, and Harry is torn apart by the fact that he is causing suffering to this man whom he has come to love as a father and a mentor. Now, we experience the horror of more dark magic as we encounter inferi, which are corpses that have been animated by a dark wizard to do his bidding. They are not alive, and they do not have free will. The inferi are an army of dead bodies, being used to do Voldemort's will. Their eyes are lifeless and cloudy. There is no sign of intelligence or soul in them. They are soulless bodies—that is something Voldemort knows a little bit about. They emerge from the water to threaten Harry, who seems to be powerless against them, and Dumbledore summons his strength one last time to defend his "son," but, having done so, he is desperately weakened, and we feel the torch about to be passed.

This moment brings us back to an important allusion to the Arthurian quest. In the beginning of the Grail Quest, an old man, frequently referred to as the Fisher King, has been grievously injured. Although he has been a brave warrior in his time, he has reached the end of his mortal power, and he must pass the torch, or pass the responsibility for continuing the larger quest to a younger man. Probably the first Fisher King could be said to be Joseph of Arimathea, the man who paid for Jesus' body to be entombed in a freshly hewn rock tomb. The story says that Joseph brought the Holy Grail, either a dish or a chalice used by Jesus at the Last Supper, to Britain. The Grail was supposedly preserved by a long line of Grail-keepers, and its whereabouts is enveloped in mystery. The story has been worked and reworked by hundreds or thousands of storytellers over the years, but there are certain elements that remain constant. The Fisher King has been seriously injured, maybe even maimed. The land is suffering storms and darkness, or maybe even a drought, because their king is dying, and the young warrior must pick up the challenge and pursue the quest. He will usually be given a sacred sword that will assist him in his trials. The sword may be given by some supernatural power. It may only be kept for a while; it must in time be returned. The imagery of the Grail is always under revision, but it clearly symbolizes God's grace. In the Arthurian quest, two very important knights are Perceval and Galahad, both of whom are pure of heart.

In the Potter quest, certainly Dumbledore can be seen as the Fisher King, and Harry, Ron, Hermione, and Neville can all be seen as knights involved in this portion of the universal quest. Although many knights are on their own personal quests, the focus of our story has been Harry Potter. However, it could have been Neville—that is for sure. And in some ways, it certainly is Ron's story too. The old Fisher King passes the responsibility of finishing the quest to young Perceval, or Galahad, and Dumbledore passes the responsibility to Harry. Listen to Harry when Dumbledore tells him he is too weak to go home: "Don't worry, sir...Don't worry, I'll get us back...Lean on me, sir...It's going to be all right, sir"(578). When Harry says this, Dumbledore smiles, just a little, and says that he is not worried, because he is with Harry. This might be the precise moment that marks the shift in the roles of Dumbledore and Harry. Dumbledore had always been saving Harry and transporting him back to safety, but now it is the exact opposite of that. Harry is now physically in charge and must take on the role that Dumbledore had previously fulfilled. Although Harry is scared of this weird place and even more frightened for Dumbledore, he finds the strength to protect him and take care of him. Harry tries to assure him that everything will be all right, even if he suspects that it will not be true. Dumbledore knows that his mortal strength is rapidly waning; in fact, he suspects that death is very near at hand. He knows that he is sharing precious moments with Harry.

But not for much longer. Harry manages to get Dumbledore back to Hogwarts, the place he so loved and the place where he will die. Dumbledore repeatedly tells Harry that he needs Severus Snape. Not wants—needs. Harry runs to get him, but before he can return, young Draco Malfoy comes face to face with an opportunity to fulfill his deadly promise. Finally, as he stands there sobbing and trembling, we understand the kind of pressure and fear that have possessed him all year. He tells Dumbledore: "I haven't got any options!...I've got to do it! He'll kill me! He'll kill my whole family...I've got no choice"(591). Dumbledore quietly asks Draco to come over to the side of goodness and mercy, but the young man is afraid to even consider that, believing that if he does so, he will be effectively murdering his mother and his father. The decision is taken out of his hands when four Death Eaters, eager for glory, arrive, each wanting to be the one that fulfills the Dark Lord's command. However, Dumbledore had foreseen that, and Severus Snape arrives, in the nick of time.

This moment is so carefully written that it is ambiguous enough to fool us as readers, until we know the last book. After having read the final novel in the quest, it is a good idea to go back and look at this scene again. Remember that Dumbledore has put Harry in a full body bind spell, so that he cannot move, no matter what. This spell will not be released until Dumbledore is dead. At this point, Dumbledore has collapsed, too weak to stand, and he is in mortal agony, the cancerous poison that leached out of the horcrux he had destroyed coursing through his aging body, causing him unthinkable pain. He gazes at Severus, who has just arrived on the scene, with a desperate pleading on his face and whispers, "Severus...

please…"(595. It is easy to misunderstand this moment and think that Dumbledore is pleading for protection and for mercy. Actually, he is pleading for mercy, but that mercy means that he wants to be killed by Snape, his friend, rather than by Draco, a young man who would be irreparably harmed if he keeps this promise to Lord Voldemort and kills Dumbledore. Beyond that, he does not want to be tortured and killed by the despicable Death Eaters who surround him in the room at the tower. Dumbledore's final words are almost a prayer, asking Severus Snape to sever the sacred thread of earthly life.

Of course, that is not how Harry sees it. Nor do we, upon a first reading. All Harry knows is that Dumbledore, the greatest and wisest man he has ever known, is dead, and at the hand of Severus Snape, a man whom Harry despises and distrusts. The minute Dumbledore dies, Harry is released from the full body bind spell, and he chases Snape, crying and daring him to fight. There is nothing for Snape to do but leave now; no one knows the secret bargain that he and Dumbledore had made—that he would kill him and thereby hopefully save Draco from the irrecoverable damage that would have been done to his soul. Obviously, both Dumbledore and Snape believed that Draco can be saved. Besides that, Dumbledore was already dying—the evil poison was coursing through his system, and he was suffering beyond all understanding. His death was already certain. Still, when Harry chases Snape down and tries to work the cruciatus curse on him, Snape blocks it, saying: "No Unforgivable Curses from you, Potter"(602). Although at the time it seems that he is mocking Harry, he is, in fact, trying to protect him from the damage he would cause himself by learning to hate like that. When the Death Eaters surround Harry and want to kill him, Snape protects him again, saying that the Dark Lord wants to be the one to kill Harry. We are deceived because of how carefully and cleverly the scene is written. It is written with such an eloquent ambiguity that we can believe, with Harry, tht Snape has betrayed Dumbledore. When we later understand everything and reread the scene, we see that J. K. Rowling has written the scene so that we can now see that Snape has actually honored Dumbledore's wishes. As Snape storms away, in the company of Death Eaters, we believe him to have acted on behalf of the Dark Lord, and we believe that Dumbledore was deceived about him. We think that Dumbledore was, in fact, dead wrong. But we should remember how wise our fallen Fisher King always was.

Still, it seems as if the very heart has gone out of Hogwarts. In the aftermath of his death, Harry discovers that the locket they had retrieved was not even a real horcrux, and it seems to him as if Dumbledore has died for nothing. As he kneels by Dumbledore's body, he cannot move. He is empty of all life and all desire to live. J. K. Rowling then teaches us, once again, about the redemptive power of love, the greatest magic of all: "A much smaller and warmer hand had enclosed his and was pulling him upward. He obeyed its pressure without really thinking bout it...it was Ginny who was leading him back into the castle...Harry and Ginny walked on, back up the steps into the entrance hall"(611). This is not to say that the loss of a loved one does not hurt, almost beyond all understanding. It does. And we have a right and a duty to grieve, to hurt, to acknowledge that loss. Still, the love between a man and a woman can, at least at some level, ameliorate that loss, making it manageable, if such a word can be used for something so intensely personal, so life altering.

We are given a hint that even this moment of suffering is blessed: "Somewhere out in the darkness, a phoenix was singing in a way that Harry had never heard before: a stricken lament of terrible beauty. And Harry felt, as he had felt about phoenix song before, that the music was inside him, not without: It was his own grief turned magically to song that echoed across the grounds and through the castle windows. How long they all stood there, listening, he did not know, nor why it seemed to ease their pain a little to listen to the sound of them mourning"(615). There are so many ideas here. First of all, death is a part of life, with all of its "terrible beauty," and it is announced by the heavens here with an almost ethereally beautiful music. Once again, remember that tears are sacred—are, in fact, a kind of holy water. Mourning is sacred. It is our duty to our loved ones, and it is proper for us to hurt. There is an ascension-like quality to this music, which lifts up their souls, even as the soul of Albus Dumbledore is lifted up, as he "goes on." We can picture choirs of heavenly voices singing him along on his passage. For, that is what death is—not a destination, but a passage. "And the last enemy to be destroyed is death."

LOSS

In the final scene, Harry thinks about all the things he wishes he would have asked Dumbledore, knowing sadly that the opportunity to do so has passed forever. That must certainly be a universal experience of losing a loved one. He remembers that the torch has now been passed, and that Dumbledore said "to fight, and fight again, and keep fighting, for only then could evil be kept at bay, though never quite eradicated"(645). How brilliant. We come right back to St. Paul: "So we are always of good courage; we know that while we are at home in this body we are away from the Lord, for we walk by faith, not by sight"(2 Corinthians 6-7). Harry comforts himself with the idea that we have discussed before, that our loved ones never leave us. He tells Rufus Scrimgeour, "He will only be gone from the school when none here are loyal to him" and he declares himself to be "Dumbledore's man through and through"(649). Armed with this greatest power of all, he prepares to do battle with Voldemort one final time, and the quest focuses in on the horcruxes that are still to be destroyed. Harry tells Ron and Hermione: "If Dumbledore was right— and I'm sure he was—there are still four of them out there. I've got to find them and destroy them, and then I've got to go after the seventh bit of Voldemort's soul, the bit that's still in his body, and I'm the one who's going to kill him"(651). Harry has suffered the loss of so many people who loved and cared for him—James and Lily, Sirius, and now Dumbledore. All of them have been killed, either directly or indirectly, by Voldemort, the incarnation of evil. Harry knows what he must do, and he is more than willing to do it. We feel him get himself ready to march into that arena, with his head held high.

And thus, we turn our attention to the last part of the Potter Quest, the Deathly Hallows.

Harry Potter and The Deathly Hallows

We open this final novel in the Potter quest with a scene in the inner sanctum of the Dark Lord, who has taken over the Malfoy mansion as his own residence at this time. He is clearly exasperated and quietly desperate, even though he is still arrogantly convinced that he will win the ultimate battle. Voldemort blames his earlier defeats on his own carelessness and on his tendency to underestimate his young adversary: "That Potter lives is due more to my errors than to his triumphs…I have been careless, and so have been thwarted by luck and chance, those wreckers of all but the best-laid plans. But I know better now. I understand those things that I did not understand before. I must be the one to kill Harry Potter, and I shall be"(7). In so doing, he underestimates Harry's grit and skill. We see him, in this first chapter, surrounded by his loyal, if frightened Death Eaters. He sits on his cold throne, talking about cutting out the poisons and impurities that threaten his "kingdom," and by this remark, he means people that he intends to kill. As if to illustrate his determination to do so, the chapter ends with his cold blooded and vicious murder of Charity Burbage, a professor of Muggle Studies at Hogwarts, who is at this moment, a prisoner of war. Voldemort announces that she must die for her heresy: "Not content with corrupting and polluting the minds of Wizarding children, last week Professor Burbage wrote an impassioned defense of Mudbloods in the Daily Prophet... The dwindling of the purebloods is, says Professor Burbage, a most desirable circumstance"(12). Perhaps intending to illustrate his power and underscore his hatred of such tolerance, Voldemort then kills her and feeds her body to his snake Nagini. We cannot help but feel our blood run cold.

Then, we move back to the Dursley residence, where Harry is spending his final days under the reluctant protection of his Aunt Petunia, Lily Potter's sister. He is mourning for, aching for Dumbledore, and for opportunities missed: "He had been forced to recognize that he had barely known him at all. Never once had he imagined Dumbledore's childhood or youth; it was as though he had sprung into being as Harry had known him, venerable and silver-haired and old"(21). Throughout the Potter quest, we are subtly reminded that knowing another person, really knowing him or her, is a lifelong mission, and one that can never be fully accomplished. However, when taking the measure of a man or a woman, it helps to find out about their past, where they came from, what are the important forces that shaped their lives. This idea will be very important in this novel, as Dumbledore tried to suggest to Harry in the previous one—that what Lord Voldemort will do now as a man depends to a significant extent on values he developed as a child. Not only will we be coming to terms with that idea with regard to Voldemort, but also with regard to Albus Dumbledore. As Harry mourns for the opportunity lost, we ought to learn a lesson. If there is someone in your life right now that you love very much, do not let the opportunity go by to have them tell you the story of their life. Be an attentive listener. We all need someone to be a witness to the moments of our lives. Someone to care.

In these final moments with the Dursleys, as Harry prepares to leave their care and their "protection" once and for all, a good thing happens between him and Dudley. His cousin acknowledges that Harry saved his life, and extends his hand in a farewell greeting. There is hope that this young man can escape the poison of his parents' evil prejudices. We will keep this idea in mind later in the novel as we follow Draco Malfoy's story more closely.

We now move to the memorable scene where Harry tries to escape Number Four Privet Drive and get to safety before his protective charm runs out. There will be seven Harry Potters flying out of the house this night, six of whom will be decoys, in an attempt to confuse the Death Eaters. Ron, Hermione, Fred, George, Fleur, and Mundungus all drink a polyjuice potion in order to deceive the Death Eaters who are hovering nearby, just outside the charmed circle, waiting to capture Harry. Each of them will be in the protection of a member of the Order of the Phoenix, and they hope, with so much carefully planned misdirection, to get Harry to safety. Harry is terrified, not for himself, but for these good people, all of whom are putting their lives at risk to save him. In the escape scene, Harry's owl Hedwig is killed. She has been his companion and friend for six years now, and he mourns her passing. J. K. Rowling chose her name carefully, for St. Hedwig is the patron saint of orphaned children. We suddenly realize that all of Harry's protections are dropping away one after the other, in rapid succession—Albus Dumbledore, his mother's protective charm, and Hedwig. During the course of the escape, Harry shows mercy to an enemy, refusing to do anything more than disarm Stan Shunpike, who is with the Death Eaters. When Lupin scolds Harry for not finishing him off, Harry says that he suspects that Stan may be under an Imperius Curse. He remembers the awkward young man who rescued him with the Knight Bus, so long ago. And like a true knight, Harry shows mercy: "I won't blast people out of my way just because they're there...That's Voldemort's job"(71). It may not be Voldemort's job, but it certainly has been his chosen response many times during the quest.

When they arrive safely at the home of Mr. and Mrs. Tonks, they count up their losses and injuries, and they try to understand how it could be that Mad-Eye Moody has been killed. It just doesn't seem possible. He had seemed almost indestructible, and they are overwhelmed with a sense of loss. It is hard for all of them to even pull themselves together, and the finality of the death of Mad-Eye Moody seems to echo all around them. What is even worse is that they cannot locate Moody's body. Because of this, they don't even get a feeling of closure. They cannot hold a proper ceremony to honor their fallen instructor. This makes their pain even worse. Sadly, this kind of thing can happen in our world too, and it hurts. This attempt to come to terms with the reality of death will be a recurring theme in this final novel. We have hinted at it before, but the losses will mount as the final battle approaches, and each time, we are keenly aware that the world is forever diminished by the loss of a loved one.

However, when they congratulate Harry on once again eluding Voldemort, with whom he had come face to face in the course of their flight, he must confess something even he cannot believe: "It wasn't me...It was my wand. My wand acted of its own accord...The bike was falling, I couldn't have told you where Voldemort was, but my wand spun in my hand and found him and shot a spell at him, and it wasn't even a spell I recognized. I've never made gold flames appear before"(83). All of his friends try to come up with reasonable or believable explanations for this, but Harry knows in his heart of hearts that it really happened. He cannot explain it, and neither can poor old Mr. Ollivander, of whom Harry has a vision. In this vision, it feels to Harry as if he is looking through Voldemort's eyes once again, and he sees the poor old man being tortured by Voldemort because he cannot explain what has just occurred with the wands. Although it is tempting for us to try to hazard an answer, to do so at this point would be premature. We watch and listen.

Soon afterwards, Ron, Hermione, and Harry are summoned to an audience with Rufus Scrimgeour, the new Minister of Magic. He is finally releasing the things that were bequeathed to them in Albus Dumbledore's will. Ron receives Dumbledore's Deluminator; Hermione receives a copy of a book for children—The Tales of Beedle the Bard; and Harry receives the golden snitch that he caught in his first-ever quidditch game. It has an inscription on it: "I open at the close." Dumbledore's will also left Harry the Sword of Godric Gryffindor, but Scrimgeour refuses to surrender that, saying that it is priceless and that, furthermore, it was never Dumbledore's to give. Harry knows that things have value in other ways, beyond any measure of silver or gold, but the Minister of Magic does not possess this wisdom.

After Scrimgeour leaves, the three young heroes express their bewilderment about these strange inheritances. They wonder if these things will have any practical application as they go forward with their quest, and Harry cries out, "Why couldn't he just have told me?"(134). He feels uncertain about what he is supposed to do, and how he is supposed to do it. He guesses that he, Ron, and Hermione must attempt to destroy the horcruxes that Voldemort has created, but where are they? And what are they? We will spend the rest of the novel answering these questions. But Harry's question can be addressed on a larger thematic level as well. Why didn't Dumbledore tell him what to do? The answer is simple and eloquent. Each one of us must find out for ourselves—that is the nature of the quest. We can have loved ones guide us and point us in the right direction, but each person's quest is a free will adventure, and the wisdom won hard through the school of experience is the most precious wisdom of all.

At this point in the novel, we have the lovely interruption provided by the wedding of Bill Weasley and Fleur Delacour, and it presents us with the last almost carefree moment in the novel. Although Harry must attend the ceremony in disguise in case of an attack, he has the opportunity to spend some time with Elphias Doge, a member of the Order of the Phoenix who has written a beautiful obituary honoring Albus Dumbledore. Harry reveals who he is to Elphias, and then he begs him for more information about his mentor. Their conversation is particularly important to Harry because there are many people who seem to feel emboldened to attack Dumbledore now that he is dead, people like Rita Skeeter and Ron's Auntie Muriel. Their mean-spirited attacks have caused Harry to wonder if he may have exaggerated Dumbledore's goodness in his own mind, perhaps out of a kind of wishful thinking. So, he is very interested in what Elphias Doge has to say about his old friend. Although their conversation is repeatedly interrupted by Ron's annoying Auntie Muriel, who keeps butting in rudely, Doge is adamant about one thing: Dumbledore was a good man, as good a man as ever there was, and Harry should not let anyone make him doubt that. Then, a more deadly interruption comes. Kingsley Shacklebolt's Patronus appears suddenly, halting the dancing and announcing: "The Ministry has fallen. Scrimgeour is dead. They are coming"(139). So begins the flight and the final part of the quest for our three young warriors. Not only is this the final part of the quest, in many ways, it is the part that everything else has been building to, preparing us for. We are approaching the part of the narrative where J. K. Rowling will make literary magic.

This may be a good moment to talk about Hermione Granger, who has certainly been incredibly important throughout the whole quest, but who will be absolutely indispensable in this final part. It does not state the matter too strongly to say that the chance of a victorious conclusion would be almost nil without her. Hermione's quick thinking, careful planning, and steadfast brilliance repeatedly saves both Ron and Harry, and she is much more than one of the minor characters accompanying the young knight on his quest. If she had not prepared so thoroughly for the eventual moment of their departure, the trio would have been in terrible trouble. Besides that, she is absolutely unflinching in her support of Harry. It never wavers, even when to keep faith with him is something that costs her a great deal personally. When the order to run comes from Shacklebolt, Hermione is ready. She grabs Harry and Ron, and with her magical beaded bag already slung around her neck, whispers the words that will carry them away from the wedding, and into the streets of London, where they try to disappear into the anonymity of a crowded city.

When they escape, at least temporarily, Harry admits to Ron and Hermione that he has started to experience visions through Voldemort's eyes again. Speaking about the mental connection between the two of them, he says: "I—I think it's started opening again whenever he loses control, that's how it used to be"(173). The visions overwhelm and physically sicken him: "he grasped his pounding head and fell to the floor, then in an explosion of agony, he felt the rage that did not belong to him possess his soul"(174). He sees that Voldemort now forces Draco Malfoy to torture people that have upset or disappointed him, and he experiences a revulsion, and almost a pity for him: "Harry felt sickened by what he had seen, by the use to which Draco was now being put by Voldemort"(175). Draco is obeying out of fear for his own family, but it looks to Harry as if he is an unwilling and terrified servant of the Dark Lord. Nonetheless, we see that Dumbledore's worst fear for Draco has been realized—he is being used by Voldemort to further the cause of evil, and Harry has enough wisdom to consider that idea with pity for Draco, whom he has perceived as an enemy for many years.

The three of them take refuge at the old Black residence, which Sirius had bequeathed to Harry, and weak and exhausted, Harry comes upon a treasure—a portion of a handwritten letter from his mother to "Padfoot," or Sirius Black. His mother seems to come to life in his very hands, as he hears her voice, speaking proudly of Harry and his accomplishments on his first birthday. He is overcome with a powerful mixture of a sense of loss, of mystery, of joy, and longing: "The letter was an incredible treasure, proof that Lily Potter had lived, really lived, that her warm hand had once moved across this parchment, tracing ink into these letter, these words, words about him, Harry, her son... It was like listening to a half-remembered voice"(181). Anyone who still treasures a letter written by a lost loved one knows exactly what Harry is feeling at this moment. However, the voice of a lost loved one can be a Siren song if we listen too long. That has been one of the most powerful lessons of the Potter quest. We must remember the warning that Dumbledore gave Harry so long ago, in the first novel of the series: "It does not do to dwell on dreams and forget to live, remember that."

And so, it is with a pang that Harry wrestles himself back to the mission at hand. He tells Hermione that in Lily's letter, she was talking about Bathilda Bagshot, the author of A History of Magic, and some of the weird stories that this old woman had told her about Albus Dumbledore. That brings Harry back to the question of Dumbledore's character, a question that, in spite of his better judgment, still haunts him because of remarks made by Auntie Muriel and the obnoxious

Rita Skeeter. When Hermione points out that he should not allow the mean-spirited remarks of old gossips like that bother him, Harry seems unable to shake off his doubts. And so it is that we will be pursuing our knowledge of the man that Albus Dumbledore was and came to be. In an indirect way, we are back to our three primordial questions— who am I? Why am I here? Is my life directed by free will or fate? If we can agree that Albus Dumbledore became a kind of surrogate father for Harry, then Harry's dogged pursuit of an honest examination of Dumbledore's past is a pursuit of self-knowledge. Remember—who is my father is just another way of saying, at least at some level, who am I?

Harry now enlists the help of Kreacher, the Black house elf who has been anything but helpful so far in the quest. There are several elves who play an important part in this quest narrative: Dobby, Winky, and Kreacher. House elves are small humanoids who possess their own kind of magic, which can be used with or without the permission of their human masters. The house elves exist to serve their masters, and they are fiercely loyal. There are many wizards in the story that treat their house elves with nothing more than contempt, and sadly, Sirius Black seems to have been guilty of this kind of treatment to Kreacher. This heartless treatment probably contributes to Kreacher's betrayal of Sirius at the end of book five, when he finds a loophole in Sirius' command "Get out!" and feels that he can do just that—get out of the house and warn Bellatrix Lestrange of what is happening at the Ministry. In book two, we saw how Lucius Malfoy treated Dobby with contempt, and we have witnessed this same cruelty from Bartie Crouch toward Winky.

Although Hermione's efforts at house elf liberation have been clumsy and almost comical, there is a grain of truth to what she has repeatedly insisted—that wizards habitually treat their house elves with cruelty, and that it is wrong, even sinful. Perhaps Harry was listening after all, because he now enlists Kreacher's help successfully. Of course, Kreacher's name is a thinly disguised "creature," which seems to be a pejorative term, but, on the other hand, maybe not. We are all God's creatures, part of his mighty creation, and perhaps his name calls this connotation to mind too. Harry discovers that Kreacher was, and still is, fiercely loyal to Sirius' younger brother, Regulus Black. Harry figures out that Regulus is the RAB who left the note in the fake locket. We discover that Regulus had been a Slytherin who played seeker for their quidditch team. Supposedly, he had become a Death Eater while he was still a teenager, having been seduced by the vision of pure blood supremacy that Voldemort was preaching. When he discovered that Voldemort was making horcruxes in an attempt to achieve immortality, he defected. He died while attempting to destroy Salazar Slytherin's locket, but before he died, he left the fake one in its place. Harry knows that he and Ron and Hermione must find this locket and complete Regulus's mission. He asks Kreacher to go and find Mundungus Fletcher: "We need to find out where the locket—where Master Regulus's locket is. It's really important. We want to finish the work Master Regulus started, we want to—er—ensure that he didn't die in vain"(199). Harry gives Kreacher the fake horcrux, the substitute locket in which Regulus had left his note for Voldemort, the note that Harry read at the end of the previous novel after Dumbledore had died. This gesture shows Harry's respect for the genuine love that can exist between people and elves, something he will learn even more about himself during the course of this novel. When he does this, Kreacher is so overwhelmed with gratitude that he can hardly stand, and from this moment on, he will be fiercely loyal to Harry Potter. In this quest narrative, kindness and mercy are rewarded. We are, time and again, encouraged to try to consider the situation from the other person's side. Eventually, Kreacher will lead the house elves into battle, fighting for Harry Potter's cause. We will see, once again, the transformative power of kindness and gentleness.

As they wait for Kreacher to bring Fletcher to them, Remus Lupin pays them a visit. He asks Harry what the nature of the mission is that he is pursuing, and he further asks them if he can come along. We see that Harry has become a man, and he seems to regard Lupin as a fellow warrior, but one whose mission is not the same as his: "I can't, Remus. I'm sorry. If Dumbledore didn't tell you I don't think I can"(211). Lupin confesses his fears about Tonks; she is carrying his child right now. This revelation only cements Harry's position. As far as Harry is concerned, no father should willingly desert his child. This conviction probably grows from his own experience. Harry lost his father when he was only a baby. James could not control that because he was killed by Voldemort as he attempted to defend his wife and child. It would obviously upset Harry that Lupin would consider willingly putting his child through that kind of pain. He sends Lupin back to Tonks. Soon afterwards, Kreacher shows up with the cowardly Mundungus Fletcher in tow, and we see an entirely different creature in Kreacher: "Kreacher apologizes for the delay in bringing the thief...Fletcher knows how to avoid capture, has many hidey-holes and accomplices. Nevertheless, Kreacher cornered the thief in the end"(220). Although Fletcher is very self-righteous and absolutely furious about being arrested by a house-elf, he is quickly subdued by Harry, Ron, and Hermione. They make him explain his betrayal the night of Harry's escape and his thievery of the treasure left behind in the Black house, to which Fletcher has unconscionably helped himself. When Harry asks about a certain locket, Fletcher admits that he gave it away to a little old witch from the office of the Ministry of Magic, someone who looked rather like a toad, and who threatened him with punishment for "trading in magical artifacts"(222). We have a Dolores Umbridge shiver.

Hermione packs her magical bag with items she thinks that they might need in the course of their journey, and they leave Number 12 Grimmauld Place and any kind of creature comforts as they set out on the quest for the missing horcruxes. Hermione and Ron express their reservations about their readiness for their mission. They feel so unprepared and uncertain. Harry says that it is time to act: "He could tell from Ron's and Hermione's faces that they were scared; he was not particularly confident himself, and yet he was sure the time had come to put their plan into operation"(231). William Shakespeare has a very famous quote in his play entitled Julius Caesar where Brutus says just about the same thing. Cassius is advocating that they wait and let the enemy come to them, but Brutus says that he thinks they need to move forward now:

> There is a tide in the affairs of men,
>
> Which, taken at the flood, leads on to fortune;
>
> Omitted, all the voyage of their life
>
> Is bound in shallows and in miseries.
>
> On such a full sea are we now afloat.
>
> And we must take the current when it serves,
>
> Or lose our ventures(4.3.218-224).

Things do not work out that well for Brutus and his colleagues for many reasons, but we still can understand and identify with what he is saying, and it is the same idea that Harry seems to be expressing.

Harry suspects that they could plan and plan and find ways to convince themselves that they are never ready. And that won't do. So, in spite of their very real misgivings, they set out. And so, the dangerous journey begins.

Their first stop is the Ministry, where Dolores Umbridge has installed herself as the Senior Undersecretary to the Minister, responsible for the registry of Muggle borns. Harry sees that he has been declared the Number One Undesirable, and he feels the presence of Dementors in the Ministry building. Voldemort has his hate-filled followers taking control of the reins of power. Harry and Hermione, disguised with the help of polyjuice potion, witness the trial of Mary Cattermole, a Muggle born witch who is accused of stealing a wand from a pure-blood wizard. In spite of the fact that she is the mother of two small children, Dolores Umbridge is about to sentence her to Azkaban when Harry and Hermione interrupt the trial in a blaze of glory. Hermione, disguised as Mafalda Hopkirk, a Ministry official, has spotted the locket on Umbridge's toadlike body. Dolores lies about it, saying that it is an old family heirloom. That lie is enough to send Harry into a rage and into action: "It was Umbridge's lie that brought the blood surging into Harry's brain and obliterated his sense of caution…He raised his wand…There was a flash of red light; Umbridge crumpled and her forehead hit the edge of the balustrade"(261). Hermione grabs the locket, and Harry helps the

Muggle-borns who are being held for trial to escape. Furthermore, he tells Mrs. Cattermole to get her children and run for her life, to leave the country until it is safe for their return. We never find out what happened to the Cattermoles, but Harry and Hermione have at least given them a chance. Once again, this episode speaks to Harry's stalwart character. He knows that he is number one on the Ministry's "most wanted" list, and he is in grave personal danger every minute he is in the building. Still, he does all he can to free the people who are in harm's way, unjustly targeted by the Ministry, rather than worrying only about himself and leaving immediately. Harry repeatedly tries to do the right thing, even if it is inconvenient for him personally. We cannot help but hear echoes of other "ethnic cleansing" horrors of our modern world in this episode. Harry, Ron, and Hermione disapparate quickly, landing in the middle of nowhere, a forest, and they realize that they cannot go back to Number 12 Grimmauld place. They are outcasts, homeless, and on the run.

Furthermore, they are hungry, cold, and miserable. In spite of Hermione's brilliant magical bag, in which she has packed a tent and which they now set up, she had packed no food, believing they would be able to return to Number 12. The three of them spend most of this novel miserably hungry, and we, as readers, are forced to realize that relentless hunger brings on desperation of spirit.: "This was their first encounter with the fact that a full stomach meant good spirits; an empty one, bickering and gloom"(287). In Harry's weakness and exhaustion, he has another vision. This time it is of another wand maker being tortured—Gregorovitch. He awakens from the nightmare screaming, and Ron insists that Harry must stop saying Voldemort's name. We have heard this warning before, but this time, Ron's instincts are good. There is a magical trace placed on the name. In Harry's terrible vision, he had seen Voldemort kill Gregorovitch, and he had seen a merry faced thief make away with something Voldemort wanted very badly: "Harry could still see the blond-haired youth's face; it was merry and wild…He had soared from the windowsill like a bird, and Harry had seen him before, but he could not think where…With Gregorovitch dead, it was the merry-faced thief who was in danger now, and it was on him that Harry's thoughts dwelled"(283). Perhaps, Harry is forced to realize, he has allies that he does not even know about yet. In this quest narrative, as in all such stories, there are countless acts of bravery and courage from minor characters. It is as if, underneath it all, there is a constant pull toward the powers of goodness and mercy, or, at least, against evil. Sometimes, it is hard to see the presence of these forces, but the Harry Potter story asks us to consider the possibility that these forces for good are always there.

However, in their weakened condition, our three warriors are hard pressed to believe in such a benevolent undercurrent. Always on the move, desperate and hungry, they take turns wearing the Horcrux since wearing it brings an elevated level of fear and anxiety to the person who carries this talisman of evil: "Harry's scar kept prickling. It happened most often, he noticed, when he was wearing the Horcrux. Sometimes he could not stop himself reacting to the pain"(291). It has the same effect on Ron and Hermione; wearing the horcrux takes a toll on all three of them. We are reminded of Frodo's ring in the Lord of the Rings trilogy.

It seems that many good people are on the run at this point in the story, and one night, Ron, Harry, and Hermione overhear a conversation involving an odd assortment of fugitives—their old classmate Dean Thomas, Ted Tonks, and a couple of goblins. They are speaking of an attempt on the part of some Hogwart's students, Ginny included, to steal the sword of Godric Gryffindor, which Severus Snape then removed from the school and hid in a vault at Gringotts, the goblin bank. In spite of the fact that the goblins say that they are taking no sides in this wizarding war, they chuckle about Snape's misinformation. The sword he hid is a fake. Griphook says: "It is a copy—an excellent copy, it is true—but it was Wizard-made. The original was forged centuries ago by goblins and had certain properties only goblin-made armor possesses. Wherever the genuine sword of Gryffindor is, it is not in a vault at Gringotts bank"(298). We know what those special properties are, and we know that this sword will become very important in the final stages of the quest.

Although Ron has been a steadfast friend to Harry throughout the quest, he is overcome by thoughts of despair and confusion. Wearing the horcrux has worn down his usually cheerful spirit and left him morose and weary. Back at their tent, the darkness pours out of him, and even Hermione cannot stem the flow of his angry words. Frustrated and hungry, he yells at Harry: "We thought you knew what you were doing…We thought Dumbledore had told you what to do, we thought you had a real plan"(307). Hermione tells him immediately to take off the locket, but the damage is done. Ron says that he is sick of the whole thing and storms out of there, in spite of the fact that he loves both Harry and Hermione, and Harry feels angry, alone, and betrayed: "Harry felt a corrosive hatred toward Ron: Something had broken between them…Harry felt dazed. He stooped, picked up the Horcrux, and placed it around his own neck"(310). Thus begins a desperately dark hour of the soul for all three of them, each of them locked in their own misery.

Hermione's plight is particularly poignant at this moment in the quest. She loves Ron, and she knows that she wants to spend the rest of her life with him. So, when Ron turns to her and asks her if she is coming with him, leaving Harry behind, she is absolutely torn in two. With an anguished look on her face, she says, "Yes—yes, I'm staying, Ron. Ron, we said we'd go with Harry, we said we'd help—"(309). He sneers at her, angry and hurt, and says, "I get it. You choose him"(310).

He storms out of the tent, and Hermione sobs quietly all night long. Ron has oversimplified and misunderstood her very difficult decision. Hermione has not chosen Harry over Ron as a lover. It is more complex than that. She has chosen to see the quest through; she has chosen to keep her promise. She is desolate about Ron leaving her behind.

Finally, it is time to talk more fully about her name. J. K. Rowling has told us that Hermione is named after a character in William Shakespeare's play entitled The Winter's Tale. This is one of the most unique plays Shakespeare ever wrote; sometimes it is called a comedy, but it does not really fit into that category. Some critics call it a romance, but that description is also misleading. The first three acts of the play are a mini-tragedy. A man named Leontes has a beautiful wife named Hermione. She is the kind of woman that men definitely find attractive. She is a faithful wife, but she is no wallflower. She is an independent thinker who is actively engaged in life. A lifelong friend of Leontes, who is a king from a neighboring country, comes to stay at their palace. Leontes says that he wants his friend, Polixenes, to stay longer. After he is unable to convince him to do so, he sends Hermione to try to change Polixenes' mind. She is able to accomplish this task easily, and this makes her husband suspicious. Although Hermione never betrays her marriage vow, Leontes becomes convinced that she has been unfaithful to him and secretly had an affair with this friend. Polixenes barely escapes from Sicilia, but Leontes puts Hermione on trial for treason and infidelity. She is defended at her trial by an oracle who proclaims her innocence. After being acquitted, Hermione apparently "dies" of grief. Leontes grieves for her for sixteen years, and, through great pain and sorrow, learns humility. After all this time, he goes to visit a "statue" of Hermione, and miraculously, the "statue" comes to life and he is given a second chance at love. Although this little synopsis doesn't really do The Winter's Tale justice, we can see a connection. Hermione is in love with Ron, and she has chosen him with her heart as the man she will marry, the man whose children she wants to bear. However, she has also chosen to be faithful to her promise to Harry to see their increasingly dangerous and difficult quest through to its conclusion. Her decision to stay with Harry is an absolutely selfless one, and she does so at great personal cost. Although Harry is aware of her great sadness, he doesn't really appreciate the enormity of what she has done for him. Understandably, he is preoccupied with many other mysteries, and although her sadness registers on the periphery of his awareness, he does not really understand how much she is hurting as they stumble on in the darkness and confusion that seems to surround them at this point.

In spite of their mounting despair, and the intensifying cold as winter moves in, Harry and Hermione keep thinking. It is a measure of their enormous strength of character that they do so. Together, they decide that they must go to Godric's Hollow, for a number of reasons. Harry, at some intuitive level, wants to confront his own past. He knows that his parents died there, trying to protect him. He has recently discovered that Albus Dumbledore lived there with his family, once upon a time. It was the home of Godric Gryffindor—everything seems to add up and Harry knows that he must see this little town for himself. Hermione knows that Bathilda Bagshot, the author of A History of Magic, lived there, and she wonders if maybe Dumbledore hid the real sword there: "You and your parents aren't mentioned...because Professor Bagshot doesn't cover anything later than the end of the nineteenth century. But you see? Godric's Hollow, Godric Gryffindor, Gryffindor's sword; don't you think Dumbledore would have expected you to make the connections"(319). Harry is overwhelmed with the idea of coming face to face with the remains of what he lost: "He was about to go home, about to return to the place where he had had a family...The life he had lost had hardly ever seemed so real to him as at this moment, when he knew he was about to see the place where it had been taken from him"(321).

Hermione has reservations about the wisdom of this trip, in spite of the fact that she can argue the logic of their going, so she arranges disguises for the two of them, and they practice using the invisibility cloak together. When they arrive in Godric's Hollow, it is Chrismas Eve. Several of the most important scenes in the Potter quest take place against a backdrop of important Christian feasts, and this is certainly one of them. As they walk into the town, Hermione notices a war memorial that transforms the moment they pass it into a different kind of war memorial. Harry sees the image of what he lost in stone: "As they passed it, it had transformed. Instead of an obelisk covered in names, there was a statue of three people: a man with untidy hair and glasses, a woman with long hair and a kind, pretty face, and a baby boy sitting in his mother's arms. Snow lay upon all their heads, like fluffy white caps...How strange it was to see himself represented in stone, a happy baby without a scar on his forehead"(324). What a poignant moment this is for Harry, but he summons his courage and his determination and plunges on to see what else Godric's Hollow has in store for him.

As they enter the graveyard, the voices of churchgoers rise up in the distance, singing Christmas hymns, as if to bless their being here. They find the graves of Dumbledore's mother and sister, and engraved on the stone, an inscription from the Bible: "Where your treasure is, there will your heart be also"(325). It is a good idea to look at the passage that surrounds this powerful line, so we turn to Luke, chapter 12 to do so. Jesus says this to his disciples: "Consider the lilies, how they grow; they neither toil nor spin; yet I tell you, even Solomon in all his glory was not arrayed like one of these. But if God so clothes the grass which is alive in the field today and tomorrow is thrown into the oven, how much more will he clothe you, O men of little faith!....

provide yourselves with purses that do not grow old, with a treasure in the heavens that does not fail…for where your treasure is, there will your heart be also"(Luke 12:27-34). This is an enormously powerful passage, and the message is clear. Commit yourself to a life of faith and let your faith turn into action. In other words, commit yourself to doing the best you can under the circumstances, knowing that your Father in heaven loves you and will take care of you, in ways you cannot even begin to imagine. Your earthly treasure is as nothing to the treasure that is stored up for you in heaven. Your loved ones who have gone before are waiting for you, watching over you. In the meantime, you must soldier on, keeping your courage and your heart strong. You must walk by faith. We are never told who chose the inscription for the tomb, but we can guess that it was Dumbledore. If so, then his message to himself and to Harry is a powerful one. We all make mistakes, but we must admit when we are wrong, and try to do better. Our real treasure is being stored up for us in ways we cannot know at this time.

But the cemetery has more to teach us. Two rows behind the graves of Dumbledore's family, Hermione finds the graves of James and Lily Potter. They were only 21 years old when they died. The dates of their life and death are given, and underneath those dates are these words: "The last enemy that shall be destroyed is death"(328). Harry is brought to his knees, his tears flow freely, and he is confused and bewildered by the inscription, not knowing how to translate its meaning. Hermione helps him: "It doesn't mean defeating death in the way the Death Eaters mean it, Harry...It means...you know... living beyond death. Living after death"(328). She is right, of course, but once again, it helps us to look at the passage in the Bible that gives us these powerful words. This time, we turn to St. Paul's first letter to the Corinthians: "But in fact Christ has been raised from the dead, the first fruits of those who have fallen asleep. For as by a man came death, by a man has come also the resurrection of the dead... But each in his own order...The last enemy to be destroyed is death"(1 Corinthians: 20-26). St. Paul is trying to tell us about the heavenly reward that is waiting for us, where our "treasure" ought to be. We feel ourselves burning with questions, wanting to know how this can happen, desperate for some reassurance, as confused as Harry is when he stands in front of two cold stones, trying to understand what it all means. If we press on in St. Paul's letter, we come to some of the most powerful writing he ever did, as close as he ever comes to giving us a glimpse of heaven:

Lo! I tell you a mystery.
We shall not all sleep, but we shall all be changed.
In a twinkling of an eye,...When the perishable puts on the
Imperishable, and the mortal puts on immortality...

Then it shall come to pass the saying that is written:
"Death is swallowed up in victory.
O death, where is thy victory?
O death, where is thy sting?"
(1 Corinthians: 36-55).

Several times during the story, J. K. Rowling has indicated that death is a passage, a moment of transport to our next life. We remember the scene at the Ministry of Magic at the end of book five, where Sirius, killed by Bellatrix, fell through the veil. He had "gone on." Our heavenly Father is presented as a mighty God, a warrior king, and we are his foot soldiers in an ongoing battle. However, we must keep our hearts strong, as best we can, knowing that with God all things are possible. The Potter quest is firmly rooted in the best traditions of the Judeo-Christian faith, and Harry's parents' gravestones give us ample proof of that. Of course, J. K. Rowling does not hammer us over the head with this. She never lectures. It would be inappropriate for her to do so, and it would lessen the universal appeal of her story. However, as scholars, it is appropriate for us to search for the connections, and although she does not explain them, it enriches our study of the stories if we do. Although Harry has not understood the inscription as well as we would like him to, it sounds like Hermione has, and together they plan to return to see this fight through to the finish. Once again, we see the importance of Hermione to this story. She never gives up on Harry, and their friendship is a perfect example of the kind of love that the Potter quest celebrates. Arm in arm, Harry and Hermione leave the cemetery.

They then seek out the remains of Harry's boyhood home, and they find this legend inscribed on a secret sign that reveals itself with a touch of their hands: "On this spot...Lily and James Potter lost their lives. Their son, Harry, remains the only wizard ever to have survived the Killing Curse. This house, invisible to Muggles, has been left in its ruined state as a monument to the Potters and as a reminder of the violence that tore apart their family"(333). Beneath the sign, many people have scrawled words of encouragement to Harry, words which fill him with a sense of support and hope. However, this ruined cottage is a powerful image in another way. It underscores the importance of what the Biblical passages we have just looked at are telling us. Your treasure had better not be earthly wealth. That is the greatest folly. Time passes here on earth, and physical treasure eventually crumbles. But there is that treasure which surpasses and overcomes all earthly ruin, and that is the greatest magic of all—love. It comes from believing, from choosing to believe, that there is something immortal in all of us, and from living a life committed to acting on that faith. This is such an important idea, and it is easy to underestimate the difficulty of what we have just said. There is nothing easy about

278

it. It is the very essence of the quest—to walk by faith. We have been given abilities, but it is the decisions we make and the things we do that determine who we are and what we stand for. Faith goes hand in hand with action. Finally, when all is said and done, the only treasure that lasts is love.

Soon they are on their way to Bathilda Bagshot's house, but this place is a trap. As Harry enters her house, which smells of decay and rot, he feels the Horcrux that he wears around his neck start to prickle and pulse, which should let him know that he is in the presence of evil. There is the dreadful scene where the snake comes out of the dead Bathilda's neck and attacks Harry. As the snake bites Harry, he is whisked away to the most powerful memory of all—the night so long ago that Voldemort killed his parents and tried to kill him. Once again, he experiences the moment from Voldemort's perspective: "He pointed the wand very carefully into the boy's face…He wanted to see it happen, the destruction of this one, inexplicable danger"(345). What kind of a man is that? We are at the heart of evil. However, as Harry sees Voldemort speak the killing curse, he feels it backfire and mangle him instead. Voldemort is broken into nothing but pain and terror, a remnant of what he had been. The vision leaves Harry exhausted, almost beyond recall. The horcrux had sealed itself to Harry's chest and he was essentially unconscious. Hermione grabbed Harry with an almost superhuman effort and, using a Blasting Curse, got them out of there. Once again, Harry is saved by Hermione's quick thinking and unfailing courage. When she gets them to safety, she makes Harry lie down. He is too weak to argue. Hermione says that Lupin had told them that they might run into magic they had never seen before, and they certainly have. In the aftermath of the attack, Harry discovers that his beautiful wand has been broken—past all mending. Sadly, Harry feels a little bit like that himself. Hermione's eyes fill with tears, and we realize that she is very nearly at the end of her prodigious strength.

Without his faithful wand, Harry feels more exposed than ever, and he, secretly and illogically, blames Hermione, even though he knows he should not hold her accountable for this loss: "No, Hermione, I know it was an accident. You were trying to get us out of there alive, and you were incredible. I'd be dead if you hadn't been there to help me"(352). And this is true. Meanwhile, however, Hermione has figured out the identity of the merry faced thief that haunts Harry—Gellert Grindelwald. She has discovered the answer while reading the annoying Rita Skeeter's biography of Dumbledore, which Skeeter has entitled The Life and Lies of Albus Dumbledore. In the book, Skeeter has reprinted some of Dumbledore's letters from his youth, where he arrogantly proclaims the superiority of wizards to non-magical people: "Yes, we have been given power and yes, that power gives us the right to rule, but it also gives us responsibilities over the ruled. We must stress this point...Where we are opposed, as we surely will be, this must be the basis of all our counterargument. We seize control FOR THE GREATER GOOD"(357). We are right at the heart of a very dangerous idea here—the idea of the greater good.

Who has the right to determine what is the greater good? We can all think of times in the history of mankind when these words have been the rationalization for unspeakable cruelties. It seems that Albus Dumbledore met Gellert Grindelwald one summer after Gellert had been expelled from Durmstrang, a wizarding school that supposedly was more accepting of the pursuit of dark magic. But young Grindelwald went too far in his pursuit of the dark arts even for the headmaster and teachers of his school; they apparently saw in him the danger of dark magic unchecked. Grindelwald was a very handsome person, with a merry looking face, and it is clear that he was arrogant and narcissistic. When he met the young Albus Dumbledore, he immediately recognized that he was finally in the presence of someone as brilliant as he, and he began to seduce Dumbledore with his seductive philosophy of wizard supremacy. It is easy to fall into this trap. Even as far back as Plato, the notion of a philosopher king existed. Those who were the most intelligent should rule because they would know how to lead the lesser mortals to "the greater good."

However, underneath it all there can be a dangerous hubris— an arrogance whereby a man thinks himself only slightly less than a god, if less at all. Grindelwald and Dumbledore, as young men, decide

hubris

to acquire the Deathly Hallows, and with them to mark their power, to create a world of wizarding supremacy. Eventually, Dumbledore's brother, Aberforth, realizes that his brother has lost perspective, and he challenges Grindelwald to a duel. It ends up being a three-way duel, one in which their younger sister Ariana is accidentally killed. Although Grindelwald runs for his life, both of the Dumbledore brothers are heartbroken at the sacrifice of this sweet innocent, and Albus Dumbledore learns the danger of lying to himself about "the greater good." This concept is not intrinsically bad; in fact, it may be used to accomplish much good. However, what is absolutely critical is that the person who is determining the greater good is a good person who is wise and selfless. There can be no secret agendas or false pride in the decision. This description does not accurately describe Grindelwald, who clearly had his own agenda to advance and who was motivated by narcissism and hubris. Eventually, as legend has it, Albus Dumbledore and Gellert Grindelwald face off in the greatest duel ever witnessed between two wizards, and Dumbledore defeats him. It is said that his defeat of Grindelwald historically coincided with the fall of Nazi Germany, so, on both fronts—the forces of darkness are temporarily beaten back.

As a result of this triumph, Albus Dumbledore is the rightful possessor of the Elder Wand, but he no longer pursues the possession of the Deathly Hallows. We will discuss the Deathly Hallows when

Harry finds out what they mean, but for now, we will remember that the Elder Wand is one of those Hallows. At this point in his life, having been indirectly responsible for his sister's death, Dumbledore becomes a very humble man. From this time forth, he recognizes the limits of his own wisdom and the danger of arrogance. From this moment on, he is a changed man. It takes Harry a long time to fight his way through all of this conflicting information, and for a while he feels betrayed and confused about who Dumbledore really was. When he cries out in his anguish and confusion, Hermione quietly speaks her defense of him. She knows that the Dumbledore they knew was not a glory seeker, and she knows that he loved and respected Harry. She says: "He loved you...I know he loved you"(362). Once again, Hermione is the voice of reason and the steadfast presence of a quiet, yet powerful faith.

As Harry stands guard that night, desperate and alone, a bright light gleams on the snow. He follows the source of the light and comes upon a Patronus, a beautiful silver doe, not a stag, and she leads him to a pool of water, frozen in the December cold, under which gleams a great gift. Once again in this quest, a sword is delivered to a young hero who is in desperate need of help: "He dropped to his knees at the pool's edge...A glint of deep red...It was a sword with glittering rubies in its hilt...The sword of Gryffindor was lying at the bottom of the forest pool"(367). Not knowing what else to do, he jumps into the pool, and immediately, the horcrux that he is wearing

horcrux

around his neck in comes to life and starts to try to strangle him. The evil of the horcrux apparently feels the presence of goodness and is frantically trying to fend this connection off, and Harry is in desperate trouble. Then suddenly, a miracle happens, or at least it seems like a miracle to Harry. Ron is there to save Harry, and he pulls him from the water, rips the horcrux off Harry's neck, and humbly apologizes and asks Harry to take him back. Harry suddenly knows what has to be done. The horcrux must immediately be destroyed with the Sword of Gryffindor, and Ron must be the one to do it: "He was not being kind or generous. As certainly as he had known that the doe was benign, he knew that Ron had to be the one to wield the sword. Dumbledore had at least taught Harry something about certain kinds of magic, of the incalculable power of certain acts"(374).

It will, however, be a joint effort. Harry will ask the locket to open, using parseltongue, and then Ron must stab it. What follows is a very interesting and clever scene, where a voice hisses out of the horcrux, speaking Ron's most secret fears aloud, saying that he is always second best and that Hermione really loves Harry. The evil genius of the horcrux is attacking Ron's confidence, trying to unman him. Harry, seeing Ron fall prey to his own doubts (remember—we make our own prisons) yells at Ron to act, and suddenly "the sword flashed, plunged: Harry threw himself out of the way, there was a clang of metal and a long, drawn-out scream. Harry whirled around,

284

slipping in the snow, wand held ready to defend himself; but there was nothing to fight"(377). This moment is huge. With this action, Ron defeats his own demons and finds the courage to destroy the horcrux. In doing so, he not only kills a part of Voldemortbut also takes power over fears that have haunted him. He recognizes them as foolish fears and destroys the thoughts that have eaten away at him. We are again reminded that Harry is not the only hero of this quest. He is certainly the most prominent one or the one on whom we have focused, but he is surrounded and helped by many heroes throughout it all. And, finally, another seventh of Voldemort's fractured soul is destroyed. At this moment, everything changes for the better. When Ron's vision clears, he asks Harry if he loves Hermione. And Harry finally tells Ron, once and for all, what we have already come to know: "She's like my sister…I love her like a sister and I reckon she feels the same way about me. It's always been like that. I thought you knew"(378). The two of them make up like long lost brothers, and we heave a sigh of relief.

Harry then leads Ron back to Hermione, who joyfully takes him back into her arms after she is done clobbering him for leaving, and Ron tells the wild story of how he found them—with the aid of the Deluminator which Dumbledore had bequeathed him in his last will and testament. Ron explains: "The little ball of light was hovering there, waiting for me, and…it sort of floated toward me…right to my chest, and then—it just went straight through…I could feel it, it was hot. And once it was inside me, I knew what I was supposed to do, I knew it would take me where I needed to go"(384). This, of course, means that Dumbledore, in all his wisdom, knew that Ron would eventually desert the quest, and just as importantly, knew he would want to come back. Luckily, Ron has also brought Harry a new wand, and our three heroes have survived a very challenging dark hour of the soul. We will later discover that the silver doe Patronus had been cast by Severus Snape, obeying orders from Dumbledore which he is able to issue from his portrait in Hogwarts. According to legend, the sword must be acquired by a true Gryffindor in an hour of extreme need, and there must be some danger in that acquisition. Therefore, Snape had placed the sword at the bottom of the frozen pool, so that Harry would have to risk everything to get it. Our young heroes do not know this at this moment in the quest, although they will find it out much later. It is interesting to note that Lily Potter's Patronus was also a silver doe, and this is the tempting interpretation for a while—that Lily is somehow reaching back into the world of the living to protect her son. But that cannot be, as we learned at the end of book three. Once a person has gone on, he or she has gone on. However, having said that—clearly, the fact that Snape's Patronus is the exact same as Lily's Patronus could be said to be a quiet testimony of his love for her. And, at least at some level, Lily had loved Severus Snape. Love is the greatest magic of all, and the power of that love can reach beyond the veil, as it does at this moment of the quest. Love never dies. So, in a way, Lily's love is reaching back to her son.

Ron explains to Harry and Hermione that they must definitely not speak Voldemort's name out loud. His instincts about that have been very good: "Using his name breaks protective enchantments, it causes some kind of magical disturbance—it's how they found us in Tottenham Court Road!"(389). We remember that when they disapparated from Bill and Fleur's wedding, Hermione had taken them there, and they were bewildered as to how they could have been found by Death Eaters so quickly. Now, they understand. With this higher level of precaution among them, they seek out Xenophilius Lovegood, Luna's father, whom they remember had worn the sign of the Deathly Hallows around his neck at the ill-fated wedding party. We are finally going to hear the legend that gave this final novel its name. It feels like a story right out of Chaucer's Canterbury Tales; it has that tone and that power. Deathly Hallows!

The crucial story involves three brothers who were traveling along a lonely road where they reach an impassable river. They work together to make a magical bridge, and halfway across, they meet a hooded figure, who pretends to congratulate them on their successful magic but really is angry at having been deprived of three victims. He says that he will grant a wish to each of them. The eldest asks for an unbeatable wand, which of course, is the Elder Wand. The second asks

287

for a resurrection stone, which could bring the dead back to life, and the third asks for a way to hide from death, since he did not trust him. The first two come to grief, and the youngest son, using the invisibility cloak, is able to hide from death for a long time and live a rich, full life. When he is ready to "go on," he "finally took off the Cloak of Invisibility and gave it to his son. And then he greeted Death as an old friend, and went with him gladly, and, equals, they departed this life"(409). These are the Deathly Hallows. There is logic behind all of it.

The first two gifts—to be completely invincible or to be able to resurrect the dead—are inappropriate and therefore bound to fail. They supposedly bequeath powers to a person that are beyond the province of mankind. Men are, by definition mortal, and they therefore cannot defeat physical death. The last gift, the cloak of invisibility, asks only to hide from death for a while, not forever. It is the wisest request, and it is within the province of man. So, it is the only request that can be honored. The third brother eventually passes the cloak of invisibility, or the cloak of time to his son, and "exits this life" with Death, whom he greets as an old friend. That is within the province of man. Xenophilius Lovegood tells them, in conclusion, that legend has it that the Peverell brothers were the young men in the story, and they therefore were the original owners of the Deathly Hallows. The name Peverell sounds vaguely familiar. Perhaps it is meant to echo the name Percival, one of the important knights in the quest for the Holy

Grail. In time, we will discover that these Peverell brothers are actually Harry Potter's ancestors, so the Invisibility Cloak, passed to Harry from James, is an appropriate inheritance. Harry will wear the cloak of invisibility from time to time until he too, some day, will surrender it to his son and heir. The quest goes on.

Before we move on, let us consider the words "deathly hallows." When we think of the word "hallow," most of us would immediately think of the Lord's Prayer—Our Father, who art in heaven, hallowed be thy name. The word means "holy" or "blessed." Death is hallowed for a person who has completed his earthly quest. It is a sacred passageway to the next life—a life that has been planned for us and waiting for us ever since we entered this earthly stage, this earthly quest. Again, we are at the heart of the mystery here.

Before they leave the Lovegood residence, they visit Luna's bedroom, and see that she has decorated her room with their portraits—and all around the pictures, she has inked the word "friends." Mr. Lovegood tries to detain them, and they soon suspect that his doing so is some kind of a trap. He is a desperate man. He eventually admits that he intends to hand the three warriors over to the Death Eaters, in a desperate attempt to get his daughter back from the powers of evil: "They took my Luna...Because of what I've been writing. They took my Luna and I don't know where she is, what they've done to her. But they might give her back to me if I—if I"(419).

We cannot entirely blame him for what he has done, that is, contacting the Death Eaters. Any parent would do almost anything to save his or her child, but Mr. Lovegood does not understand that there is no mercy in Voldemort and his followers.

Harry, Ron, and Hermione escape just in time, and Harry does some hard thinking. He remembers that the youngest Peverell boy is his distant forefather; he is buried in Godric Hollow, and he realizes, all at once, that Voldemort is seeking the Elder Wand, an unbeatable wand with which to finally defeat him. When he puts all of this together, Hermione mocks him, saying that the story is only a fairy tale, and that if it were really true, Dumbledore would have told him so. Harry responds that she should have been listening to herself earlier: "But you said it, Hermione! You've got to find out about them for yourself. It's a Quest!...Dumbledore usually let me find out stuff for myself. He let me try my strength, take risks. This feels like the kind of thing he'd do"(433). We can translate the metaphor easily. Life is a quest, and although, as parents we can guide our children when they are young, helping them to learn the difference between right and wrong, eventually we must step back and let them figure things out for themselves. It is the only way they will acquire lasting knowledge. From the moment children are born into this earthly life, or as St. Paul would say, perishable body, they are on their own quests. We may not be thinking in those terms; when they are little, they seem wholly dependent on their parents. However, soon they rapidly start to "be about their Father's business," and begin shaping the course of their lives themselves. Experience is the best teacher, and sometimes the most painful. All any parent can try to do is guide their child, helping them to distinguish right from wrong. Eventually, they must leave the rest of the quest up to them.

The spring approaches, and our three heroes are still on the run and still bewildered about what their next step should be. One evening, they hear an underground broadcast, an interview hosted by Lee Jordan, their classmate who used to do the commentary for the Hogwarts quidditch matches. They hear Kingsley Shacklebolt insist that the fight against the powers of darkness must go on, that Muggles and wizards are all human beings, and that each human life is sacred. Then, and it seems like balm to Harry's broken spirits, he hears the voice of Remus Lupin. Lupin says that the Boy who Lived "remains a symbol of everything for which we are fighting: the triumph of good, the power of innocence, the need to keep resisting…I'd tell him we're all with him in spirit…And I'd tell him to follow his instincts, which are good and nearly always right"(441). It is almost as if Lupin is hoping that Harry has somehow tuned in, and it is easy to hear what Lupin is trying to tell Harry—that he is happy he went back to Tonks, that Harry is wise beyond his years, that he is so grateful that he chose to stick by his family. Harry has saved another family from the damage he suffered—at least for now. As Harry listens, his eyes fill with tears, which as we have said before, are sacred. And these words give a lift to Harry's soul—they give him courage, maybe too much courage.

He willingly speaks Voldemort's name, allowing the magical trace to work, and although he, Hermione, and Ron are in disguises that Hermione has hastily conjured, they are quickly picked up by Death Eaters and taken to Malfoy Manor. There, they are interrogated, and Draco, threatened by the Death Eaters, is forced to examine them, and testify whether he is looking at the most famous "undesirables" in the world, perhaps simply disguised by polyjuice potion. Although Draco probably recognizes Harry, he will not say that the person standing before him is, in fact, Harry Potter. Harry, Ron, and Hermione are thrown into the Malfoy dungeon, as the Malfoys try to decide what to do. There they find Luna, Dean, the goblin called Griphook, and Mr. Ollivander, who is very weak, in fact, almost dead.

Many things happen very quickly here. Harry convinces Griphook to tell the Malfoys that the sword they have is a fake. Then, in fear and desperation, he calls out for help, hoping that help will be given, even though he is not at Hogwarts. We remember that house elves have magic of their own, and suddenly help arrives, in the form of Dobby. It seems that elves can apparate into the Malfoy dungeon, and even more importantly—out of it. Harry tells Dobby to get Luna, Dean, and Mr. Ollivander out of there and come back as quickly as he can. The loud "crack" of his apparating summons Wormtail into the dungeon where he sees Harry and Ron. Although he almost turns them in, Harry reminds him that he saved his life, showed him mercy several years ago, and that mercy now reaps its reward. Wormtail does not speak against them, and they have a chance to escape. However, his silver hand, given to him by Voldemort in the cemetery long ago, and therefore wedded to evil, turns itself on him and kills him. Arguably, Peter Pettigrew (Wormtail) redeems himself with this final act of mercy. Certainly, Harry's act of mercy long ago is repaid a hundred fold.

Immediately thereafter, they are face to face with Bellatrix Lestrange who tells them that she has summoned the Dark Lord. However, Dobby returns, and Ron and Harry grab Hermione and Griphook, and holding on to Dobby, apparate out of Malfoy Manor and into freedom. When they land on solid earth, Harry's heart breaks, for Dobby is dying. Before they escaped the Malfoy house, Bellatrix Lestrange threw a dagger at them, and that dagger found its mark— Dobby. Harry is heartbroken. He feels responsible for Dobby's death. Bellatrix has caused so much sadness for Harry. She killed Sirius, and now she has killed Dobby. Harry kneels in the sand, sobbing as Dobby dies in his arms. Dobby's last words are "Harry Potter": "And then, with a little shudder the elf became quite still, and his eyes were nothing more than great glassy orbs, sprinkled with light from the stars they could not see"(476).

Now comes one of the most important moments of the quest. Harry digs Dobby's grave, all by himself, by hand, using nothing but his strength as a young man. It is easy to miss the significance of this moment, but, on a symbolic level, it is huge. Overcome with rage and grief, Harry once again takes refuge in physical action, saying that he wants to dig the grave properly. Although his hatred for Bellatrix is almost overwhelming, his love for Dobby is even greater. We see, once again, that love is much more powerful than hatred: "His rage was dreadful and yet Harry's grief for Dobby seemed to diminish it, so that it became a distant storm that reached Harry from across a vast, silent ocean…He dug with a kind of fury, relishing the manual work, glorying in the non-magic of it, for every drop of his sweat and every blister felt like a gift to the elf who had saved their lives. His scar burned, but he was master of the pain; he felt it, yet was apart from it. He had learned control at last, learned to shut his mind to Voldemort…his thoughts could not penetrate Harry now, while he mourned Dobby. Grief, it seemed, drove Voldemort out…though Dumbledore, of course, would have said that it was love"(478). J. K. Rowling sets up an interesting definition here—grief is a kind of love. Harry sees a big difference between grief and love, but maybe the point is this—we grieve because we have loved. Since Voldemort felt no love, he could never feel grief for those he has killed. Again, through the experience of love, Harry becomes more powerful than Voldemort.

We are right back at some of the most sacred lessons of the Potter quest, of any human quest. The most powerful magic of all is love—true, unselfish love. When we love, we approach the divine—we truly are, in those moments, made in the image and likeness of God. Tears are sacred. They are a language of their own, and they spring from a place deep in our hearts, deeper than words can ever reach. And—we must walk by faith. We must soldier on, trusting in the power of love, in the love of our heavenly Father, and in our purpose here to be his hands, eyes, hearts, and words in this, our time on earth. We cannot know the answers to all of our questions now. We must choose to believe and to trust and to keep doing what we believe to be the right thing. And in this moment of loss, Harry chooses to believe. Anyone can find reasons to doubt that this earthly quest makes sense. Life is full of such temptations. Since we cannot know the answers to some of the most difficult questions, eventually, each person must choose whether or not to believe, to make a leap of faith. And Harry does that right here. From this moment on, he is a different man—stronger and more determined than ever to finish this battle. He walks away from Dobby's grave, "his mind full of those things that had come to him in the grave, ideas that had taken shape in the darkness, ideas both fascinating and terrible"(481). What Harry realizes is that we cannot know the answers to all of our burning questions, and that sooner or later—you have to make a decision to trust in the power of love, and in the presence of a divine providence, and do the right thing. Knowing that you cannot know everything, you keep up the quest and persist. Sometimes, it really is that simple, and complicated, all at the same time.

Harry is joined by the others, and they give Dobby a proper funeral. Harry marks Dobby's grave with the words, "HERE LIES DOBBY, A FREE ELF"…and then walked away, but with a new sense of determination and focus. He is done with the dark hour of the soul. He has made peace with his own doubts about Dumbledore and about himself. It seems as if, from this moment on, he really takes command of the troops preparing for battle. Dawn is breaking over the landscape, and Harry remembers that Dumbledore had promised him that help would always be given, if he asked. Ask, and you shall receive: "He looked out over the ocean and felt closer, this dawn, than ever before, to the heart of it all…What did you know about me, Dumbledore? Am I meant to know, but not to seek: Did you know how hard I'd find that? Is that why you made it this difficult? So I'd have time to work that out?"(483). It is clear, with these words, that Dumbledore is a stand-in for God, and Harry must "choose to believe" in Him, as do we. We hunger for facts, for answers to our questions, for proof. Understandably, there is a little bit of the Doubting Thomas in all of us. Remember, Jesus appeared to his disciples after his resurrection, and Thomas refused to believe until he had placed his fingers in His wounds and had seen him for himself. Jesus gently scolds him when next he appears to his disciples, and says,"Have you believed because you have seen me? Blessed are those who have not seen and yet believe"(John 20:28). This is the impossible leap of faith that our heavenly Father asks of each one of us on our quest—to choose to believe. And, as Harry digs Dobby's grave, he makes the decision to do just that. He recalls this moment for us later. On Easter morning, a moment obviously replete with resurrection imagery, "he had made his choice while he dug Dobby's grave, he had decided to continue along the winding, dangerous path indicated for him by Albus Dumbledore, to accept that he had not been told everything that he wanted to know, but simply to trust. He had no desire to doubt again; he did not want to hear anything that would deflect him from his purpose"(563). It is this choice—to put aside doubts, to walk by faith, to trust and believe in our heavenly Father's divine plan and unsurpassed love, and to do the best he can that makes all the difference.

There is a similar moment in the Grail legend. There are countless versions of the Grail quest, so there is some uncertainty about many of the details here, but in the quest lore, one of the young knights who is on the quest for the Holy Grail (in some versions it is

Gawain and in some it is Perceval) is exhausted, and has come to the end of his rope. Suddenly, he happens upon a chapel, in the middle of a primeval forest, where none had been before. But, the chapel does not look quite right—the doors are hanging open, weirdly. Still, there is light inside, and so he rides into the chapel. There he finds the remains of a Black Mass, that is to say, an act of sacrilege—a disembodied hand throwing the Eucharist on the floor, a dead body dissected and placed on the altar—absolute horror. And the young knight takes all this in, makes the sign of the cross to bless himself and reaffirm his faith, and backs out of the chapel. He knows that the destruction he sees before him is not the act of a person of faith but rather the act of someone committed to evil, the heart of darkness. And yet he believes. He goes on, knowing that his heavenly Father will guide his steps and see him through this time of danger. In other words, in the course of your quest, there will come moments of horror, and evil people who will attack your faith. In spite of these reasons to doubt, you have to make a conscious decision to choose to believe, and to go forward in faith.

T. S. Eliot gives us a modern retelling of this important moment in his modernist poem "The Waste Land:"

In this decayed hole among the mountains
In the faint moonlight, the grass is singing

> *Over the tumbled graves, about the chapel,*
>
> *There is the empty chapel, only the wind's home,*
>
> *It has no windows, and the door swings,*
>
> *Dry bones can harm no one*
>
> *Only a cock stood on the rooftree*
>
> *Co co rico co co rico*
>
> *In a flash of lightning. Then a damp gust*
>
> *Bringing rain*
>
> *(The Waste Land: lines 385-395).*

Notice that, as we have said before, the rooster calls out, announcing the dawn of a new day, and in this case, bringing rain—for which the waste land is desperate. Similarly, Dobby's death is like a clarion call to Harry's soul, giving him the strength and the desire to finish his task. In Eliot's poem, the rooster is like a herald that announces that we are about to hear God's voice. Here, Eliot uses a technique from Hinduism, where the Hindu priests would listen to the thunder and interpret for their followers what God has said. So, God's voice comes in the form of thunder. At this point in the poem, the thunder speaks and the speaker of the poem (working like a Hindu priest) hears three commands from his God—Give, Sympathize, and Control Yourself. Taken together, these commands sum up the lesson of the quest. Give your heart in love. Give of yourself. Eliot's speaker defines love as the "awful daring of a moment's surrender." What a beautiful definition, and we notice that love demands surrender of one's self. To surrender is to choose to believe, to walk by faith. The second command is to sympathize. Do not rush to judgment. And, finally-control yourself. Keep to the middle way. As St. Thomas Aquinas says, "Virtu est en media." The virtuous way is in the middle. Keep your balance, and trust. Choose to believe and move forward in your quest.

Harry's decision to bury Dobby moves Griphook, a goblin who does not usually trust human beings, to help him. Harry has figured out that Bellatrix's panic at the thought that their vault at Gringott's had been broken into suggests that a horcrux, a piece of Voldemort's broken soul must be guarded there. We cannot be sure if Bellatrix understands the true nature of the horcrux. It is hard to picture Voldemort trusting her, or anyone else, enough to explain what he is attempting to do. Still, Harry remembers that she is in mortal terror of something that Voldemort had entrusted to her having been taken in the break-in. Harry figures all of this out, and the fact that he does this shows his increasing understanding of the way Voldemort works, whereas Voldemort does not seem to be achieving an increasing understanding of Harry. That would require Voldemort understanding the power of love, and that is something he has chosen not to do.

At this point in the story, Harry, Ron and Hermione must break into Gringott's, which they do with the somewhat reluctant help of Griphook. Just before they leave on this perilous journey, Harry notices that "small green shoots were forcing their way up through the red earth of Dobby's grave now; in a year's time the mound would be covered with flowers"(522). J. K. Rowling is reminding us that life goes on. The regenerative power of the earth and her mysterious cycles of life and death underscore our every moment here. This earthly body will not last; the earth will swallow every one of us up, in time. However, love lasts. It is the mighty power that can even conquer death. And Dobby's love moves in Harry as he begins this dangerous mission to Gringotts. Griphook, who is always wary of human beings, now treats Harry with a cautious but newfound respect, saying, "I should climb up now, Harry Potter, I think?"(524). Hermione has disguised herself as Bellatrix Lestrange, with the help of polyjuice potion, and Harry and Griphook conceal themselves under the Invisibility Cloak. Hermione alters Ron's appearance so that he does not look like himself, and they invent a completely new identity for him, hoping that Bellatrix's malevolent aura will carry the day. Harry has to remind Hermione to be rude and arrogant with everyone they meet since that is how Bellatrix would conduct herself. Several times, Hermione slips, finding it difficult to act so cruel and contemptuous to people they pass. They must run the gauntlet of several protective charms, but since Griphook knows what is coming, he can advise them. Finally, they are in the Lestrange vault, and they run into an ingenious and dangerous curse. Every time they touch any piece of treasure in the vault, it multiplies itself into a cascade of enchanted doubles, all burning hot to the touch: "Hermione screamed in pain, and Harry turned his wand on her in time to see a jeweled goblet tumbling from her grip. But as it fell, it split, became a shower of goblets, so that a second later, with a great clatter, the floor was covered in identical cups rolling in every direction, the original impossible to discern amongst them. 'It burned me!' moaned Hermione, sucking her blistered fingers. 'They have added Gemino and Flagrante Curses!' said Griphook. 'Everything you touch will burn and multiply, but the copies are worthless—and if you continue to handle the treasure, you will eventually be crushed to death by the weight of expanding gold'"(537). What an interesting metaphor that is! If you allow yourself to be distracted by gold and riches during your time on earth, you will eventually be crushed by it, having lost everything. Know that the real treasure is your loved ones, and invest your time and energy in that. Nothing else matters as much, certainly not gold and silver.

Suddenly Harry just knows, as he sometimes does, that he can touch the treasure with the Sword of Gryffindor, and the duplicating and burning charms will be neutralized. Hermione uses the old levitating charm of "Levicorpus" to lift Harry to Hufflepuff's goblet, and then, he has to fight to hang on to it, since Griphook grabs the sword away from Harry once he falls: "The tiny golden cup, skewered by the handle on the sword's blade, was flung in to the air. The goblin still astride him, Harry dived and caught it, and although he could feel it scalding his flesh he did not relinquish it, even while countless Hufflepuff cups burst from his fist…Hardly aware of the pain from the burns covering his body, and still borne along on the swell of replicating treasure, Harry shoved the cup into his pocket and reached up to retrieve the sword…Slipping on hot metal, Harry struggled to his feet and knew that the only way out was through"(541). There are several interesting ideas here—the importance of teamwork, the power of persistence, and the often underestimated effectiveness of intuition. All of these are in play in the scene of their amazing escape from Gringotts.

When they find the dragon chained in the vault, meant to bar their escape, they release him from his chains, and he roars his way out of the dungeon, carrying our three heroes on his back. Once again, Hermione's quick thinking kicks in, as she shouts out the charm that helps the dragon enlarge the passageway that he is making for their flight from the vault: "She was helping the dragon…carving out the ceiling as it struggled upward toward the fresher air, away from the shrieking and clanking goblins: Harry and Ron copied her, blasting the ceiling apart with more gouging spells. They passed the underground lake, and the great crawling, snarling beast seemed to sense freedom and space ahead of it…And then at last, by the combined force of their spells and the dragon's brute strength, they had blasted their way out of the passage and into the marble hallway…it staggered into Diagon Alley and launched itself into the sky"(543). Once again, a magical creature has come to the aid of the young heroes. It is not the last time that this will happen.

Eventually, Hermione destroys Helga Hufflepuff's cup with the sword of Gryffindor, and another portion of Voldemort's fractured soul is also destroyed. In the aftermath of her destruction of the horcrux, Voldemort knows, with fearful certainty, that they are coming for him, that he is under attack, that the final battle is approaching. Help for our young heroes appears from many different sources now—it can and it does frequently in a quest. It is almost as if the forces for good amass a certain kind of weight that can no longer be denied. Aberforth Dumbledore, who is Albus's brother, pulls Ron, Hermione, and Harry to safety when they arrive in Hogsmeade. He is the barman at the Hog's Head pub, and his pub has a secret passageway by which he has been assisting students in entering and leaving Hogwarts. It is this passageway that Harry will use to enter Hogwarts for the great final battle. Harry, looking at Aberforth's piercing blue eyes, realizes that his is the eye he has been seeing, not Dumbledore's. Aberforth confirms the story about Ariana's death, how she was killed accidentally when a stray curse killed her during a three-way fight between Grindelwald, Albus, and Aberforth. Aberforth believed that

Albus was being seduced by evil, and fought to keep his brother from being sucked into Grindelwald's twisted interpretation of "the greater good." Actually, Albus was seduced by Grindelwald's intellect, rather than by evil. Albus was a brilliant young man stuck at home, trying to take care of his family. Grindelwald's ideas provided intellectual stimulation for Dumbledore, and the promise of a way out of Godric's Hollow. Apparently, the young Grindelwald was a very handsome and very articulate young man, and for a while, Albus fell under his spell. Neither Albus nor Aberforth has ever been able to forgive himself for Ariana's death, for which they both felt culpable. Although Aberforth seems coarse and gruff, he will be a huge help to Harry as he finishes this quest, and he will fight bravely at the battle of Hogwarts.

The castle is under attack, and Dumbledore's real army assembles to fight to the death, if need be. In one heartwarming moment right before the disastrous battle, Percy Weasley, having seen the error of his ways, returns to the fold. He approaches his mom and dad, as well as his brothers and sister, and apologizes for his stupidity and arrogance: "I was a fool!...I was an idiot, I was a pompous prat, I was a –a—I'm sorry, Dad…I managed to make contact with Aberforth and he tipped me off ten minutes ago that Hogwarts was going to make a fight of it, so here I am"(606). Arthur and Molly Weasley are overwhelmed with joy, and they welcome their son back into the heart of the family, with no further scolding or embarrassment. We are reminded once again of one of the most famous parables of all—the parable of The Prodigal Son. You know the story. A man has two sons, and the younger one asks for his share of the inheritance, leaves home and spends his fortune prodigally. Having fallen into a state of desperation, he goes home, begging his father to allow him to work as a laborer, knowing full well that he does not deserve forgiveness. Instead, the father welcomes him home with open arms: "And the son said to him 'Father, I have sinned against heaven and before you; I am no longer worthy to be called your son.' But the father said to his servants, 'Bring the best robe, and put it on him; and put a ring on his hand, and shoes on his feet; and bring the fatted calf and kill it, and let us eat and make merry; for my son was dead, and is alive again; he was lost, and is found.'"(Luke 15: 21-24). Here we have one of the most famous metaphors for the love of our heavenly Father for us. We are, each of us, at some time during our lives, like this Prodigal Son. We turn our backs on our faith, on the love of our heavenly Father. And He is waiting, always, to welcome us back with this kind of love. And this is exactly how the Weasleys behave at this critical moment. Unfortunately, there will be no feast for them on this day, and the day's battle will cost them the earthly life of another son. Still, we cannot for one moment miss the importance of Percy returning to full membership in his family before the battle begins.

Harry's focus is absolutely clear now as the battle approaches;

he must find and destroy the remaining horcruxes. With the destruction of each horcrux, Voldemort becomes ever more mortal. With the aid of Luna Lovegood, he finds the Ravenclaw diadem, in which Voldemort has also hidden a portion of his soul. We remember that Dumbledore had theorized that Voldemort would search for a piece of priceless treasure from each of the four houses of Hogwarts. For the Ravenclaw house, that icon is the famous diadem. It has been residing quietly in the Room of Requirement, where Harry had actually seen it long ago, although at the time, he had not realized its significance. When he gets to that room with his friends and fellow warriors, he finds Draco, Crabbe, and Goyle. He is actually saved the trouble of having to destroy the diadem by Vincent Crabbe, who tries to use fiendfyre on them. However, since this is very hard to control, he ends up actually killing himself with it as well as accidentally destroying the horcrux, and with it, another portion of Voldemort's soul.

Although Crabbe dies in the fiendfyre that he has summoned, Harry, Ron, and Hermione are able to save Malfoy and Goyle. Their act of mercy follows the code of the true knight. Harry has long ago come to believe that Draco is not as bad as he seems, and he is probably right. Draco has been under terrible pressure, essentially blackmailed by Voldemort into doing evil. Although Harry and Draco have never been friends, Harry saves him. Harry is usually willing to give a person the benefit of the doubt, and his act of kindness will eventually be rewarded, once again. Using his skills as a seeker, he dives through the fire: "Malfoy saw him coming and raised one arm…Malfoy clambered up behind Harry….Harry made a hairpin swerve and dived. The diadem seemed to fall in slow motion, turning and glittering as it dropped toward the maw of a yawning serpent, and then he had it, caught it around his wrist—"633-4). When they emerge from the Room of Requirement, Harry sees a dark, tarry, bloodlike substance leak out of the broken diadem. And as it does, he hears a faint scream, and he knows that this portion of Voldemort's soul has been destroyed by the fiendfyre. Hermione points out that what this means is that all they have left to do is to destroy the snake, and then Voldemort will be nothing but a mortal man. A very powerful wizard, true, but mortal in every ordinary sense.

So, we feel the final confrontation between Harry and Voldemort approaching rapidly. All around Harry, Dumbledore's Army is assembling now, and they know they are approaching a fight to the death. The siege of Hogwarts is breathtaking reading. Readers can almost feel themselves holding their breath as it all comes down. All at once, the castle seems to explode, and in the moment after the explosion, we make a terrible discovery. Fred Weasley is dead. This loss almost undoes Harry. He just can't get his mind around the idea of the world without Fred Weasley in it: "The world had ended, so why had the battle not ceased, the castle fallen silent in horror, and every combatant laid down their arms? Harry's mind was in free fall, spinning out of control, unable to grasp the impossibility, because Fred Weasley could not be dead"(638). This passage seems to express a universal truth that we will probably all experience, if we have not already. Almost all of us can fill in the blank where the words Fred Weasley are with the name of someone we have lost, and because of that loss, the world is forever altered, forever diminished. And again, there is a lesson here. We have to go on. We have to grieve, when we get the time, and then keep going, because that is what the quest is all about. As the wise speaker in Ecclesiastes tells us, there will be a time for every purpose under heaven: "A time to weep, and a time to laugh; a time to mourn, and a time to dance; a time to cast away stones, and a time to gather stones together...a time for war, and a time for peace"(Ecclesiastes 3: 4-8). There will be a time to mourn Fred, and the many other friends they will lose this day, but first, it is a time for war.

Harry allows his mind to open to Voldemort's, and he discovers that Voldemort is in the Shrieking Shack, waiting for Harry to come to him, knowing that Harry will come to him. There, he is interrogating Snape, asking him why the Elder Wand will not work for him. Harry, Ron, and Hermione make their way there, under the invisibility cloak, and they witness Voldemort's murder of Severus Snape. Voldemort has convinced himself that the Elder Wand will not do his bidding because Snape is the true master of it: "The Elder Wand cannot serve me properly, Severus, because I am not its true master. The Elder Wand belongs to the wizard who killed its last owner. You killed Albus Dumbledore. While you live, Severus, the Elder Wand cannot be truly mine…It cannot be any other way…I must master the wand, Severus. Master the wand, and I master Potter at last"(656). With cold-blooded finality, Voldemort then orders Nagini to kill Snape, and he leaves the chamber to take charge of the fight. Harry rushes to Snape, and he sees a silvery blue liquid pouring out of him. Hermione gives Harry a flask, and Snape orders Harry to examine these memories. His last words are incredibly poignant, when we know the full story. As Snape dies, he says to Harry: "Look…at…me…"(658). We will come back to these words after we examine, with Harry, these crucial memories.

It seems an odd time for a "time-out" in the narrative. It is a very clever and very daring decision by J. K. Rowling. She accomplishes it by having Voldemort declare a one-hour reprieve, in order for the valiant warriors of Hogwarts to bury their dead. He warns them that at the end of that hour, they must prepare to surrender Harry, or they will all die. Harry looks in at the Great Hall, where the wounded are being tended to and the slain are being laid out. The toll is too high already. Among the dead, he sees Lupin, Tonks, and Fred. In a daze of grief, he makes his way to Dumbledore's office, pours Snape's memories into the Pensieve, and is swept away into the past.

310

There, he learns a lot about Snape. He was an awkward, unattractive, and unloved child, who never really fit in and who hid his insecurity behind a sneering countenance. He had only one love in his whole life—Lily Evans. We witness their childhood friendship, and we witness Snape's unspeakable grief on the night that Voldemort killed Lily Potter. Overcome with grief, Snape tells Dumbledore that he wishes he had died rather than Lily. Dumbledore tells him how to honor her with his love: "If you loved Lily Evans, if you truly loved her, then your way forward is clear…You know how and why she died. Make sure it was not in vain. Help me protect Lily's son"(679). Severus Snape groans at this suggestion, because Harry is not only Lily's son—he is also James Potter's son, and James is still, in Snape's mind, his only true nemesis, since he won Lily's heart. Still, he agrees to Dumbledore's plan since his love for Lily is far greater than his contempt for James. We now know why Dumbledore trusted Snape so completely. Love is the most powerful magic of all—much more powerful than support for evil, loyalty to Voldemort, or even fear of punishment. Snape makes Dumbledore swear to never tell that he has given his word to protect Harry, a promise that Dumbledore makes reluctantly. Dumbledore tells Snape that it seems odd to him to be forbidden to speak of Snape's good heart.

In that memorable scene at the end of book six, we saw Dumbledore, with his ruined hand, asking Snape for help. Snape controls the curse, but he tells Dumbledore that he cannot undo it: "That ring carried a curse of extraordinary power, to contain it is all we can hope for; I have trapped the curse in one hand for the time being… There is no halting such a spell forever. It will spread eventually, it is the sort of curse that strengthens over time"(681). It is haunting to hear how much this curse sounds like an aggressive cancer, which can be controlled, but never completely beaten back. Evil is a cancer. Dumbledore then asks Snape if he will kill him when the time comes, rather than allow Draco Malfoy to do it. He says that if Snape will do him this final honor, Draco may yet be saved: "That boy's soul is not yet so damaged…I would not have it ripped apart on my account…I ask this one great favor of you, Severus, because death is coming for me…I confess I should prefer a quick, painless exit to the protracted and messy affair it will be if, for instance, Greyback is involved"(683). Dumbledore has no illusions about what is coming for him. He would like to die with his dignity intact, and that is not likely to happen if a villain like Greyback is in charge of ending his life.

Then comes the most shocking revelation of all. Dumbledore tells Snape that when the moment comes, Snape must tell Harry something very important: "Tell him that on the night Lord Voldemort tried to kill him, when Lily cast her own life between them as a shield, the Killing Curse rebounded upon Lord Voldemort, and a fragment of Voldemort's soul was blasted apart from the whole, and latched itself onto the only living soul left in that collapsing building. Part of Lord Voldemort lives inside Harry, and it is that which gives Harry the power of speech with snakes, and a connection with Lord Voldemort's mind that he has never understood. And while that fragment of soul, unmissed by Voldemort, remains attached to and protected by Harry, Lord Voldemort cannot die"(686). And so, Harry learns that he must die in order to kill Lord Voldemort. Harry considers this idea, with a kind of bizarre and almost other-worldly objectivity, after he gets through a momentary panic.

He realizes that life is precious, and that his body is a miracle: "Slowly, very slowly, he sat up, and as he did so he felt more alive and more aware of his own living body than ever before. Why had he never appreciated what a miracle he was, brain and nerve and bounding heart? It would all be gone...or at least, he would be gone from it. His breath came slow and deep, and his mouth and throat were completely dry, but so were his eyes(692). As we read this passage, we find ourselves pausing to consider the miracle of our own bodies, and we realize, that like Harry, we take too much for granted. Back at Hogwarts, it is almost four in the morning, and everyone is exhausted. So many people have died already, and Harry knows that he must give his life to save the others. His friends have steadfastly refused to surrender Harry, but he can see no way around this necessity. It breaks his heart to think that he will never laugh again with Hermione,

Ron, Luna, and Ginny. Most of all Ginny: "It was nearly four in the morning, and the deathly stillness of the grounds felt as though they were holding their breath, waiting to see whether he could do what he must"(695). What he must. It is very clear that while Harry does not want to die, he never considers not sacrificing himself. He will do anything, even give his own life, to destroy Voldemort and save all those he loves. Greater love hath no man. Harry will carry his cross, not joyfully, but willingly.

Harry finds Neville and tells him that no matter what happens during the battle, when the moment comes, he must kill the great snake Nagini. Neville doesn't understand the command, but he gives his word. True friendship does not require an explanation. He accepts Harry's command, and then Harry walks away. Harry wants to make sure that his death does not mean the end of the quest unless the mission is complete. He is overcome with sadness, with the weight of opportunities for love that will never now be his, and he is just worn out: "The long game was ended, the Snitch had been caught, it was time to leave the air"(698). Once again, we realize that quidditch is being used here as a metaphor for life, and Harry feels like his game is just about over. Suddenly, he has an epiphany, as he often does. He pulls the Snitch from his pocket that Dumbledore had left him in his will, presses his lips to it and whispers that he is about to die. We remember the inscription on the snitch—I open at the close. And it does. As Harry faces death, the metal shell breaks open! Suddenly, Harry is surrounded by the spirits of those who have "gone on" but who still love him—James, Lupin, Tonks, Sirius, and Lily, whose smile is the widest of all. We realize that both Lupin and Tonks have died that very night, at the hands of Lord Voldemort, leaving a small child behind. Teddy Tonks is Harry Potter all over again. It reminds us that Harry's story is our story, that evil will always continue to exist in our world, and that people will always suffer losses and hurts. However, just as certainly, good people will rise up and fight against evil, the same way Harry did, the same way we all do.

The images of his lost loved ones encourage him to finish the quest, and he asks them to stand by his side and see him through it. His father answers, "Until the very end"(700). When Harry asks if anyone else can see them, Sirius tells him that they are a part of him, invisible to anyone else. Once again, we realize—love never dies, and our loved ones never leave us. They are in our hearts and minds and souls, and all we have to do is ask them to be present with us and they will. Harry quietly says, "Stay close to me"(700). And they are— "He glanced sideways, and his mother smiled at him, and his father nodded encouragement"(701).

Thus encouraged, Harry strides into the clearing in the Forbidden Forest where Voldemort, surrounded by his Death Eaters, has been awaiting his appearance. With his heart hammering against his ribs, he announces his presence, and Voldemort smiles a deadly smile, filled with arrogance and contempt: "Voldemort and Harry looked at each other, and now Voldemort tilted his head a little to the side, considering the boy standing before him, and a singularly mirthless smile curled his lipless mouth…None of the Death Eaters moved. They were waiting: Everything was waiting…Harry thought inexplicably of Ginny, and her blazing look, and the feel of her lips on his"(704. In other words, at this crucial moment, Harry thinks of love. Almost immediately, Voldemort raises his wand, the Elder Wand, and speaks the words of the Killing Curse. We see a flash of green light, and then everything is gone. Remember—Harry has not raised his own wand to defend himself. He has willingly given his life to save the ones he loves—or so he thinks.

Then comes one of the most wonderful chapters in the whole of the Potter Quest—the scene at King's Cross. Harry comes to consciousness, lying facedown, and listening to the silence. He realizes slowly that he is naked, and although he is not frightened or concerned about this, he wishes for some clothing, and immediately, he is clothed. What an interesting idea. If we are being given an imaginative glimpse of the passage to heaven, and we might be, then we should be reassured that "every tear will be wiped away." We will only have to think of something we need to be more comfortable, and it will be done. The place where he has landed has an other-worldly feeling to it: "He lay in a bright mist, though it was not like mist he had ever experienced before...The floor on which he lay seemed to be white, neither warm nor cold, but simply there, a flat, blank something on which to be"(706). Later in the scene, Harry tells us that this place seems to be King's Cross Station, only cleaner and brighter. We know by then that it is a temporary holding place for Harry and Dumbledore to meet, as Harry decides whether to "go on" or return and fight Voldemort to the death. Now, the religious significance of King's Cross comes to us. Jesus is the King of kings, and he died on a cross to save us. Time and again, he told us to take up His cross and follow Him, to live our lives in the service of others. No greater love has any man except he will lay down his life for his brothers and sisters. And that is exactly what Harry is willing to do.   Jesus

Harry becomes aware that there is someone or something lying there next to him: "He recoiled. He had spotted the thing that was making the noises. It had the form of a small, naked child, curled on the ground, its skin raw and rough, flayed-looking, and it lay shuddering under a seat where it had been left, unwanted, stuffed out of sight, struggling for breath...He ought to comfort it, but it repulsed him"(707). Suddenly, Albus Dumbledore appears, beautiful and whole, and he tells Harry that this wounded thing is beyond the scope of their help. We begin to suspect that this ugly, wounded thing is Voldemort's soul, suffering for his commitment to evil in his days of life on earth. At the moment of death, the soul goes on, but Voldemort's soul is going on to suffering. It is the path he has repeatedly chosen, and neither Harry nor Dumbledore can help him. He has run out of chances. When Harry sees Dumbledore "alive" and well, he is shocked and joyful, and he asks his beloved headmaster for an explanation of where they are and what is going on:

> *"But you're dead," said Harry.*
> *"Oh yes," said Dumbledore matter-of-factly.*
> *"Then...I'm dead too?"*
> *"Ah," said Dumbledore, smiling still more broadly. "That is the question, isn't it? On the whole, dear boy, I think not"(707).*

Harry is bewildered by his answer, and he tells Dumbledore that he meant to let Voldemort kill him. "And that...will, I think, have made all the difference"(708). Harry survives another killing curse because he did exactly what Lily Potter did—he lay down his life for others. Greater love hath no man except that he will lay down his life for others. The last enemy to be destroyed is death. Love is the most powerful magic of all. Love conquers all—even death. The man who does not fear death is the man who conquers death.

Then comes a kind of catechism, a systematic question and answer session between Dumbledore and Harry, where he helps Harry to think out what has just happened. Dumbledore guides Harry, but Harry arrives at the understanding mostly by himself. He realizes that part of Voldemort's soul had been hidden in him and that Voldemort has now killed that portion of his own soul. He realizes further when Voldemort took his blood to rebuild his body, part of Lily Potter's protection had transferred with it. And then, Harry gets confused—and so do we: "I live...while he lives? But I thought...I thought it was the other way round! I thought we both had to die? Or is it the same thing?"(709). Even at this very intense moment, Harry is distracted by the pitiful state of this creature at his feet, and moved by its suffering, he asks Dumbledore if there is anything they can do for it. Once again, Dumbledore tells Harry that it is beyond the scope of their power to help it, and we are beginning to suspect that we know what it is. Then Dumbledore answers Harry's question: "You were the seventh Horcrux, Harry, the Horcrux he never meant to make. He had rendered his soul so unstable that it broke apart when he committed those acts of unspeakable evil, the murder of your parents, the attempted killing of a child. But what escaped from that room was even less than he knew. He left more than his body behind. He left part of himself latched to you, the would-be victim who had survived...He took your blood believing it would strengthen him. He took into his body a tiny part of the enchantment your mother laid upon you when she died for you. His body keeps her sacrifice alive, and while that enchantment survives, so do you and so does Voldemort's one last hope for himself"(709).

It is a time for truth, and Harry and Dumbledore talk at length about the Elder Wand, and they consider the reasons why it never really belonged to Voldemort. They speak also about the Resurrection Stone, the Deathly Hallow that can raise someone from the dead. This stone was the stone in Marvolo Gaunt's ring, and Dumbledore had been tempted to use it to raise his mother and his sister from the dead so they could be reconciled. As we have said earlier, raising someone from the dead is not the province of man. It is the province of God alone. Beyond that, when Voldemort created a horcrux of the ring, he put an evil curse upon the stone, and that curse could not be stopped. Like a cancer, it would have killed Dumbledore in time, and it would have been a horrible and painful death had Snape not saved him from this by killing him at the end of the sixth novel. Through this conversation with Harry, we are privileged to see Dumbledore as a man, with a man's flaws and desires, and it actually makes us love and admire him even more. He confesses to Harry that he, particularly as a young man, had been sorely tempted by hubris: "I had proven, as a very young man, that power was my weakness and my temptation. It is a curious thing, Harry, but perhaps those who are best suited to power are those who have never sought it. Those who, like you, have leadership thrust upon them, and take up the mantle because they must, and find to their own surprise that they wear it well"(718). In saying this, he makes us think of Plato and his philosopher kings. Plato says, in his very famous essay entitled "The Allegory of the Cave," that those who are most eager for the power of ruling are likely to be those who are motivated by a secret greed and a desire for power and glory. Those who are not desirous of ruling may actually be the ones who could rule best.

In conclusion, Dumbledore tells Harry that he is the right man to possess the Deathly Hallows, simply because he does not want them. That is why Harry was able to defeat death—because he welcomed it if it meant that he could save his loved ones. We will each carry our cross, just as Jesus told us. We are reminded of the Sorceror's Stone from book one: "You are the true master of death, because the true master does not seek to run away from Death. He accepts that he must die, and understands that there are far, far worse things in the living world than dying"(721). We think of the youngest son in the tale from Beetle the Bard. He hid from Death for a while, lived a full and happy life, and then, surrendering the cloak to his son, went away with Death, greeting him like an old friend. Harry understands, and so do we. Then, it is time to say farewell to Dumbledore and to King's Cross, for a while. Harry suddenly understands that he must go back and finish his quest on earth, that his heavenly Father has not called him home just yet. He looks at Dumbledore and says, "I've got to go back, haven't I?"(722). Dumbledore tells him that the choice is entirely his own, and that, since they are at King's Cross, if Harry desires, he could probably 'board a train' and go on. How tempting that must be for Harry, at least for a moment, to be reunited with his loved ones. However, he knows, in his secret heart of hearts that his earthly quest is not yet finished. He asks Dumbledore is he thinks that he should go back, and Dumbledore answers respectfully: "I think…that if you choose to return, there is a chance that he may be finished for good. I cannot promise it. But I know this, Harry, that you have less to fear from returning here than he does…Do not pity the dead, Harry. Pity the living, and, above all, those who live without love. By returning, you may ensure that fewer souls are maimed, fewer families are torn apart. If that seems to you a worthy goal, then we say good-bye for the present"(722). What a brilliant and thought provoking speech. Do not pity the dead—if they have lived a good life, committed to doing the best they can, they are in a place of sweetness and light, where every tear has been dried away. In our Father's house, there are many mansions. Pity the living—they are still trying to make their way through the maze that is their life, filled with challenges, trials, and losses. Most of all, pity those who live without love, for they are the loneliest people in the world.

Harry nods and sighs. He feels a kind of bittersweet sadness as he knows he must leave this place of gentle peace. We understand that this interview has taken place in a temporary holding place, before the final judgment that will take place for Harry when he finally does "go on." We recall the words from the 23rd Psalm, written approximately 3,000 years ago:

The Lord is my shepherd, I shall not want;
He makes me lie down in green pastures.
He leads me beside still waters; he restores my soul.
He leads me in paths of righteousness for his name's sake.
Even though I walk through the valley of the shadow of death,
I fear no evil; for thou art with me.
Thy rod and thy staff, they comfort me.
Thou preparest a table before me in the presence of my enemies;
Thou anointest my head with oil, my cup overflows.
Surely goodness and mercy shall follow me all the days of my life;
And I shall dwell in the house of the Lord forever
(Psalms 23:1-6).

It really is that simple. Our loving Father in heaven has prepared a place of sweetness and light for us, a place where every tear will be wiped away, but this earthly body cannot inherit this place. We will leave this body behind when we complete our earthly quest, and be welcomed home to the presence of our loved ones who have gone on before us. We are all invited to the banquet, and we must walk by faith until our quest is done and we are called home. Harry now willingly returns to the valley of the shadow of death, to do what has to be done.

One last wonderful comment from Dumbledore is worth noting. Harry asks if this scene which we have just witnessed is real, or has it been happening inside his head. Dumbledore answers with the enigmatic wisdom of Solomon and heaven: "Of course it is happening inside your head, Harry, but why on earth should that mean that it is not real?"(723). How utterly brilliant. We have spoken of this idea before. What you think is happening, your perception of reality, your honest understanding of what is going on is what is real to you. You constantly reevaluate that understanding, of course. That is what it means to be a living, sentient being. However, we live in our own bodies and minds, while we are here on earth. Eventually, our body wears out, but our mind and our soul are inextricably interwoven, and our soul goes on.

After this incredibly intense chapter, and the high that comes with it, we come crashing down, with Harry, back into the clearing in the forest, back into a body filled with pain. As Harry slowly regains consciousness, he becomes aware of the fact that both he and Voldemort apparently collapsed during the suspended animation of the scene at King's Cross. Voldemort reveals that he is

324

conscious once again, refuses any assistance, and tells Narcissa Malfoy to examine Harry's body and discern whether or not Harry is alive or dead. Narcissa leans close to Harry, feels his heart thumping wildly, and whispers to him, asking if her son Draco is still alive. Draco is alive, thanks to Harry who saved him from the fiendfyre, and he whispers back to her "yes." Once again, Voldemort underestimates the power of a mother's love, and Narcissa lies to Voldemort, announcing that Harry is dead. Voldemort never understands the power of love; almost any mother would do anything to save her son's life. That is what love means. Narcissa's announcement causes Voldemort to excitedly drop his guard, and flushed with triumph, he orders Hagrid to carry Harry's body back to Hogwarts so that he can put it on display and announce his evil triumph before the defeated army of Hogwart's defenders.

Hubris will, once again, be his undoing. He orders Hagrid to put Harry's corpse at his feet, and he arrogantly proclaims his victory to the bedraggled assembly of Hogwart's defenders: "Harry Potter is dead! Do you understand now, deluded ones? He was nothing, ever, but a boy who relied on others to sacrifice themselves for him... He was killed while trying to sneak out of the castle grounds...killed while trying to save himself"(731). He is in for a big surprise. With great effort, Harry lies still, allowing Voldemort to tell these lies, to arrogantly proclaim his power and victory. Harry lies there, waiting for the right moment. He doesn't quite know what it will be, but he somehow knows that he will recognize it when it comes. That perfect moment suddenly arrives when Voldemort sneeringly forces the old Sorting Hat down on Neville's head, and sets it aflame, intending to torture Neville and make an example out of him for his disrespect and disobedience. We remember that Neville was sorted into the house of Gryffindor for a reason, and that a true Gryffindor can always call for the Sword of Gryffindor when in dire need. We remember also that Neville has an unparalleled faith in what Harry told him to do, and that he will do all he can to ensure that he successfully carries out the task that Harry has assigned him. He has grown in confidence immeasurably from the timid boy we knew in book one. Voldemort is no longer facing a frightened boy who can be easily intimidated. He is facing a powerful young warrior who is committed to doing the right thing. Once again, Voldemort completely underestimates the man.

At this point, J. K. Rowling writes a very simple sentence that perfectly sums up the moment: "And then many things happened at the same moment"(732). The last fifteen pages of this chapter, teasingly called "A Flaw in the Plan," suggest that, as Hamlet says, "There's a divinity that shapes our ends, rough hew them how we will"(5.2.11-12). In other words, although things may not turn out exactly the way we plan them, there is a plan—a divine providence. And that divine providence kicks in right now.

Harry pulls the Invisibility Cloak from underneath himself and swings it over his shoulders, seeming to disappear. The Sorting Hat hands over the Sword of Gryffindor to Neville, who, with one smashing blow, decapitates the snake Nagini, thereby destroying the last horcrux: "With a single stroke Neville sliced off the great snake's head, which spun high into the air, gleaming in the light flooding from the entrance hall, and Voldemort's mouth was open in a scream of fury that nobody could hear, and the snake's body thudded to the ground at his feet"(733). We cannot help but remember how throughout literature, ever since the Old Testament, the snake has been connected to the imagery of hell. Neville's deathblow for Nagini seems to foreshadow the fall of evil that is fast approaching. Suddenly, the defenders of Hogwarts are joined by an army of centaurs, house elves, hippogriffs, and thestrals. Kreacher, completely transformed by Harry's earlier act of kindness, leads the house-elves into battle, crying: "Fight! Fight! Fight for my Master, defender of house-elves! Fight the Dark Lord, in the name of brave Regulus! Fight!"(734). Aberforth Dumbledore is there, fighting bravely and effectively against the Death Eaters. Mr. Weasley and Percy fight side by side, the father and son reunited. The Death Eaters fall back, inundated by the tide of the diverse army of Hogwarts defenders, and we see it all come down to two main battles. In one circle, Voldemort is battling McGonagall, Slughorn, and Kingsley all at once, and there is a cold sneer of arrogant hatred on his face. They cannot take him down; he is too powerful.

In the other circle, Bellatrix Lestrange is dueling Hermione, Ginny, and Luna, and her evil magic is powerful enough to hold them all at bay. In fact, we have the terrible impression that she is, once again, like a cat, toying with her food before she devours it. We remember how she killed Sirius so easily. Harry is caught in the middle of the two duels, wanting to help, not knowing which way to move. Suddenly, Molly Weasley explodes on to the scene. All through the quest, we have loved Molly, and seen in her the epitome of a mother's love, but we have perhaps not thought of her as much of a warrior herself. One thing this story suggests is that we are all warriors on a quest. And if it comes to it, we must fight for our loved ones. We are forced to reconsider our impression of Molly as she charges over to Bellatrix, waving the three young women away: "NOT MY DAUGHTER, YOU BITCH!...OUT OF MY WAY!...You—will—never—touch—our—children—again!"736. Molly makes short work of her, and Voldemort's best lieutenant is dead. Then, Harry presents himself to Voldemort, telling everyone to step aside and let him face Voldemort alone, insisting that it must be that way: "I don't want anyone else to try to help...It's got to be like this. It's got to be me...There are no more Horcruxes. It's just you and me. Neither can live while the other survives, and one of us is about to leave for good"(737).

Then, Harry behaves as a true knight—he offers his opponent mercy, and a chance to make an act of contrition. Voldemort sneers at this, believing, that he is still invincible, since he holds the Elder Wand in his hand. Harry gives him full warning that things may not be as he thinks they are: "You won't be killing anyone else tonight...Haven't you noticed how none of the spells you put on them are binding? You can't torture them. You can't touch them. You don't learn from your mistakes, Riddle, do you?...I know things you don't know, Tom Riddle. I know lots of important things that you don't. Want to hear some, before you make another mistake?"(738). We notice that Harry addresses Voldemort as Tom Riddle, showing complete contempt for his self-created title of "Lord Voldemort," reducing him to his essential, frail, human identity. Voldemort thinks that Harry is talking about love, which Dumbledore always believed to be the most powerful magic of all. We learned this in book one of the quest, and even in these final moments, this message echoes very powerfully; still, as we know— Voldemort does not believe in love, which is exactly what he tells Harry: "It is not love that will save you this time...you must believe that you have magic that I do not, or else a weapon more powerful than mine"(739).

Harry tells him that he is right on both counts, and a shadow of fear and doubt crosses Voldemort's snake-like face. Then Harry explains that the Elder Wand, which is in Voldemort's hand, will not truly obey him; it does not recognize him as its true master. When Voldemort sputters with disbelief, Harry tells him what he does not know—that Severus Snape was not the master of the wand because he did not really defeat Dumbledore. He killed him, but he did not defeat him, because Dumbledore's death was planned between the two of them: "Aren't you listening? Snape never beat Dumbledore! Dumbledore's death was planned between them! Dumbledore intended to die undefeated, the wand's last true master! If all had gone as planned, the wand's power would have died with him, because it had never been won from him!...You still don't get it, Riddle, do you? Possessing the wand isn't enough! Holding it, using it, doesn't make it really yours. Didn't you listen to Ollivander? The wand chooses the wizard...The true master of the Elder Wand was Draco Malfoy...But you're too late...You've missed your chance. I got there first. I overpowered Draco weeks ago. I took the wand from him"(743). Once again, Voldemort's fatal error is predicated on his inability to understand the power of the greatest magic of all—love. When Severus Snape had begged that Voldemort spare Lily's life, Voldemort had laughed at him. We remember that Lily was the one great love of Severus Snape's life, and from the moment Voldemort killed her, Snape's allegiance belonged to Dumbledore, and by extension (although Snape was usually reluctant to express it openly) to Harry, Lily's son.

So, Voldemort stands face to face with his nemesis, and all the false securities of his riddles and mysteries have been stripped away.

This moment reminds us of the final scene in William Shakespeare's Macbeth, where it all comes down to a final battle between Macbeth and Macduff. Macbeth had heard three predictions from the witches—that he should fear Macduff, that he would be safe until Birnam Wood marches on Dunsinane hill, and that no man born of woman could harm him. Macbeth acknowledges that Macduff is a worthy adversary, so that prediction rings true to him. However, he is terrified when Birnam Wood does march on his castle, situated on the top of Dunsinane Hill. Young Malcolm, the slain king's son has his men cut down branches from the forest of Birnam, in order to camouflage their approach as they attack the castle. When this happens, he suspects that he has been played for a fool, and that the witches who gave him these riddling predictions may have been deceiving him on purpose.

Riddles are often meant to deceive. Remember the sphinx? How perfect that Voldemort's true name is Tom Riddle, and he will be undone by a riddle he has failed to understand, just like Macbeth was. Macbeth confronts Macduff, and he tells him that he cannot be defeated by any man born of woman. He has misunderstood this to mean that he is safe; after all, every man is born of woman, right? That depends what you mean by the word "born." Macduff tells him that he was "from his mother's womb untimely ripped"(5.8.16). This means, of course, that she could not "give birth" to him. Perhaps she was even already dead, and he was taken from her womb by a Caesarean section. Therefore, he was not "born" in the typical sense. And so, Macbeth, stripped of all illusions of immortality and invincibility, faces the man who will defeat him.

We have much the same feeling in this scene between Harry and Tom Riddle. Voldemort holds the Elder Wand, the Deathly Hallow that is supposedly an unbeatable wand. The question is—is holding the wand tantamount to owning the wand and controlling it? Harry whispers to Voldemort, probably terrifying him, "So it all comes down to this, doesn't it?...Does the wand in your hand know its last master was Disarmed? Because if it does...I am the true master of the Elder Wand"(743). And, yelling "his best hope to the heavens," Harry shouts "Expelliarmus," his signature spell(743). Notice that, even in this final moment, Harry does not speak an unforgivable curse. Voldemort screams the words of the killing curse, but Harry does not: "Harry saw Voldemort's green jet meet his own spell, saw the Elder Wand fly high, dark against the sunrise...spinning through the air toward the master it would not kill, who had come to take full possession of it at last. And Harry, with the unerring skill of the Seeker, caught the wand in his free hand as Voldemort fell backward....Tom Riddle hit the floor with a mundane finality...killed by his own rebounding curse, and Harry stood with two wands in his hand, staring down at his enemy's shell"(744). Notice how cleverly J. K. Rowling has written this passage. Lord Voldemort was never really anything more than Tom Riddle, and he is undone by his own evil. His death is "mundane," and ordinary, and his corpse is nothing but a "shell" for his soul and mind, which have now "gone on" to judgment. And that judgment, is, of course, beyond the province of man. We remember Dumbledore telling Harry that the thing in obvious pain at their feet in their scene at King's Cross Station is beyond their power to help. It is not for us to judge. That is the province of God, not man, and so we do not go there.

In closing, there is jubilation and sorrow, in equal parts, and the defenders of Hogwarts gather in the Great Hall to celebrate their victory and to mourn their dead. Even the three Malfoys are there, reunited, and apparently humbled. The bodies of those who have given their lives in the battle are laid out and honored, and the cost has been so dear. Among the dead are Lupin, Tonks, Colin Creevey, and Fred. Those who are wounded have their wounds dressed. There is a time to dance, and a time to mourn. Harry wants very much to be with Ginny, and he will, but he has a bit of unfinished business to take care of first. Luna understands that Harry must want some privacy, so she distracts everyone's attention, allowing Harry to find Ron and Hermione, and to get themselves up to Dumbledore's office. There, our three warriors are greeted by all the old headmasters applauding their victory from their talking portraits.

However, Harry only has eyes for Albus Dumbledore, and he needs his wisdom one last time. He confesses to Dumbledore that he dropped the Resurrection Stone in the forest, and that he is not going to go looking for it. Dumbledore heralds this as a wise and brave decision. Furthermore, Harry tells him that all he wants the Elder Wand to do for him is mend his own broken wand, the pieces of which he still carries in the pouch around his neck. He says that he was always happier with his own wand than with this one. Harry proves himself to be the very thing that Dumbledore had said—the Master of Death because he does not fear death. He does not desire powers that are beyond the scope of a mortal man. He does not want to bring the dead back to life in this earthly incarnation—he understands that they are waiting for him, and will be reunited with him when he "goes on." Furthermore, he does not want an unbeatable wand, which by extension suggests that he does not have the heart of a tyrant. He is not tempted by visions of grandeur. He wants to love Ginny, and raise a family. He will keep the Invisibility Cloak, like the wise youngest brother in the legend of old, and he will pass it to his own son, in time, when it is time for him to "go on."

Although Ron sputters with disbelief—we remember, the Elder Wand is the one Deathly Hallow he coveted—Harry says that he has no desire to wield it. He hopes to die, someday, as the true master of the wand, having not used it, so its power would be broken: "That wand's more trouble than it's worth…And quite honestly…I've had enough trouble for a lifetime"(749). We cannot help but smile at this gentle wisdom.

And so, we leave the Potter quest. In an epilogue, J. K. Rowling gives us a glimpse of all of our beloved friends nineteen years later. Harry and Ginny are married, and they have three children—Albus, James, and Lily. Ron and Hermione are married, and they are at the platform with their two children, Rose and Hugo. Draco Malfoy and his wife are also there, with their son Scorpius. Draco nods curtly to Harry as the children bound for Hogwarts board the train. Just before he gets on the train, Harry's younger son pulls his father aside, worried about the possibility of not being chosen for Gryffindor House, and Harry tells him something very important: "Albus Severus…you were named for two headmasters of Hogwarts. One of them was a Slytherin and he was probably the bravest man I ever knew…It doesn't matter to us, Al. But if it matters to you, you'll be able to choose Gryffindor over Slytherin. The Sorting Hat takes your choice into account….It did for me"(758). We remember what we heard at the end of book two of the quest—"It is our choices, Harry, that show what we truly are, far more than our abilities." And this powerful idea echoes here in the final moments of the quest.

This epilogue closes with some interesting words. As the parents watch the Hogwarts Express pull out of the station with their children on board, they whisper reassurances to one another… they will be all right. Harry's hand moves reflexively to the scar on his forehead: "The scar had not pained Harry for nineteen years. All was well"(739). This quest is concluded. That does not mean that evil is completely and forever eradicated. We are not naïve enough to believe that. It does mean that good has triumphed over evil at this moment and in this setting. And that is a good reason to celebrate. Evil is quiet—for the moment. The powers of darkness can be beaten back, but they lie dormant only for a while, and the Dark Lord, in some other guise, will rise again. However, so will a new Harry Potter rise up, a warrior who, although flawed and terribly human, will fight for others who are unable to defend themselves, will fight in a just cause, and will show mercy to an enemy if and when he is defeated, giving him a chance to choose differently and experience remorse.

The Potter quest is a multi-faceted story, and it is not only Harry's story—not by a long shot. In fact, one of the most important ideas that the story shows us is the sacred power of love and friendship. Harry defeats Voldemort largely because of the help of his friends and loved ones. In fact, Harry only destroys one horcrux. It may be that J. K. Rowling did this on purpose to show the importance of opening ourselves to others and recognizing that we can accomplish little by ourselves. Dumbledore, Ron, Hermione, and Neville all destroy horcruxes. In an interesting aside, Voldemort and Crabbe accidentally destroy horcruxes, not ever meaning to do so. It is almost as if J. K. Rowling is suggesting that evil will eventually, left to its own devices, destroy itself.

Furthermore, Voldemort destroys himself because of his inability to recognize the power of the love and magic that surround him. He could have chosen differently at so many moments in his life. We remember when Dumbledore came to the young Tom Riddle, offering him a whole different life, but he refused that outstretched hand. Dumbledore describes it in this way: "That which Voldemort does not value, he takes no trouble to comprehend. Of house-elves and children's tales, of love, loyalty, and innocence, Voldemort knows and understands nothing. Nothing. That they all have a power beyond his own, a power beyond the reach of any magic, is a truth he has never grasped." These words are a reminder to us to look for and value the magic that exists in our world—the beautiful earth that blesses us with her gifts every day, the miracle of children, our loved ones. We will, each of us, face our trials and tribulations. No one is exempt from sorrow and suffering in this life. However, we must keep our hearts centered on what is important, do the best we can, and treasure our loved ones. Then, we can say with Harry, "All is well."

The Lessons of The Potter Quest

The journey of the Potter quest has taught us many things, most of which we already knew in our secret heart of hearts. The thing is—this story makes us take these treasures out and look at them again, and maybe appreciate them in a whole new way. That is not to say that J. K. Rowling is breaking new ground here. On the contrary, she is telling us a delightful story that makes us think about what is really important in life. The brilliant writer C. S. Lewis once said, "Even in literature and art, no man who bothers about originality will ever be original; whereas, if you simply try to tell the truth (without caring twopence how often it has been told before) you will, nine times out of ten, become original without ever having noticed it." That is the secret to every great writer's success, and it is certainly in play in the Potter quest. Yes, J. K. Rowling has thrilled us with her imaginative settings and magical charms, but the true charm of the Potter story goes deeper than that. J. K. Rowling has presented us with a story about what matters.

Probably the most important lesson of all is that the greatest magic of all is something we are all capable of—love. We are talking about the kind of love that St. Paul describes for us in his famous passage from Corinthians, which we have spoken of at length already.

When we love someone, we participate in the divine. It is as close as we can come to showing that we truly are made in the image and likeness of God. To be loved is to be changed forever; you are marked with that love. There is a passage in the Old Testament book entitled the Song of Solomon that gets to this idea: "Set me as a seal upon your heart, as a seal upon your arm; for love stronger than death... Many waters cannot quench love, neither can floods drown it"(Song of Solomon 8:6-7). Love is like a seal on our hearts. Love marks us— not with a scar, but with a power to defeat even death.

Perhaps it is time to listen one more time to St. Paul on love: "If I speak with the tongues of men and of angels, but have not love, I am a noisy gong or a clanging cymbal. And if I have prophetic powers, and understand all mysteries and all knowledge, and if I have all faith, so as to remove mountains, but have not love, I am nothing. If I give away all I have, and if I deliver my body to be burned, but have not love, I gain nothing. Love is patient and kind; love is not jealous or boastful; it is not arrogant or rude. Love does not insist on its own way; it is not irritable or resentful; it does not rejoice at wrong, but rejoices in the right. Love bears all things, believes all things, hopes all things, endures all things. Love never ends; as for prophecies, they will pass away; as for tongues, they will cease; as for knowledge, it will pass away. For our knowledge is imperfect and our prophecy is imperfect; but when the perfect comes, the imperfect will pass away...For now we see in a glass darkly, but then face to face. Now I know in part; then I shall understand fully, even as I have been fully understood. So faith, hope, love abide, these three; but the greatest of these is love"(I Corinthians 13:1-13). Love is the most powerful magic of all, and it gives back to you a hundredfold. That is the most important lesson of the Potter Quest. And we are talking about the kind of love that St. Paul describes in this passage. It is the kind of love that helped Lily Potter to stand in front of Voldemort's killing curse. It is the kind of power that emboldened Harry to do the same. It is the kind of love that made Molly confront Bellatrix Lestrange. There are countless other examples of this powerful magic in the course of the Potter quest. *immortal / loss*

Secondly, this story has a lot to say about the question of immortality. There is something in us that is immortal, something that lasts beyond this earthly incarnation, something that "goes on." There is no reason to fear death; death is only a transition to that next life, which is what we have all been moving toward from the moment we are born. In his poem entitled "Song of Myself," Walt Whitman uses the symbol of grass for the promise of our immortality. Grass grows everywhere around the earth, and although it is sometimes dormant, it always returns to life. It covers the scars of battlefields, and its beautiful green is like a flag, or like a handkerchief dropped by our heavenly Father, inviting us into a more personal relationship with him. We never really lose the ones we love. The grass proves that. He writes, "Look for me under your bootsoles. I stop somewhere waiting for you."

We have been told from thousands of years ago in Psalm 23 that we are all invited to the heavenly banquet, that our heavenly Father has invited us to lie down in a verdant green valley, where every tear will be dried away. The Harry Potter stories quietly echo these ideas. We should live this life as fully as we can. We should not fear death. Death is but a moment, a passage, a veil that we will pass through on our way to our next life. And, 'it does not do to dwell on the past—or the future—and forget to live.'

knights / proie

Thirdly, the classic lessons of the knights of old echo in this story. The Knights of the Round Table took an oath to always fight in just causes, to protect widows and children, and those too weak to protect themselves, and to show mercy. These lessons are repeated throughout the quest. Even as Harry is approaching the last battle with Voldemort, he gives him a chance to experience remorse, and to save his own soul. He, in fact, invites him repeatedly to do so, telling him that he is making his final mistake, and that he has once again failed to learn from his previous mistakes. He says to Tom Riddle: "It's your one last chance…it's all you've got left. I've seen what you'll be otherwise…Be a man…try…Try for some remorse"(Hallows 741). Notice that in order to be a man, you must be capable of remorse, of knowing when you are wrong and admitting it. Of course, if Voldemort were capable of any kind of remorse, he could not even attempt to do what he does—speak the words of the killing curse which will ultimately backfire on him on this final occasion.   However,   Harry gives him a chance to save his soul, his mind from the utter desolation that awaits him. Harry is merciful on many occasions during the quest, and every single time, the mercy comes back to him. It reminds me of a very famous quote from William Shakespeare's play entitled The Merchant of Venice: "The quality of mercy is not strained. / It droppeth as the gentle rain from heaven / Upon the place beneath. It is twice blessed. / It blesseth him that gives and him that takes"(4.1.183-187). Sadly, of course, Voldemort refuses this mercy. However, we are shown, very quietly, the benefits of showing mercy to others in the course of the Potter quest.

Fourthly, the story shows us the importance of choice. You must choose what you will believe in, what you will fight for. Yes, there are things that happen in the course of your life that you cannot control, but free will matters. You must choose, every day of your life, to keep on fighting for what you believe to be the right thing. You must choose to love and to show mercy and to struggle on bravely, sometimes in the face of seemingly insurmountable odds against you. Do the best you can to "brighten your little corner of the world," every day. Commit yourself to a life of service to others. When you feel overwhelmed with a dark hour of the soul, direct your thoughts and energies to those around you. Ask your heavenly Father for the strength and courage to go on, and know that He hears your prayer. At Hogwarts, whenever you ask for help, it will be given. And we are at Hogwarts every day of our lives. Ask, and you shall receive. Live your life actively, choosing to believe, choosing to love, choosing to do what is right, as best you understand it. *friendship*

And then, these novels speak to us about the importance, the sacredness, of friendship. Although these stories have focused on Harry Potter, the truth is—he is nothing and can do nothing without Ron and Hermione. And not only them—in the siege of Hogwarts, everyone is working together. All of Dumbledore's Army is there, fighting side by side, putting their lives on the line to defeat the powers of darkness. And fighting with the young warriors are all the adults who have helped to shape them into the fiercely good people they are—including Molly and Arthur Weasley, Tonks and Lupin. Several of them lose their lives in the battle. Without our friends we are nothing. This idea is connected to the idea of the sacredness of love. We remember that Dumbledore told Harry that it is one of the chief differences between himself and Tom Riddle. Riddle refused to let people into his life, arrogantly convinced that he is far superior to any of them. He would use them, but he would never trust them. Harry knows that he would be dead on many occasions without the help of his friends, and he is humbly grateful for the love and support they give him throughout his quest. As we should be. No man is an island. We stand on the shoulders of those who have come before us, who have sheltered us and taught us, and brought us to this point in our lives. When any good thing happens to us, we need to remember that there are many people who worked behind the scenes to bring us to this opportunity and to this moment of triumph. And we too must be humbly grateful. *magic is real*

Another important idea we can take away from the Potter quest is the notion that magic is real. It is all around us. In fact, we are magic, and we are capable of creating the mightiest magic of all—love. Life itself is a miracle. Consider the stars in the heavens at night. Consider a newborn baby, or a child taking his first steps. Consider the wonderful feeling of being hugged, held closely in somebody's arms. Consider the joy of a cup of hot chocolate on a cold, wintry day. Walking by the seaside in the early morning. The "barbaric yawp" of a pelican. The sunrise filtering through the treetops. The thrill of freshly fallen snow covering the town at night. The list goes on and on. You should make your own list of the things of life that are magical to you—that have healing properties, that can make you feel warm and safe, if only for a little while. And in times of trouble, remember these things, these people who are so dear to you, and let them work their magic on your heart. There is no question about it—

our days are filled with magic. We are filled with magic. *humming*

Finally, live humbly. Find a time for reverence in your life. Speak quietly to your heavenly Father, and know that He is listening. Do not believe that you can solve all the problems of the world, or that anything is all your fault—or all anyone else's either. Life is not that simple. There will be times of peace, and times of battle. You must learn to gather your strength and appreciate the seasons of grace when they come, knowing full well that something will happen, soon enough, that requires you to fight for what you believe in. Respect the privacy of others—there are stories upon stories, and you cannot ever really know all the forces that have shaped that person's life and brought them to this moment. Perhaps, in closing, we can go back to the Old Testament, to the book of Isaiah, for our final bit of guidance. Written approximately 2,700 years ago, we get this spiritual guidance and the promise of peace: "There shall come forth a shoot from the stump of Jesse, and a branch shall grow out of his roots. And the Spirit of the Lord shall rest upon him, the spirit of wisdom and understanding, the spirit of counsel and might, the spirit of knowledge and the fear of the Lord. And his delight shall be in the fear of the Lord"(Isaiah 11: 2-3). What a hauntingly beautiful passage it is, and it still speaks to us today. The spirit of the Lord still rests upon us, and we open our hearts to his quiet wisdom and understanding, we will know an earthly measure of peace.

The things that are promised in this passage are the gifts of the Holy Spirit, and they are the lights that the Potter Quest encourages us to live by: wisdom based on charity, understanding, right judgment, courage, knowledge, piety, and fear and reverence for our heavenly Father. Our scars will occasionally give us great pain; we are not in heaven yet. But, if we do the best we can to live humbly and faithfully, we can say, with Harry, 'all is well.'

Dedication

This book is dedicated to the people who have taught me about the most powerful magic of all—love. That means, first and foremost, to my husband, Christopher—my best friend and my heart's delight. In a very special way, this book is also therefore dedicated to my Mom and Dad. My mom was the first person who ever told me that I should write a book—and I finally got around to it. My mom and dad have been the best teachers a little girl could ever have, and they continue to teach me today, even though I am all grown up. Next—this book is dedicated to my children—Jessica, Christopher, Benjamin, and Nicholas. When they came into my life, I learned more and more about love—how it never ends, how it strengthens us and heals us, how it is infinite. The book is also dedicated to the wonderful "adopted" children of our hearts—the people that our children have brought into our lives—Brett, Jenessa, Heather, and Michelle. They have also deepened my understanding of love in so many ways. In an almost sacred way, the book is also dedicated to our grandchildren— Brett, Tessa, Trey, Lila, and Paige (who is still on her way here at the time of this writing) and hopefully many more to come. They keep us young, and they show us, once again, that love never dies. It is also dedicated to my brothers and sisters—Carol, Mary, Eddie, Angie, and

John. And to their wonderful husbands and wives—Kurt, Wayne, Lori, Ben, and Mary. Unlike Harry, I was lucky enough to grow up in a home where I was surrounded by love. And that has made all the difference. Truthfully, it is why I was able to write this book.

I humbly dedicate this book to J. K. Rowling, whose wonderful vision has inspired so many people. Thank you for taking us on this journey with you. I will come back to it again and again, always with joy.

I also dedicate this book to my wonderful friends at St. Thomas Aquinas High School—you know who you are. Every day you make me feel appreciated and worthy. Finally, this book is dedicated to all the students who sat in my classroom, hungry for more. Here it is. Now—keep going. As Walt Whitman says, you will delight me if you go further than I have gone. I have shown you what I know—now, go further. Swim deeper. All is well.

Acknowledgements

This book never would have happened had it not been for the encouragement and insights of so many of my loved ones who took time to read the manuscript and offer detailed and thoughtful suggestions. Thank you from the bottom of my heart to my husband, Christopher Stearns, who was with me from the very first moment the idea occurred to me. Thank you to my Mom and Dad, for believing in me and telling me that someday I should write a book. I finally did. Thank you to my children—all of whom read and helped me shape this thing—Jessica and Brett Salamin, Christopher and Jenessa Stearns, Ben and Heather Stearns, Nick Stearns and Michelle Kinne. Thank you to all my friends who read rough drafts of chapers and said, "Keep going!" Finally, to Monica McNerney and AnnMarie Rodriguez, who read every single word, offered brilliant suggestions, and encouraged me to keep going. I love you and I thank you all. It has been a joy to share this part of my personal quest with all of you.

Works Cited

Rowling, J. K. *Harry Potter and the Sorceror's Stone*. New York: Arthur A. Levine
    Books, 1997.
Rowling, J. K. *Harry Potter and the Chamber of Secrets*. New York: Arthur A.
    Levine Books, 1998.
Rowling, J. K. *Harry Potter and the Prisoner of Azkaban*. New York: Arthur A.   Levine
    Books, 1999.
Rowling, J. K. *Harry Potter and the Goblet of Fire*. New York: Arthur A. Levine Books,
    2000.
Rowling, J. K. *Harry Potter and the Order of the Phoenix*. New York: Arthur A. Levine
    Books, 2003.
Rowling, J. K. *Harry Potter and the Half-Blood Prince*. New York: Arthur A. Levine
    Books, 2005.
Rowling, J. K. *Harry Potter and the Deathly Hallows*. New York: Arthur A. Levine
    Books, 2007.
Shakespeare, William. *The Complete Works of William Shakespeare*. David   Bevington,
    Ed. New York: Harper Collins. 1992.
The New Oxford Annotated Bible: The Holy Bible. New York: Oxford Univesity
    Press. 1973.

Made in the USA
Charleston, SC
26 October 2015